Human Rights and Disability

The formerly established medically-based idea of disability, with its charity-based approach to treatment and services, is being replaced by a human rights-based approach in which people with impairments are no longer considered medical problems, totally dependent on the beneficence of non-impaired people in society, but have fundamental rights to support, inclusion, and participation. This interdisciplinary book examines the diverse concerns that people with impairments face in the context of human rights, provides insights into new developments on important issues relating human rights to disability, and features new approaches and solutions to vital problems in the current debate.

John-Stewart Gordon received his MA in philosophy and history from the University of Konstanz (2001) and his PhD in philosophy from the University of Göttingen (2005), Germany. He is full professor and head of the Research Cluster for Applied Ethics at Vytautas Magnus University in Kaunas, Lithuania. From 2010–2016, he was codirector of the Hans Jonas-Institut at the University of Siegen, Germany. In addition, he has been a visiting professor at Queen's University Kingston, Canada (2009–2010), and a permanent visiting professor at Vytautas Magnus University in Kaunas, Lithuania (2012–2015). Furthermore, he has been a member of the board of *Bioethics* since 2007 and area editor and board member of the *Internet Encyclopedia of Philosophy* (2007–2014). He has written and edited several books in the context of practical philosophy and published peer-reviewed articles and special issues in leading international journals and encyclopedias, including *Bioethics, Ethical Theory and Moral Practice, Kennedy Institute of Ethics Journal, The Journal of Law, Medicine and Ethics, Baltic Journal of Law and Politics, Ethical Perspectives, Internet Encyclopedia of Philosophy*, and *Oxford Bibliographies Online Philosophy.* He has taught philosophy and bioethics at the University of Tübingen (Germany), Ruhr-University Bochum (Germany), Duisburg-Essen University (Germany), Queen's University in Kingston (Canada), Vytautas Magnus University in Kaunas (Lithuania), and the University of Cologne (Germany).

Johann-Christian Põder studied theology and philosophy in Tartu, Greifswald, and Göttingen. He graduated from Tartu University in Estonia (theology, 2001) and received his PhD in theology from Göttingen University in Germany (2010) with a thesis on the phenomenological ethics of K. E. Løgstrup. He was lecturer in ethics at the Theological Institute of the Estonian Evangelical Lutheran Church in Tallinn (2008–2011) and substitute lecturer in modern theology at Tartu University (2011). He has also worked as a chaplain at Tallinn Prison (2007–2008) and as Chaplain General of Prisons at Estonian Ministry of Justice (2009–2013). In 2011–2012 and 2014, he was a research associate for the GANI_MED-Project at Greifswald University in Germany, where he is still member of a working group in medical and theological ethics. Since 2015 he is Carlsberg Foundation postdoctoral fellow at the Faculty of Theology at Copenhagen University, Denmark, working on a book on predictive medicine, ethics, and religion.

Holger Burckhart completed his PhD in philosophy in 1990 and his postdoctoral lecture qualification in 1997. In 2008, he was appointed to the professorship for anthropology and ethics in curative education, taking a special account of people with disabilities in the faculty of human sciences at the University of Cologne. From 2007–2009, he was also prorector for teaching, studies, and study reform at the University of Cologne. He is currently the rector of the University of Siegen, vice-president of the German Rectors' Conference for the Department of Teaching, Learning, Teacher Training, and Lifelong Learning, and a member of the German Accreditation Council. In 2014, he was appointed to the professorship for the philosophy of education with a special focus in philosophical anthropology, ethics, and theory of science at the University of Siegen. In 2015, he was elected to the board of the European University Association.

"Disability human rights talk is ubiquitous, but disability human rights thought is scarce. This book helps fill that gap by subjecting human rights rhetoric to rigorous but supportive interrogation. An excellent roster of authors shows us what is needed to promote the flourishing of disabled people."

Professor Tom Shakespeare
University of East Anglia, United Kingdom

Human Rights and Disability

Interdisciplinary Perspectives

Edited by John-Stewart Gordon, Johann-Christian Põder, and Holger Burckhart

Routledge
Taylor & Francis Group
LONDON AND NEW YORK

First published 2017 by Routledge

2 Park Square, Milton Park, Abingdon, Oxfordshire OX14 4RN
52 Vanderbilt Avenue, New York, NY 10017

Routledge is an imprint of the Taylor & Francis Group, an informa business

First issued in paperback 2018

British Library Cataloguing in Publication Data
A catalogue record for this book is available from the British Library

Library of Congress Cataloging in Publication Data
Names: Gordon, John-Stewart, 1976– editor. | Põder, Johann-Christian, 1977– editor. | Burckhart, Holger, editor.
Title: Human rights and disability : interdisciplinary perspectives / John-Stewart Gordon, Johann-Christian Põder and Holger Burckhart [editors].
Description: First edition. | Abingdon, Oxon ; New York, NY : Routledge, 2017. | Includes bibliographical references and index.
Identifiers: LCCN 2016025150 | ISBN 9781472448231 (hardback) | ISBN 9781315587486 (ebook) | ISBN 9781317119876 (mobipocket)
Subjects: LCSH: People with disabilities—Civil rights. | People with disabilities—Legal status, laws, etc. | Human rights.
Classification: LCC K637 .H856 2017 | DDC 323.3–dc23
LC record available at https://lccn.loc.gov/2016025150

ISBN: 978-1-4724-4823-1 (hbk)
ISBN: 978-0-367-07567-5 (pbk)

Typeset in Galliard
by Apex CoVantage, LLC

This book has been part of the research project "Global Bioethics: Human Rights and Disability" that has been financed by the Hermann and Marianne Straniak Stiftung and the Forschungskolleg "Zukunft Menschlich Gestalten" of the University of Siegen.

Contents

Acknowledgments ix
Contributors x

1 General introduction: Human rights and disability – interdisciplinary perspectives 1
ALICIA OUELLETTE

1 Introduction 1
2 The challenge continues 1
3 The promise and limitations of a human rights approach 2
4 An interdisciplinary approach to understanding the promises and challenges of a human rights approach to disability 4
5 The contribution, as a whole 6
6 References 6

PART I
Human rights and disability: Different voices 7

2 Remarks on a disability-conscious bioethics 9
JOHN-STEWART GORDON

1 Introduction 9
2 The gap between bioethics and the disability rights community: Concepts, biases, and fears 10
3 On the possibility of overcoming the divide: Autonomy and personhood 15
4 Conclusions 19
5 References 19

3 Theology, disability, and human rights: Difficult past, promising future 21
JOHANN-CHRISTIAN PÕDER

1 Introduction 21
2 Theology and disability: Difficult past 21

3 Theological efforts at rethinking disability: Three examples 24
4 Theology and disability in relation to human rights and theories of justice 28
5 Theology and disability: Promising future 34
6 References 34

PART II
Human development and inclusion 37

4 Grounding disability and human rights with the capabilities approach 39
CHRISTOPHER A. RIDDLE

1 Introduction 39
2 The capabilities approach to justice 39
3 Human rights 41
4 Equality 43
5 Dignity 45
6 Autonomy 47
7 Concluding remarks 48
8 References 48

5 Human rights and persons with intellectual and developmental disabilities: An elusive but emerging paradigm 50
DONATO TARULLI, DOROTHY GRIFFITHS, AND FRANCES OWEN

1 Historical context and rationale for a rights agenda 50
2 The UN Convention on the Rights of Persons with Disabilities 54
3 Making the paradigm shift 56
4 Rights education 60
5 Relationships and rights 62
6 Conclusions 65
7 References 65

6 On human rights and human duties: Is there a moral obligation to inclusion? 68
HOLGER BURCKHART AND BENNET JÄGER

1 Introduction 68
2 Inclusion: A human right 68
3 Inclusion as an area of responsibility in society as a whole 70
4 Conclusion 72
5 References 72

7 **The right to inclusive education: Practical implications in German schools** 74
PETR FRANTIK

1 Introduction 74
2 Preliminary remarks 75
3 Current difficulties 77
4 Promising approaches 83
5 Conclusion and final remarks 88
6 References 89

PART III
Justice and legal protection 93

8 **Disability rights, legal and moral** 95
HANS S. REINDERS

1 Introduction 95
2 Moral and legal rights 97
3 Signification and ratification 99
4 Promotion and protection 100
5 Liberties and claim rights 101
6 Justifiable restrictions 103
7 What rights claims can do 107
8 What disability rights cannot do 108
9 Conclusion 109
10 References 110

9 **From manifesto to action: Transforming the aspiration of disability human rights into accountable government action** 111
JEROME BICKENBACH

1 Introduction 111
2 The "human rights approach" and the CRPD 113
3 Ideological obstacles to fulfilling the promise of the CRPD 116
4 Transforming aspiration into accountable action 125
5 References 128

10 **Human and civil models of rights: Healthy and ill disabled and access to health care** 132
ANITA SILVERS AND LESLIE PICKERING FRANCIS

1 Introduction 132
2 Humanity as a basis for rights ascription 133

3 Collective agreement as a basis for rights justification 137
4 Health care rights in a civil rights frame 139
5 Group-differentiated rights and the problem of clashing models of disabilities 140
6 Disability as a medical problem 141
7 Disability as a social problem 143
8 Disability identity: Healthy versus ill? 145
9 Regarding robustness 147
10 Disability rights as civil rights 148
11 Conclusion 150
12 References 151

11 Agency and disability: A rights-based approach 154
MICHAEL BOYLAN

1 Central definitions 154
2 Environmental disability 157
3 Disability and stigma 159
4 Eliminating negative liberty and enhancing positive liberty 167
5 Community support 168
6 Conclusion 168
7 References 169

12 Afterword 171
AKIKO ITO

Bibliography 175
Index 177

Acknowledgments

The present volume, *Human Rights and Disability: Interdisciplinary Perspectives,* contains ten original and challenging chapters on human rights and disability written by well-known philosophers, bioethicists, theologians, and scholars working in the field of disability studies and special education. The contributors are Jerome Bickenbach, Michael Boylan, Holger Burckhart, Leslie Pickering Francis, Petr Frantik, John-Stewart Gordon, Dorothy Griffiths, Akiko Ito, Bennet Jäger, Alicia Ouellette, Frances Owen, Johann-Christian Põder, Hans S. Reinders, Christopher A. Riddle, Anita Silvers, and Donato Tarulli. We are very thankful to all of them for their great work and their willingness to contribute a chapter to this fine volume. A special thanks goes to Alicia Ouellette, who has written the general introduction, and to Akiko Ito, Chief Secretariat for the Convention on the Rights of Persons with Disabilities, who has written the afterword. Their support is greatly appreciated. We would also like to thank Routledge for their interest in and willingness to publish the book, and in particular, Alison Kirk for her excellent support from the early to the final stages of this volume. Last but not least, we would like to thank our former research assistants, Paula Segler and Felice Tavera-Salyutov, for their great help. They provided outstanding support with regard to the book's editorial work; without their help, we certainly would have been lost in the details of the project.

John-Stewart Gordon
Vytautas Magnus University Kaunas and University of Cologne, May 2016

Johann-Christian Põder
University of Copenhagen, May 2016

Holger Burckhart
University of Siegen, May 2016

Contributors

Jerome Bickenbach (PhD) is a professor at the University of Lucerne and Swiss Paraplegic Research, Nottwil, and Emeritus Professor at Queen's University, Canada. He is the author of *Physical Disability and Social Policy* (1993) and the co-editor of *Introduction to Disability* (1998), *Disability and Culture: Universalism and Diversity* (2000), *A Seat at the Table: Persons with Disabilities and Policy Making* (2001), *Quality of Life and Human Difference* (2003), *Ethics, Law, and Policy: The SAGE Reference Series on Disability* (2012), and *Disability and the Good Human Life* (2014) as well as numerous articles and chapters on disability studies, focusing on the nature of disability and disability law and policy. He was the editor of the joint World Health Organization and International Spinal Cord Society report titled *International Perspectives on Spinal Cord Injury* and more recently the World Bank/World Health Organization manual *ICF and Disability Assessment*. Since 1995, he has been a consultant with the World Health Organization working on the preparation and implementation of the ICF. Most recently, his research includes disability quality of life and the disability critique, disability epidemiology, aging and well-being, universal design and inclusion, modeling disability statistics for population health surveys, the relationship between disability and health, and the ethics and application of ICF to the development of human right indicators for monitoring the implementation of the UN Convention on the Rights of Persons with Disabilities.

Michael Boylan (PhD, University of Chicago) is professor and chair of philosophy at Marymount University in Arlington, Virginia. He is the author of twenty-eight books, the most recent of which are *Natural Human Rights: A Theory* (2014), *The Origins of Ancient Greek Science: Blood – A Philosophical Study* (2015), *Morality and Global Justice: Justifications and Applications* (2011), and *A Just Society* (2004). He has more than 130 published articles and has given invited lectures in fourteen countries on five continents. Boylan's work has been the subject of a book, *Morality and Justice: Reading Boylan's A Just Society* (2009), and several doctoral dissertations. On a practical level, he has been a public policy consultant for the US government and helped establish a center for clinical bioethics in Valparaiso, Chile.

Holger Burckhart completed his PhD in philosophy in 1990 and his postdoctoral lecture qualification in 1997. In 2008, he was appointed to the professorship for anthropology and ethics in curative education, taking a special account of people with disabilities in the faculty of human sciences at the University of Cologne. From 2007–2009, he was also prorector for teaching, studies, and study reform at the University of Cologne. He is currently the rector of the University of Siegen, vice-president of the German Rectors' Conference for the Department of Teaching, Learning, Teacher Training, and Lifelong Learning, and a member of the German Accreditation Council. In 2014, he was appointed to the professorship for the philosophy of education with a special focus in philosophical anthropology, ethics, and theory of science at the University of Siegen. In 2015, he was elected to the board of the European University Association.

Leslie Pickering Francis, PhD, JD, holds joint appointments as distinguished Alfred C. Emery professor of law and distinguished professor of philosophy at the University of Utah, where she also directs the Center for Law and Biomedical Sciences. Her primary fields of interest are health law, bioethics, and disability ethics and law. Francis is immediate past co-chair of the Subcommittee on Privacy, Confidentiality, and Security of the National Committee on Vital and Health Statistics, a member of the Ethics Committee of the American Society for Reproductive Ethics, and Secretary-General of the International Association for Philosophy of Law and Social Philosophy. Recent publications include Stein, Michael Ashley, Anita Silvers, Bradley Areheart, and Leslie P. Francis, 2014, "Accommodating Every Body," *University of Chicago Law Review* 81(2), 689–757. She is the editor of the *Oxford Handbook of Reproductive Ethics* (Oxford, 2016) and is co-authoring (with John Francis) *Sustaining Surveillance: The Ethics of Public Health Data Collection and Use* (Springer, forthcoming 2016) and *Privacy: What Everyone Needs to Know* (Oxford, forthcoming 2016).

Petr Frantik graduated in special education from the University of Cologne in 2005. During his studies, he was involved in a project of the *Autismus Therapie Zentrum/ Therapy Center for People with Autism*, supporting children with autism to help structure their free time and thereby to participate in society. Between 2005–2009, he worked as a teacher for children with learning disabilities. In addition, he conceptualized and implemented a program at some selected special needs schools to help graduates manage their apprenticeships (2007–2009). In 2013, he worked as an academic assistant on the research project Die Gelingensbedinungen von Inklusivem Unterricht (The Conditions of Successful Inclusive Education) at the University of Cologne and Dresden University of Technology. He has taught at the University of Cologne since 2009, and his main topics are intercultural education and ethics in rehabilitation sciences. He is also a member of the Hans Jonas Institut in Siegen, where he conducts research on the ethics of responsibility against the background of current social and technological challenges.

John-Stewart Gordon received his MA in philosophy and history from the University of Konstanz (2001) and his PhD in philosophy from the University of Göttingen (2005), Germany. He is full professor and head of the Research Cluster for Applied Ethics at Vytautas Magnus University in Kaunas, Lithuania. From 2010–2016, he was Co-director of the Hans Jonas-Institute at the University of Siegen, Germany. In addition, he has been a visiting professor at Queen's University Kingston, Canada (2009–2010), and permanent visiting professor at the Vytautas Magnus University in Kaunas, Lithuania (2012–2015). Furthermore, he has been a member of the board of *Bioethics* since 2007 and an area editor and board member of the *Internet Encyclopedia of Philosophy* (2007–2014). He has written and edited several books in the context of practical philosophy and published peer-reviewed articles and special issues in leading international journals and encyclopedias, including *Bioethics, Ethical Theory and Moral Practice, Kennedy Institute of Ethics Journal, The Journal of Law, Medicine and Ethics, Baltic Journal of Law and Politics, Ethical Perspectives, Internet Encyclopedia of Philosophy,* and *Oxford Bibliographies Online Philosophy*. He has taught philosophy and bioethics at the University of Tübingen (Germany), Ruhr-University Bochum (Germany), Duisburg-Essen University (Germany), Queen's University in Kingston (Canada), Vytautas Magnus University in Kaunas (Lithuania), and the University of Cologne (Germany).

Dorothy Griffiths (PhD) is a professor in the Department of Child and Youth Studies and the Centre for Applied Disability Studies at Brock University. She has published extensively and presented throughout North America and abroad on issues related to human rights of persons with disabilities, in particular deinstitutionalization as well as on issues related to persons with intellectual disabilities who have mental health or challenging behaviors, including sexual offending. Griffiths is a recipient of both the Order of Ontario and the Order of Canada for her work with persons with intellectual disabilities.

Akiko Ito is Chief of the Secretariat for the Convention on the Rights of Persons with Disabilities/DSPD/DESA at UN Headquarters in New York. She is also the UN Focal Point on Disability and the Departmental Focal Point for Women of Department of Economic and Social Affairs (DESA), as well as the DESA Focal Point for Human Rights Mainstreaming for UNDG – the United Nations Development Group. Ms. Ito has extensively lectured and published on issues concerning disability and human rights. Prior to her current posting at UN Headquarters, she worked in the Legal Affairs Section of the United Nations Drug Control Programme in Vienna, Austria. Her academic background is in international law and the area of interest is domestic application of international law, with a focus on the rights of minorities and other disadvantaged groups. Ms. Ito has an LL.B. in International Legal Studies from Sophia University, Tokyo, an M.A. in International Relations from the University of Chicago and an LL.M. from Boalt Hall School of Law, University of California at Berkeley.

Bennet Jäger completed his studies at the University of Cologne in history and German in 2006 and his PhD in Anglo-American history (about organized crime and the creation of its image in postwar America) in 2012. From 2004–2013, he worked at the Historical Institute and the Department for Campus Management at the

University of Cologne. From 2013–2015, he was the research and personal assistant of the rector of the University of Siegen. He has been employed at the Centre for Quality Assurance at the University of Siegen since 2015.

Alicia Ouellette is president and dean of Albany Law School, where she also served as associate dean for academic affairs and intellectual life and a professor of law, as well as professor of bioethics in the Union Graduate College/Mt. Sinai School of Medicine Program in Bioethics. Her research focuses on health law, disability rights, family law, children's rights, and human reproduction. Her book, *Bioethics and Disability: Toward a Disability Conscious Bioethics*, was published in 2011 by Cambridge University Press. She has authored numerous articles published in academic journals such as the *American Journal of Law and Medicine, Hastings Center Report, American Journal of Bioethics, Hastings Law Journal, Indiana Law Journal*, and *Oregon Law Review.* Before joining the law faculty, Ouellette served as an assistant solicitor general in the New York State Attorney General's office, where she briefed and argued more than one hundred appeals on issues ranging from termination of treatment for the terminally ill to the responsibility of gun manufacturers for injuries caused by handguns. Before that, she worked in private practice and served as a confidential law clerk to Judge Howard A. Levine on the New York State Court of Appeals. She has continued her advocacy work in select cases and was lead counsel on the law professors' brief submitted in support of same-sex couples who sought the right to marry in New York State.

Frances Owen is professor of Child and Youth Studies and is cross-appointed to the Centre for Applied Disability Studies at Brock University in St. Catharines, Ontario, Canada. She is a psychologist interested in the relationship between organizational systems and clinical practice as well as issues related to mental health promotion and intervention. She has professional experience in children's mental health, developmental services, and schools. Her research focuses on human rights and community engagement of persons with intellectual and developmental disabilities, deinstitutionalization, and interorganizational and interdisciplinary partnerships in community services.

Johann-Christian Põder studied theology and philosophy in Tartu, Greifswald, and Göttingen. He graduated from Tartu University in Estonia (theology, 2001) and received his PhD in theology from Göttingen University in Germany (2010) with a thesis on the phenomenological ethics of K. E. Løgstrup. He was lecturer in ethics at the Theological Institute of the Estonian Evangelical Lutheran Church in Tallinn (2008–2011) and substitute lecturer in modern theology at Tartu University (2011). He has also worked as a chaplain at Tallinn Prison (2007–2008) and as Chaplain General of Prisons at Estonian Ministry of Justice (2009–2013). In 2011–2012 and 2014, he was a research associate for the GANI_MED-Project at Greifswald University in Germany. Since 2015, he has been a postdoctoral research fellow at Copenhagen University in Denmark, working on a book on predictive medicine, ethics, and religion.

Johannes (Hans) S. Reinders is professor emeritus at VU University Amsterdam. He has written extensively on ethical issues regarding disability within the context of Christian theology. Through participation in international colloquia and conferences, he has contributed to the academic and public discussion of ethics in this field. Reinders took up the study of theology at the Vrije Universiteit in Amsterdam in 1975 and held a research fellowship at the Dutch Organization of Advanced Scientific Research and earned his PhD in theology in 1988. Appointed a lecturer in ethics and promoted to full professor in 1995 at his alma mater, he has been a visiting scholar in philosophy at the University of Notre Dame and a resident scholar at the Center for Theological Inquiry in Princeton. A former member of the board of directors of the Dutch Society of Ethics, the institutional review board of the Royal Institute for Medical Research, and the Health Council of the Netherlands, he served on the scientific council of the International Association for the Scientific Study of Intellectual Disabilities until 2014. In 2010, he became the general editor of the *Journal of Disability and Religion*. Reinders is the author of many articles published in academic journals. Among his most well-known books are *The Future of the Disabled in Liberal Society: An Ethical Analysis* (University of Notre Dame Press, 2000) and *Receiving the Gift of Friendship: Profound Disability, Theological Anthropology, and Ethics* (Erdmans, 2008). He also edited a volume titled *The Paradox of Disability: Responses to Jean Vanier and L'Arche Communities from Theology and the Sciences* (Erdmans, 2010).

Christopher A. Riddle (PhD) is an Associate Professor & Chair of Philosophy and the Director of the Applied Ethics Institute at Utica College, NY. Previously, he held positions at Concordia University and Queen's University at Kingston. His work has been published in journals such as *The Journal of Social Philosophy*; *The American Journal of Bioethics*; *Essays in Philosophy*; *Medicine, Healthcare, & Philosophy*; *Topoi*; and *Disability Studies Quarterly*. He is also the author of "Disability & Justice: The Capabilities Approach in Practice" (2014) and "Human Rights, Disability, and Capabilities" (2016).

Anita Silvers, professor and chair of philosophy at San Francisco State University, has published six co-authored or co-edited books, as well as more than 150 articles and chapters on topics in ethics and political philosophy, philosophy of art, bioethics, feminist philosophy, and philosophy and disability. Among the honors she has received are the APA Quinn Prize, the Phi Beta Kappa/APA Lebowitz Prize, and the California Faculty Association's Human Rights Prize. She served for many years on the American Philosophical Association's board of officers and was appointed to the National Council on the Humanities by the president of the United States.

Donato Tarulli is an associate professor in the Department of Child and Youth Studies at Brock University. He is a developmental psychologist with interests in theoretical and meta-theoretical issues in child and youth development and disability studies. He has published on the topics of child rights, as well as rights for persons with intellectual disabilities, in each case foregrounding the philosophical, sociorelational, and cultural underpinnings of human rights and rights discourse.

1 General introduction

Human rights and disability – interdisciplinary perspectives

Alicia Ouellette

1. Introduction

In 2016, the UN General Assembly adopted the Convention on the Rights of Persons with Disabilities (CRPD) to "promote, protect and ensure the full and equal enjoyment of all human rights and fundamental freedoms by all persons with disabilities, and to promote respect for their inherent dignity." Adoption of the CRPD marked and seeded a political and cultural shift by and for people living with impairment, representing an express and legally potent recognition that the presence of a physical or mental impairment should not diminish human dignity or access to opportunity. In large measure, adoption of the CRPD was monumental. For much of history, and throughout much of the world, laws and societal practices have systematized the mistreatment and isolation of individuals living with physical or intellectual impairments. With its promise of inclusion, respect, and dignity, adoption of the CRPD marked significant progress in a decades-long struggle for legally enforceable human rights protections by and on behalf of persons living with physical, mental, and intellectual impairments. Yet a decade later, the CRPD's effects are neither as pervasive nor as concrete as proponents had envisioned.

2. The challenge continues

Ensuring human rights and equal opportunities for persons living with disabilities remains an enduring challenge. Despite significant social, legal, and political progress made by and on behalf of the hundreds of millions of people who live with disabilities, the challenge is complex and deep. Although most humans will experience temporary or permanent impairments during their lifetimes, and as many as a billion people, or 15 per cent of the world's population, are estimated to currently live with a disability, understanding of the meaning of disability and a path to full inclusion remains elusive. Individuals, their families, and communities struggle to understand the meaning of impairment in the lives of those living with them. Physical, legal, social, and architectural barriers continue to limit access to education, housing, employment, health, family, and reproduction. These barriers affect the ability of many individuals living with impairment to realize their full human potential.

Some statistics illustrate the scope of the problem. In Europe, people with disabilities are two to three times more likely to be unemployed than their nondisabled counterparts. About 38 per cent of disabled people aged sixteen to thirty-four have an earned income, compared with 64 per cent of nondisabled people. In the United States in 2015, 17.1 per cent of persons with disabilities were employed, compared to 64.6 per cent of those without a disability (US Department of Labor 2016). Throughout the world, people with disabilities are particularly vulnerable to deficiencies in health care services, yet people with disabilities have greater unmet health needs and worse outcomes than people without disabilities. For example, a survey of people with serious mental health disorders showed that between 35 and 50 per cent of people in developed countries and between 76 and 85 per cent in developing countries received no treatment in the year prior to the studies. Women with mobility disabilities receive less screening for breast and cervical cancer than women with full mobility, and people with intellectual impairments are less likely to have their weight checked (World Health Organization 2015). In developing countries, 90 per cent of children with disabilities do not attend school, and the global literacy rate for adults with disabilities is as low as 3 per cent, and 1 per cent for women with disabilities (International Labour Organization 2003). Compounding issues with health, education, and employment (and as detailed later in this volume), bias, stigma, isolation, and forced institutionalization continue to present human rights challenges for individuals living with disabilities.

3. The promise and limitations of a human rights approach

Recognition that disability is a human rights issue has several advantages. Human rights are universal, inalienable rights belonging to all human beings. They cross boundaries and carry moral and legal force. Recognition of human rights empowers individuals and organizations to claim and enforce rights and encourages institutions and governments to provide means and mechanisms to fulfill the promise and corresponding duties of human rights.

With respect to disability, the CRPD was formulated with extensive participation of people with lived experiences with disabilities and their representative organizations to ensure the full and equal enjoyment of human rights by persons with disabilities. The inclusive nature of the drafting process gives the CRPD moral authority for disability advocates who frequently implore others to remember the mantra "nothing about us without us." The CRPD recognizes eight guiding principles: (1) respect for inherent dignity, individual autonomy, including the freedom to make one's own choices, and independence of persons; (2) nondiscrimination; (3) full and effective participation and inclusion in society; (4) respect for difference and acceptance of persons with disabilities as part of human diversity and humanity; (5) equality of opportunity; (6) accessibility; (7) equality between men and women; and (8) respect for the evolving capacities of children with disabilities and respect for the right of children with disabilities to preserve their identities.

The CRPD uses these principles to derive general obligations and rules applicable to its state parties. The obligations imposed on the states under the CRPD are sweeping, comprehensive, and suggest priority areas for disability work. Participating states are obligated to introduce measures that promote the human rights of persons with disabilities, such as antidiscrimination legislation and laws that ensure inclusion of persons with disabilities in services, goods, and facilities. In this way, the CRPD, which did not recognize new rights, addressed human rights in the particular context of disability, draws into sharp focus the failure of many nations to provide adequate services and protections to meet the human rights needs of individuals living with disabilities.

Having entered force in 2008, the United Nations established a Committee on the Rights of Persons with Disabilities to monitor its implementation. Countries that ratified the CRPD must report regularly on their progress to the committee. An optional protocol allows citizens in those countries that ratified the protocol the possibility of launching an individual complaint to the committee after exhausting national options.

Translating the promise of the CRPD into practice has been complicated. As explored more fully in this volume, at least three categories of obstacles – theoretical, practical, and implementation based – impede and confound realization of universal human rights for individuals with disabilities.

First, the meaning of disability in the lives of individuals living with impairment is not uniform. Disability in the form of a mobility impairment differs in a fundamental sense from intellectual disability. Further, those born with impairments may experience the trait differently from persons who unexpectedly develop the same trait later in life. Theorists struggle to place the disabling aspects of disability: Is it in the body of the affected injury, in socially created barriers, or in some combination of both? While the CRPD commits to a social model, "recognizing that disability is an evolving concept and that disability results from the interaction between persons with impairments and attitudinal and environmental barriers that hinders their full and effective participation in society on an equal basis with others" (CRPD Preamble (5)), the effect of that commitment is unclear. For example, the social model does not itself distinguish when, in a medical setting, the fact of physical impairment is being considered for legitimate medical reasons and when it is being used based on false assumptions about potential quality of life or as a subterfuge for disability bias. Nor does the CRPD's adoption of the social model provide clarity as to how to respect the freedom to make one's own choices for persons with severe intellectual impairment. Further exploration of these theoretical challenges as presented in this volume illuminates these difficulties.

Second, existing structures, practices, and policies impede practical implementation. The principle of accessibility includes a form of positive obligation. That is, accessibility requires a commitment of resources and actions to remove barriers and ensure full participation of persons with disabilities in societal institutions. For example, older buildings must be retrofitted to enable full inclusion to accommodate persons with mobility impairments. Educational programming needs restructuring if schools are to become inclusive of children of all abilities. Health resources must be reallocated to ensure equal access to health by all humans. All of these efforts require resources and commitment, making elusive the goals of full and effective participation, equality, and an end to discrimination. In times of scarce resources, associated costs are a practical and political barrier to implementation.

Finally, implementation itself is an issue. The CRPD is not self-executing. Nation states and regional integration organizations may join as signatories, but enforcement requires action and ratification. By signing the CRPD or optional protocol, states or regional integration organizations indicate their intention to take steps to be bound by the treaty at a later date and to refrain from acts that would defeat the object and purpose of the treaty, but ratification is necessary to create binding legal obligations under international law. Although there are 160 signatories and 161 parties to the CRPD, far fewer have ratified the convention, including the United States and the Netherlands, making its principles aspirational but not legally enforceable in much of the world. Understanding obstacles to ratification, objections to a human rights approach, and the practical challenges with implementation will inform the discussion of an effective human rights approach to disability.

4. An interdisciplinary approach to understanding the promises and challenges of a human rights approach to disability

This book provides a tool for understanding the progress toward and obstacles to ensuring the civil and human rights necessary to human dignity for persons living with impairment. As a whole, the volume challenges its readers to address critical issues surrounding a human rights approach to disability: disability identity, linguistics, law, policy, rights, theology, morality, and justice. The collection addresses central questions such as: How do theoretical models of disability help or hinder the realization of human rights for persons living with impairment? What does it mean to be a rights-bearing person? How does a human rights approach to disability affect bioethical, theological, and educational discourse and thought? What are the strengths and weakness of a human rights approach to disability – from a moral, legal, and practical perspective? Each chapter addresses the central questions through a different lens, drawing on the varied expertise of the authors, to present a panoramic view of the disability rights landscape.

The first two chapters approach disability and human rights from two related disciplines, bioethics and theology, both of which have been charged with historical intolerance for the notion that persons living with disabilities are entitled to full human dignity and rights. In chapter 2, John-Stewart Gordon responds in part to an earlier call for a disability-conscious bioethics, a bioethics that makes central a moral understanding of disability in the lives of individuals living with impairment. Documenting a lack of common understanding of historical and theoretical underpinnings by bioethicists and disability rights advocates, Gordon asks whether "one can 'do' bioethics without adhering to the concept of personhood as the prerequisite to assigning moral status – and hence the right to life." Taking a novel approach, Gordon argues that decoupling moral status from personhood will facilitate discussion and uncover common ground between bioethicists and disability rights scholars, bridging a wide and seemingly impenetrable gap between potential allies. In chapter 3, Johann-Christian Põder rejects traditional theological approaches to disability – those that couch disability as God's punishment or a test – in favor of a language of love and rights rooted in biblical text. Põder argues for a theology embracing human rights, including disability rights, on the basis of love. A love-based theology, argues Põder, encompasses and supports a human rights–based disability ethics.

In chapter 4, Christopher Riddle argues that the capabilities approach to justice, one focused on an individual's capability to function, is the conception of justice that best supports a human right to health and absence of disabling barriers. The capabilities approach, argues Riddle, endorses the values underlying human rights: equality, dignity, and autonomy. Donato Tarulli, Dorothy Griffiths, and Frances Owen demonstrate the practical elusiveness of a capabilities-based approach for persons with intellectual and developmental disabilities in chapter 5. They further advance the importance of cultivating a discourse of rights to redress the oppression experienced by people with intellection disabilities, couching their approach to rights in explicitly relational terms: "collectively creating the conditions, capacities, and communities in which the provisions, protections, freedoms, and entitlements" could emerge.

The next chapters focus more specifically on the human right to education. In chapter 6, Holger Burckhart and Bennet Jäger emphasize the importance of education for inclusion and argue that, to achieve inclusion, "we need a paradigm shift at different interacting levels." Participation, they argue, cannot be dependent on an individual's ability to adapt to the norm. Instead, educational institutions should be adapted to the individual needs of people with disabilities. It is the state's role, they argue, to create conditions necessary for inclusion. In chapter 7, Petr Frantik picks up on Burckhart and Jäger's argument by focusing on practical implications for integration in German schools. Documenting an ongoing shift from a dual system of regular and special schools to one of integration, Frantik identifies the lack of teacher training and the German educational model of teacher-centered instruction as principal challenges. He presents a model for a more inclusive educational approach that applies various learning and teaching methods, allowing for choices, collaboration, and separate work.

Turning to justice and legal protection, in chapter 8, Hans Reinders uses two cases from the Netherlands in which young people housed in facilities for persons with intellectual disabilities were chained to a wall for years to explore the potential of human rights claims to effect practical change. Specifically, Reinders distinguishes the moral from the legal authority of human rights claims. The moral power of human rights, he says, is to change hearts and minds. No one with intellectual disabilities should be chained to the wall. But in a practical sense, he says, the legal significance of human rights – that is, the ability to enforce the right in a court of law – takes precedence over moral rights. But the law was of no use in the cases studied. Nor was a human rights framework legally enforceable. The Netherlands has signed but not ratified the CRPD. Only when ratified, and when a state has adopted the optional protocol, can an individual go to court. Thus, Reinders concludes that the legal power of human rights may be weak. Nonetheless, he asserts, the moral power of a human rights claim may, in the end, be stronger than legal enforceability because of its power to change hearts and minds. Recognition of human rights abuses appeals to the shared moral consciousness in a way that may more effectively change policy on a national level than individual legal claims.

Jerome Bickenbach is less enamored of the moral persuasiveness of human rights claims. In chapter 9, he argues that the promise depends on implementation. A "true transformation in policy" can only come when aspirational ideals are transformed into actions, not merely at the level of action but at the micro-policy level where state action directly affects the lives and opportunities of persons with disabilities. What stands in the way of implementation – what he calls the "social model fetish" – is the uncompromising interpretations of human rights disability claims. Thus, Bickenbach raises the provocative claim that disability scholars and activists may impede progress toward recognition of human rights regardless of impairment by demanding too much of human rights claims.

In chapter 10, Anita Silvers and Leslie Francis take issue with the human rights model, which they believe rests on a claim that only individuals with definitive human physical or intellectual capabilities are entitled to rights. A civil rights framework, they argue, is a better approach for making progress for inclusive justice for disabled people. "Individuals with disabilities depart species typicality," but the human rights model invites a one-size-fits-all remedy. As an alternative, civil rights "should be understood in a pragmatic rather than a metaphysical framework, grounded explicitly in acknowledgement of people's differences rather than rooted in claims about how humans are essentially the same."

In chapter 11, Michael Boylan struggles with the role of environment on the value or worth of a particular trait, looking to scientific studies showing the contextual worth of various traits. An effective human rights approach to disability, he argues, will eliminate negative liberty obstacles and support positive liberty enhancements, requiring participation of a functioning community.

5. The contribution, as a whole

Each contribution in this volume stands on its own to advance and develop the discourse surrounding a human rights approach to disability, touching on theoretical, practical, and implementation-based challenges to realization of the promises of the CRPD. More significantly, however, the collection pushes the discussion to new levels – adding nuance, theory, and practical wisdom to a discussion central to the human condition but too frequently marginalized in practice. In particular, it challenges readers to understand why ensuring human rights, regardless of impairment or disability, remains an elusive goal, despite the victory of the CRPD and national and local laws. The challenge presented is theoretical and practical, legal and political, strategic and tactical, personal and public. To the extent the authors suggest solutions, the message is clear: crafting effective solutions will require a similar interdisciplinary approach. Together, the authors' collective contributions challenge readers to reexamine assumptions and think creatively and systematically to ensure that the vision set forth in the CRPD has a meaningful effect on the lives of people living with disabilities.

6. References

International Labour Organization. 2003. "Inclusion of People with Disabilities in Indonesia." http://www.ilo.org/wcmsp5/groups/public/---asia/---ro-bangkok/---ilo-jakarta/documents/publication/wcms_233427.pdf.

US Department of Labor. 2016. "Persons with a Disability: Labor Force Characteristics – 2015." http://www.bls.gov/news.release/pdf/disabl.pdf.

World Health Organization. 2015. "Disability and Health." http://www.who.int/mediacentre/factsheets/fs352/en/.

Part I

Human rights and disability

Different voices

2 Remarks on a disability-conscious bioethics

John-Stewart Gordon

1. Introduction

Alicia Ouellette, an American lawyer and bioethicist with a strong interest in disability studies, claims in her recent book *Bioethics and Disability: Toward a Disability-Conscious Bioethics* that "it is fair to say . . . that except for a small corner of bioethics inhabited by people[1] with disabilities, experts in disability studies, and disability rights advocates, there is no well-developed disability-conscious approach to bioethics" (Ouellette 2013, 14). Whether it will be possible to overcome what the well-known scholars Mark Kuczewski and Kristi Kirschner (2003) have termed a "civil war" between bioethicists and disability scholars and activists remains to be seen. According to Ouellette, however, "it seems [indeed] quite possible that bioethicists and disability experts might benefit by working together to address common areas of concern" (2013, 331) in order to develop a so-called disability-conscious bioethics – that is, "a bioethics that is mindful of and knowledgeable about the fact of disability in bioethical cases, a bioethics that works for – and with – people with disabilities" (Ouellette 2013, 316).[2]

Even though Ouellette's book contains valuable and important insights that are certainly suitable for further promoting the idea of a disability-conscious bioethics, one might question whether it is *really only* the bioethicists who need to change their attitude and "show a consciousness of disability issues and perspectives" so that the deep-rooted conflict might be resolved (Ouellette 2013, 332).[3] Rather, both camps must change and – without a doubt – scholars and activists contributing to this lively debate must engage more deeply with the opposing perspective in order to gain a better understanding of the concepts as well as of the biases and fears of the other side.

Thus, the goal of this chapter is twofold. First, I seek to highlight the differing perspectives of bioethicists and members of the disability rights community in order to

1 For example, Adrienne Asch, Anita Silvers, and Leslie Francis.

2 Ouellette states later, "Rather, a disability-conscious bioethics is a loose framework for bioethical debate that incorporates disability as a central issue and engages disability experts in the enterprise of bioethics" (2013, 333).

3 "So long as bioethics continues to be perceived as insensitive to or indifferent about the concerns of people with disabilities, however, prospects for reconciliation remain poor. In other words, until bioethicists take action to show a consciousness of disability issues and perspectives as a matter of course in their work, the conflict is likely to persist" (Ouellette 2013, 332).

show – based on the different historical and theoretical underpinnings of bioethics and disability studies – that they do not share a common ground of understanding. Second, I examine whether refraining from adherence to the important idea of autonomy and the related issues of personhood and moral status – an adherence that causes intractable problems for the disability rights community – might be a first step toward a mediating approach between the two camps.[4]

2. The gap between bioethics and the disability rights community: Concepts, biases, and fears

It seems advisable to start with a brief note regarding how I will depict the different perspectives in the debate between bioethicists and members of the disability rights community. This chapter does *not* claim that all bioethicists hold the same view or that all disability activists and scholars working in the field of disability studies hold the same view. On the contrary, many different viewpoints exist within each group. No one within the disability rights community purports to speak for every person with an impairment, nor is there any single, recognized spokesperson for the diverse views in bioethics (see Ouellette 2013, 15). However, it does seem possible to describe the main issues of controversy between the two camps and to outline the historical development of both fields, along with the biases and fears of the people involved in the debate that currently hinder reaching a common ground of understanding.

2.1 Historical observations: The rise of autonomy in medical ethics[5]

The idea of paternalism in medical ethics, which is likely best exemplified by the statement that "the physician knows best," was considered a truism since the times of the Hippocratic Oath in ancient Greece. The very idea that patients have a say in, or should be informed about, their medical treatment was completely absent until the beginning of the last century. The rise of autonomy in the context of the physician-patient relationship can thus be seen as a countermovement to paternalism in health care. The concept of personhood and the principle of autonomy pervaded debates over medical ethics, significantly shaping discussions both in academia and on the ward.

The initial demand for medical ethics was largely in reaction to some serious incidents of abuse, such as the research experiments on human subjects conducted by the Nazis and the Tuskegee Syphilis Study (1932–1972) in the United States. At that time, bioethics was essentially driven by urgent cases (i.e. "putting out fires") and did not consider systematic problems in health care, such as the issue of access to quality care. However, in reaction to these horrible events, the Nuremberg Code (1947) and the Declaration of Helsinki (1964) were created in order to provide researchers

4 Whether this mediating approach should be supported by a human rights perspective that pays attention to the different perspectives by ensuring a minimal standard of conflict resolution is something that needs to be discussed after such an approach has been established.

5 This section draws on the parts of my entry, "Bioethics," at *IEP* (2012).

and physicians with ethical guidelines on respecting the autonomy, or (as it is usually referred to in modern health care and research) the individual informed consent, of patients and research subjects.

2.2 The notion of autonomy

Since Beauchamp and Childress's pioneering work, *Principles of Biomedical Ethics* (1979), the idea of individual informed consent has been an influential and vital part of the principle of autonomy in medical ethics. As we have seen, the notion of informed consent was known long before that time, but Beauchamp and Childress were among the first to use this concept systematically for bioethical reasoning and decision making, giving it a prominent place in their theory.[6] According to them, a patient is capable of autonomous, well-informed decisions in medical contexts if the particular patient meets the threshold and information elements of individual informed consent. If the patient in question is not meeting these standards, then he or she is unable to give informed consent regarding a medical treatment and hence must be considered incompetent.[7] Beauchamp and Childress's idea of informed consent influenced the fields of medicine and medical ethics all over the world and was the gold standard for several decades.

2.3 Theories in bioethics: Utilitarianism and deontology

Contemporary bioethics is substantially shaped by two main ethical approaches, utilitarianism and deontology. Both approaches, along with the rise of the concept of autonomy in medical ethics, cause great fear in members of the disability rights community *because* bioethics links the right to life with the human capacity of rationality and autonomous decision making by ascribing moral status only to those beings who either have or potentially may have that capacity. Disability scholars and activists argue that both ethical theories promote views that lead to extreme bioethical positions on a variety of issues, such as prenatal testing and selective abortion, how to deal with fetuses and newborns who have severe impairments (see the Singer debate), and surrogate decision making in cases of people in permanent vegetative states or with severe mental impairments (see Adrienne Asch 2001). In brief, disability activists claim that

6 For the history of informed consent, see the readable work by Ruth R. Faden and Tom L. Beauchamp, *The History and Theory of Informed Consent* (1986). For some brief historical remarks on the notion of autonomy and informed consent, see also my article "Medical Paternalism and Patient Autonomy" (2013).

7 Beauchamp and Childress offer a list of seven major alternative standards of incompetence often used by health care professionals to determine the capacity of the particular patient, and they rate each one from weak to strong (2009, 114–115). They place those seven standards into three categories as follows: (1) stating a preference: inability to express or communicate a preference or choice; (2) understanding and appreciating one's own situation: inability to understand one's situation and its consequences, inability to understand relevant information; (3) reasoning through a consequential life decision: inability to give a reason, inability to give a rational reason (although some supporting reasons may be given), inability to give a risk/benefit–related reason (although some rational supporting reasons may be given), inability to reach a reasonable decision (as judged according to a reasonable person standard).

"laws that facilitate dying, whatever their form, discriminate against and hurt people with disabilities. People who advocate such laws are enemies to people with disabilities" (Ouellette 2013, 4).[8]

The following brief depiction of utilitarian and deontological reasoning in bioethics will further illuminate the gap between bioethics and the disability rights community.

a. Utilitarianism

One of the most prominent and influential forms of ethical reasoning and decision making in the field of bioethics is based on utilitarianism. In the late twentieth century, utilitarian approaches were so influential that many people outside academia – including members of the disability rights community – believed that all bioethicists were utilitarians. Utilitarianism, in fact, contains a wide range of different approaches. The general idea of maximizing the patient's well-being according to a rather simplistic idea of calculating and comparing the pleasures and pains of all affected persons seems questionable to many people, as they do not think that the outcome of these calculations necessarily leads to morally right or wrong actions. Furthermore, the claim that the killing of an innocent being, such as a fetus with a severe impairment, might be the best possible outcome in some situations – as utilitarians conclude from their understanding of "the good life" – seems to undermine some important values of communal living, such as compassion, care, responsibility for the weak, and concern for justice. In addition, the idea that minority groups, such as people with severe impairments or patients in a permanent vegetative state, can be legitimately sacrificed in some cases, has given utilitarian approaches a rather bad reputation. Utilitarians are also at odds with approaches in bioethics that appeal to human dignity and human rights. Two centuries ago, Jeremy Bentham famously stated that natural rights (or human rights) are "nonsense upon stilts," a dictum that most utilitarians still regard as reasonable (and one that is particularly relevant in the case of the UN Convention on the Rights of Persons with Disabilities).

b. Deontology

Kantian-oriented deontological approaches (or Kantianism) generally adhere to the basic Kantian ideas of respect for persons and human dignity; both central ideas are rooted in the human being's capacity to act autonomously. Kantianism has been adopted in order to provide a justification for strict truth telling in medical contexts – for example, in cases of terminal cancer, bedside rationing, and medical experiments. This development can be seen as a countermovement against previous malpractice. Despite the prima facie reasonableness of Kantian-oriented deontological approaches

8 This depiction is from Ouellette's observation of the activist disability group Not Dead Yet, which held a protest at a plenary session of a large national conference that she co-organized (2013, 4).

in cases concerning truth telling and in the context of medical exploitation, these approaches particularly suffer from using moral norms that are too general and abstract to be applied without difficulty to concrete cases. The upshot is that deontological approaches seem to be less effective at providing adequate guidance, as their application is too complex and possibly misleading (for a different view, see Altman 2011). Furthermore, the fundamental Kantian idea that moral status is assigned according to "rationality" and not according to "membership in the human species" is, from the disability perspective, a serious problem in medical contexts on issues such as abortion, euthanasia, the use of prenatal genetic diagnosis (and selection of embryos), and genetic enhancement.

2.4 The disability rights community

Since the very beginning of humankind, people with impairments have suffered from extreme social disadvantages in their nation states and communities and sometimes even in their own families. They have been shunned, socially and politically excluded, systematically denied education and employment (Gordon 2013), and at times, purposefully eliminated in national eugenics programs (e.g. in Nazi Germany). The ways in which nonimpaired people have treated (and continue to treat) persons with impairments throughout history[9] are deeply embedded in the collective consciousness of the disability community (e.g. Amundson and Tresky 2008, 113). This is why members of the disability community are, by nature, suspicious concerning so-called developments in medicine, such as the prominence of the concept of autonomy among bioethicists. Their suspicion is particularly strong in cases of end-of-life decision making or of people in permanent vegetative states or with severe impairments. As the important disability scholar Adrienne Asch (2001, 301) has stated, people with impairments are deeply concerned about the most vital issues of their "right to life" and about ensuring that society acknowledges their existence as legitimate and valuable.

The history of disability groups is a history of the total neglect of its members and their experienced injustices. Until the last few decades, there was no real progress in terms of recognizing a moral and legal right that universally protects the minority group of the disability community. In 2006, the United Nations adopted the Convention on the Rights of Persons with Disabilities, a legal milestone that provides human-rights protection for people with impairments by demanding that their member states grant them complete social, political, cultural, and economic inclusion (not integration!) in their particular societies. This is a great success and represents significant progress for disability rights – the culmination of a journey from social exclusion and denial to segregation, integration, and finally full inclusion.

9 For a brief but solid overview of the history of the disability rights community, see Ouellette (2013, 15–29).

The old and deeply felt concerns, existential fears, and feelings of neglect and worthlessness (e.g. "useless eaters") present among members of the disability community are regularly provoked by scholars who adhere to the dominant bioethical theories of utilitarianism and deontology. In brief, for many disability activists and scholars, utilitarianism is viewed as the "ethics of death," synonymous with devaluing and even questioning the right to life of people with impairments (e.g. the Singer debate and most recently the lively debate in the *Journal of Medical Ethics* concerning the contribution by Giubilini and Minerva on infanticide in 2012). Deontological approaches that adhere to the Kantian line of reasoning are commonly seen as major threats to the right to life of people with severe mental impairments, as without rationality there is no (human) personhood and hence no moral status; this stance, members of the disability rights community fear, could become a slippery slope leading to active euthanasia for people with mental impairments.

However, the well-known and influential disability scholar Tom Shakespeare (2006) offers a different voice, arguing for active physician-assisted suicide for people with impairments as a reasonable expression of individual self-determination in some rare cases. Furthermore, he approves the practice of prenatal genetic diagnosis and selective abortion, and he claims – contrary to the vast majority of members of the disability community – that these practices are not necessarily directed against people with impairments. Shakespeare's positions demonstrate that the disability rights community is not monolithic in its beliefs, but his is certainly an outlying view.

We can now understand clearly why the relationship between bioethicists and members of the disability rights community is complex and problematic. It is mainly characterized by distrust on both sides and an unwillingness to fully engage with the opposite perspective. Whether this first impression will remain is the topic of the next section, where the conflicting views of both groups are placed alongside each other in a concise way.

2.5 Conflicting views: Mapping the landscape

Given the different concepts and prevailing biases of both groups, as well as the substantial fears of members of the disability rights community, it seems rather unlikely that both camps share a common ground of understanding. This picture of sharp disagreement becomes even clearer when we study the critical reception of a book that is commonly seen as articulating the mainstream bioethics perspective: *From Chance to Choice: Genetics and Justice* (2000), written by the well-known bioethicists Allen Buchanan, Dan W. Brock, Norman Daniels, and Daniel Wikler. In two substantial and well-argued papers, Amundson and Tresky (2007, 2008) critically examine the bioethical perspective on people with impairments, and they show convincingly the currently unbridgeable gap between the two standpoints. The following nonexhaustive general overview of positions in the debate between bioethicists, on the one hand, and disability scholars and activists within the disability rights community, on the other hand, shows the deep-rooted divide between the two parties.

Bioethics	*Disability Rights Community (DRC)*
Medical model of disability.	Social model of disability. People with impairments are "normal" in the sense that the impairment is a "human variation" (e.g. the deaf community).
Right to self-determination for everyone, including people with severe impairments, also in cases of physician-assisted suicide (so long as this does not contain any discrimination against people with impairments).	The notion of autonomy as the gold standard of decision making in medical ethics is a dangerous and misleading development (e.g. surrogate decision making in end-of-life cases).
The DRC is wrong when it claims that bioethicists want to contest the right to life of persons with impairments by promoting individual informed consent, nor are bioethicists seeking thereby to infringe on the rights of persons with impairments in cases of end-of-life decision making (i.e. the objection is an exaggeration or misreading of bioethicists' intent).	The DRC members are deeply afraid of views that assign personhood and hence moral status according to the capability to reason because it is seen as depriving them of the right to life (e.g. the Singer debate).
Quality of life is a reasonable standard by which to determine a patient's overall happiness (justifying the use of concepts such as "wrongful life").	Many bioethicists (aka utilitarians) wrongly believe that the lives of people with serious impairments are less valuable and that their quality of life is low.
The DRC members are too sensitive or squeamish. Debates in academia should be rather neutral in tone and should not become emotional.	Many bioethicists – either intentionally or unintentionally – use humiliating language and provide derogatory examples. The substantial worries and deep concerns of the DRC are not taken seriously by bioethicists (e.g. fears based on historical events that reach back to the Nazi regime and eugenics programs conducted in Germany and the United States).
Many activists and scholars within the DRC lack conceptual clarity and analytical depth (e.g. with regard to the concept of personhood).	Today, disability scholars are, academically speaking, as proficient as their colleagues in bioethics.
The DRC is not a real civil rights movement.	The DRC is a legitimate civil rights movement comparable to the civil rights movements of gays, African Americans, and women.
The DRC has a deep-rooted prejudice against bioethics (viewing it as the "ethics of death").	Confrontation instead of reconciliation.

3. On the possibility of overcoming the divide: Autonomy and personhood

Alicia Ouellette has suggested establishing a disability-conscious bioethics, which can be seen as "a loose framework for bioethical debate that incorporates disability as a central issue and engages disability experts in the enterprise of bioethics" (2013, 333).

However, according to her, this requires "bioethicists, policy makers, and health care professionals to engage the work of disability scholars and participate in civil discourse with disability experts" (2013, 5). Indeed, her contribution is important in terms of facilitating a "cross-disciplinary conversation and study" (2013, 5), but one may doubt whether the underlying idea throughout her book – that only bioethicists should be expected to change in order to bridge the gap between the two groups – is ultimately convincing.

In this section, I present another way of resolving the major conflict between bioethicists and members of the disability rights community in order to pave the way for a mediating approach and provide a fresh start for a new conversation. The core question is whether one can do "bioethics" without adhering to the concept of personhood as the prerequisite for assigning moral status – and hence the right to life – to people. It seems crystal clear that debates between both camps often focus on personhood and the opposing ways in which this notion is depicted. In his paper "The Difference That Difference Makes: Bioethics and the Challenge of 'Disability'" (2004), Tom Koch shows the different perspectives of bioethics (by referring to Peter Singer) and the disability rights community (by referring to Harriet McBryde Johnson) on the notion of personhood. Whereas most bioethicists identify the capabilities of autonomous decision making, self-determination, and independence of action as establishing that a human being possesses "personhood," disability scholars and activists instead take a relational or communal approach to personhood that is not necessarily reciprocal and does not include rational decision making as the most decisive component (i.e. "caring humanity").

The two differing notions of personhood are mutually exclusive by nature and do not allow for a common ground for argumentation. Furthermore, the idea of moral status, and hence the right to life, is linked to each particular notion. Therefore, it is impossible that the two opposing perspectives can share a common basis for resolving important issues, such as end-of-life decision making (including surrogate decision making), prenatal genetic diagnosis and selective abortion, or the status of people in permanent vegetative states or with severe mental impairments. Is there any way out of this complex philosophical cul-de-sac? I think there is, and I would like to suggest three possible steps toward a more disability-conscious bioethics that is committed to mutual listening and understanding as well as to acknowledging the various fears and biases of people in the debates (see also Ouellette 2013). I do not claim, however, that the following steps are sufficient in order to fully guarantee a common ground for argumentation, nor do I claim that this is the only way to do so. Rather, I propose that these steps embody a promising start toward a mediating approach between the opposing perspectives that could overcome the so-called civil war between them.

3.1 Unlinking personhood and moral status

The very idea of linking moral status to the notion of personhood might be misleading. According to many disability scholars and activists, this notion opens the door for determining that it is morally acceptable to cause death in cases where patients lack autonomy (i.e. surrogate decision making) or where, based on their individual informed consent and severity of impairment, they have a valid claim to be euthanized. Disability scholars and activists believe that this linkage undermines their right to life and establishes a slippery slope that will affect how people with severe impairments are viewed by nonimpaired people – namely, as persons who should have been aborted in the first place.[10] This idea, according to members of the disability rights community, eventually leads to active euthanasia in cases of impaired people who may not want to die (e.g. wrongful life, genetic prevention and eugenics, human enhancement, and so on).

Given the history of society's treatment of disabilities and the existential fears of people with impairments, it seems reasonable to decouple moral status from personhood. The main consequence of such a decoupling for members of the disability community is that they would no longer have to fear that bioethicists (even if unintentionally) would be establishing a justification for involuntary euthanasia of people with impairments. Whether this decoupling rules out any request to obtain physician-assisted suicide is more questionable because to do so would also require denying the same request by nonimpaired people. A slightly different approach might propose that nonimpaired people may request physician-assisted suicide but that people with impairments, or perhaps only those with severe impairments, may not. Shakespeare (2006) has argued against this view, considering it a form of discrimination against people with impairments. As noted earlier, he claims that, in some rare cases, one should allow active physician-assisted suicide for people with impairments as a reasonable expression of their individual self-determination (2006).

In brief, scholars and activists of both camps may continue to use their particular notion of personhood while observing the pragmatic solution under which the linkage of moral status with personhood is not permitted. Still, both groups should also find a *joint* cross-disciplinary solution to allow for active physician-assisted suicide in some rare cases in order to avoid inhumane suffering.[11]

10 Tom Koch (2004, 708) cites McBryde Johnson (2003, 50), who claims that Singer "insists that he doesn't want to kill me . . . he simply thinks it would have been better, all things considered, to have given my parents the option of killing the baby I was, and to let other persons kill similar babies as they come along and thereby avoid suffering that comes with lives like mine and to satisfy the reasonable preferences of parents for a different kind of child." However, Dan Brock has argued that it is possible to respect persons with severe impairments and, at the same time, to practice prenatal genetic diagnosis and selective abortion in cases where the future child might be impaired (Brock 1995, 2005). Whether his arguments are convincing, of course, is a matter of debate.

11 Ouellette has described a convincing case in which "the patient's family and doctors submitted evidence that, although providing nutrition and hydration would extend her life, the treatment was medically inappropriate. The woman's body was no longer able to digest or metabolize caloric intake. As a result, her body bloated; her organs deteriorated; her skin stretched to the point where it fell off; and her condition made pain relief impossible. The doctors documented the patient's excruciating journey toward death in her medical chart. They argued that applying the law as written was morally wrong, even inhumane" (Ouellette 2013, 2). For more detail, see Alicia Ouellette (2004).

3.2 Avoiding extreme positions

In order to achieve viable and long-lasting cross-disciplinary solutions, one must avoid extreme perspectives and seek a common ground as a basis for discussion. It is impossible to find such a common ground between, for example, Singer's standpoint on abortion and infanticide and the perspective of the disability activists of Not Dead Yet. A pragmatic solution requires that both sides abstain from extreme positions and allow for a viable compromise. This may not necessarily do justice to the scientific truth of the matter at hand, but it will further communication on complex and seemingly unresolvable moral issues (see Shakespeare 2006).

3.3 Unfolding the perspectives: I-, you-, and third-person perspectives

One of the main topics that regularly come to the fore in debates involving disability issues concerns the differing ways of reasoning that prevail in the academic disciplines. In bioethics, scholars usually adhere to the so-called third-person perspective – that is, the impersonal way of talking about issues by adhering only to the scientific truth of the matter at hand. In contrast, disability scholars and activists commonly broaden the academic horizon by taking the first- or second-person perspective – that is, the I and You dimensions – into account. This broadening of the academic horizon by including external standpoints is an important and valuable source of information.

For example, if someone happens to have an impairment and experiences the pros and cons of his or her impairment first-hand (the I perspective), then it seems likely that this person may arrive at different conclusions from those of someone looking at the same thing impersonally. The same is true if a person's offspring has an impairment (the You perspective), as, in most cases, this experience within one's own family substantially changes the way in which one views impairments. People taking an I perspective or a You perspective can be expected to answer questions on such issues as whether people with (severe) impairments have a right to life in a way very different from the impersonal, third-person perspective of academic debates. Bioethicists who are personally unfamiliar with issues involving impairments most likely lack additional valuable and important information that is needed in order to make a well-informed decision.

In making this claim, however, I do not propose the stronger assertion that disability scholars and activists or other people who happen to have an impairment are, by virtue of their privileged position, the *only* people who have the legitimate right to discuss these issues. Rather, I suggest that bioethicists who have no personal history of impairments should make themselves more familiar with what it truly means to have an impairment and to use this enlightened or enhanced standpoint to refine their bioethical expertise (see Brody 2004).[12] Without a doubt, one necessary feature of good ethical reasoning and decision making is to be able to put oneself in the shoes of

12 http://dredf.org/public-policy/assisted-suicide/a-bioethicist-offers-an-apology/. See also Ouellette (2013, 256–257).

another person in order to activate one's own compassion with regard to other people in complex cases, particularly bioethical cases. This is a precondition for making morally adequate and sensitive decisions.

4. Conclusions

A common ground for argumentation could be reached if bioethicists share a minimum standard of understanding with disability scholars and activists. In this chapter, I have highlighted the main differences between both groups and suggested a way to bridge the gap between the opponents. I do not claim that this is the only way to bridge the gap, but it is my hope that this might be a good start toward revising former perspectives and arriving at new and more promising positions that could resolve the complex issues involving impairments.

5. References

Altman, Matthew C. 2011. "Animal Suffering and Moral Character." In *Kant and Applied Ethics: The Uses and Limits of Kant's Practical Philosophy*, edited by Matthew C. Altman, 13–37. Oxford: Wiley-Blackwell.

Amundson, Ron and Shari Tresky. 2007. "On a Bioethical Challenge to Disability Rights." *Journal of Medicine and Philosophy* 32(6), 541–561.

———. 2008. "Bioethics and Disability Rights: Conflicting Values and Perspectives." *Journal of Bioethical Inquiry* 5(2/3), 111–123.

Asch, Adrienne. 2001. "Disability, Bioethics and Human Rights." In *Handbook of Disability Studies*, edited by Gary L. Albrecht, Katherine D. Seelman, and Michael Bury, 297–326. London: Sage.

Beauchamp, Tom L. 2009. "The Concept of Paternalism in Biomedical Ethics." *Jahrbuch für Wissenschaft und Ethik* 14(1), 77–92.

Beauchamp, Tom L. and James F. Childress. 1979. *Principles of Biomedical Ethics.* New York: Oxford University Press.

Brock, Dan W. 1995. "The Non-Identity Problem and Genetic Harms – The Case of Wrongful Handicaps." *Bioethics* 9(3), 269–275.

———. 2005. "Preventing Genetically Transmitted Disabilities While Respecting Persons with Disability." In *Quality of Life and Human Difference: Genetic Testing, Health Care, and Disability*, edited by David Wassermann, Jerome Bickenbach, and Robert Wachbroit, 67–100. New York: Cambridge University Press.

Brody, Howard. 2004. "A Bioethicist Offers an Apology." http://dredf.org/public-policy/assisted-suicide/a-bioethicist-offers-an-apology/.

Buchanan, Allen, Dan W. Brock, Norman Daniels, and Daniel Wikler. 2000. *From Chance to Choice: Genetics and Justice.* Cambridge: Cambridge University Press.

Faden, Ruth R. and Tom L. Beauchamp. 1986. *The History and Theory of Informed Consent.* New York: Oxford University Press.

Giubilini, Alberto and Francesca Minerva. 2012. "After-Birth Abortion: Why Should the Baby Live?" *Journal of Medical Ethics* 39(5), 261–263.

Gordon, John-Stewart. 2012. "Bioethics." *Internet Encyclopedia of Philosophy.* http://www.iep.utm.edu/bioethic/.

———. 2013. "Medical Paternalism and Patient Autonomy." In *Medical Ethics*, edited by Michael Boylan, 72–83. Oxford: Wiley-Blackwell.

Koch, Tom. 2004. "The Difference That Difference Makes: Bioethics and the Challenge of 'Disability.'" *Journal of Medicine and Philosophy* 29(6), 697–716.

Kuczewski, Mark and Kristi Kirschner. 2003. "Special Issue: Bioethics and Disability." *Theoretical Medicine* 24, 455–458.

McBryde Johnson, H. 2003. "Unspeakable conversations: Or, how I spent one day as a token cripple at Princeton University." *New York Times Magazine* 50–55, 74–79.

Ouellette, Alicia. 2004. "When Vitalism Is Dead Wrong: The Discrimination Against and Torture of Incompetent Patients by Compulsory Life-Sustaining Treatment." *Indiana Law Journal* 79(1), 1–55.

———. 2013. *Bioethics and Disability: Toward a Disability-Conscious Bioethics.* Cambridge: Cambridge University Press.

Shakespeare, Tom. 2006. *Disability Rights and Wrongs.* London: Routledge.

Trials of War Criminals Before the Nuremberg Military Tribunals under Control Council Law. 1949. "The Nuremberg Code." https://history.nih.gov/research/downloads/nuremberg.pdf.

World Medical Association. 1964. "The Declaration of Helsinki – Ethical Principles for Medical Research Involving Human Subjects." http://www.wma.net/en/30publications/10policies/b3/index.html.

3 Theology, disability, and human rights

Difficult past, promising future

Johann-Christian Põder

1. Introduction

In this chapter,[1] I would like to contemplate the discussion of disability in modern theology while also asking about the role of human rights in this discourse. The methodological focus of the treatment – that should also help reduce complexity of this topic – is on identification of different concepts of disability entailed and described in different theological discussions. The presentation is divided into three parts. In the first part, I will provide a brief outline of those theological concepts of disability that have become, in modern theology, objects of criticism and of attempts to replace them with more adequate interpretations. In the second part, I will examine three theological interpretations of disability that, in my opinion, reflect the three different experiential dimensions of disability that must be taken into account (discrimination, normalcy/gift, and deficit). In the final part, I will establish a link between the preceding discussion and the issue of human rights, also touching on the theory of justice associated with human "capabilities" according to Martha Nussbaum.

2. Theology and disability: Difficult past

In the introduction to the collection *Disability in the Christian Tradition*, Brian Brock and John Swinton emphasize the need to learn about and explain both the negative and the positive aspects of the Christian tradition in connection with disability. Knowledge of these aspects, which have caused and facilitated stigmatization and marginalization of persons with disabilities, helps to fend off any discriminating tendencies in the modern church. Furthermore, these aspects, which have helped nurture, appreciate, and include persons with disabilities, could make an important contribution to today's theological and nontheological debates about disability (Brock and Swinton 2012, 4–5). Indeed, the church and theology have had a complex past, which includes both negative and positive elements, in connection with disability. This ambivalence does not arise solely from the historical contexts of the church's past and the predominant beliefs of those

1 This chapter is part of the research project *Global Bioethics. Human Rights and Disability*, funded by the Hermann and Marianne Straniak Foundation and the Research Centre "Shaping the Future" (FoKoS), University of Siegen.

periods but, to a great extent, also from the multiplicity of views expressed in the normative canonical texts of Christianity. This multiplicity includes several interpretation patterns, which are problematic for an understanding of disability but have played an important role in the history of the church and theology. One of the main characteristic traits, which is shared by most modern theological concepts of disability, is an attempt to criticize and reject those theologically problematic interpretation patterns.

First, we could mention the interpretation of disability as a punishment from God. This explanation, which, according to Manfred Oeming is "classical" and almost "reflex-like" (Oeming 2014, 98), has been very influential in the church tradition, having roots in both the Old and the New Testament. This is based on the so-called principles of action and consequences, which understand disability as a punishment for human sin as well as a reflection of God's wrath, damnation, and absence (Oeming 2011, 81–84). An example pars pro toto could be Deut 28:28f: "The Lord will afflict you with madness, blindness, and confusion of mind; you shall grope about at noon as blind people grope in darkness, but you shall be unable to find your way." God's absence could also be seen as being possessed by demons, especially in instances of mental disabilities. In any case, according to this interpretation pattern, disability resulted in forceful marginalization and stigmatization of a person, effectively isolation from society. A disabled person was regarded as impure and unfit for any ritual duties or participation in community life in general. Such a person was associated with sin, shame, and lack of faith. The spirit of the interpretation, which links disability with sin and punishment, is poignantly summarized in an Arabian proverb from a later period: "If you see a blind man, run up and kick him. Why should you be kinder than his Creator?" (Oeming 2011, 82; trans. by A. Helstein).

Another questionable interpretation sees disability as God's gracious choice and a test, a divine method of cleansing and education on the way to the heavenly reward. Nancy Eiesland calls this a concept of "virtuous suffering" and refers among other examples to Paul's description of the "thorn in the flesh" (2 Cor 12, 7–10), which Paul could ultimately be happy about, seeing this as a sign of special qualifications for following Jesus. However, interpreting disability as a graceful choice and test is problematic in several respects, especially when it is used as an "objective explanation" but also in cases of personal interpretation. Religious elevation of disability means that many socially unfair situations associated with it almost receive a divine seal of approval. This makes it unnecessary to speak up for elimination of social inequality – discrimination and social exclusion (Eiesland 1994, 72–73; Eurich 2008, 343–344). Most importantly, however, both concepts of disability – as a punishment or as a divine test and path to salvation – entail a problematic, non-Christian view of God ("punishing, vengeful God," "God as a proponent of 'dark education'" (Fischer 2011, 58)).

Third, we could mention a motif, which could seem utterly positive at first sight: this is the biblically rooted practice of charitable donations and care bestowed on disabled and other marginalized persons, originating from love for one's neighbor. Since early Christianity, the church has treated the issue of helping those in socially weaker positions with particular attention and responsibility, caring for the poor and the sick, building hospitals and nursing homes. The human care, medical assistance, and financial support involved should not be underestimated (Eiesland 1994, 73). However, the charitable work of the church and Christians has often been combined with a paternalistic stance, which has the unintended result of making disabled persons objects of charity without facilitating their social and religious inclusion and autonomous development. In this way, even Christian care efforts have reinforced and supported segregating beliefs and practices.

In view of the outlined problematic interpretations and their consequences, Johannes Eurich and Andreas Lob-Hüdepohl, editors of the series "Disability – Theology – Church, Contributions to Diaconal Caritative Disability Studies," published since 2011, point out that the history of the church and theology has been dominated in connection with disability "by Christian traditions, which have been rather more damaging than liberating" (Eurich and Lob-Hüdepohl 2011, 7; trans. by A. Helstein). A similarly critical assessment is expressed in one of the most important inter-confessional documents discussing persons with disabilities – namely, the interim statement "A Church of All and for All" by the World Council of Churches: "Rather, churches have generally followed the trends in society, often with distinct reluctance. Conservative structures in the churches, often related to the churches' own charitable institutions, have enforced old ways of interpreting disability. Theological ideas, like that linking disability and divine punishment for sins, remain evident in every part of the world" (World Council of Churches 2003, § 12).[2]

Indeed, the increasing focus and contemplation on disability in theology and in the church is not the result of the pioneering initiative of theology itself but is largely linked with developments outside theology. Particularly important in this context are the influences of disability studies, which have paradigmatically emphasized the significance of the social dimension in understanding disability. In disability studies, disability is understood primarily as a social construct, associated with dominant negative, discriminating social attitudes and practices, irrespective of whether the argument is based on a "criticism of normalization" or a model of individual and human rights of minority groups.[3] The first approach deconstructs the dominant stigmatizing "normalcy" in society, emphasizing and valuing instead human differences and diversity. The second approach starts from visible injustice, discrimination, and inequality, which connects many diverse marginalized minority groups as a shared experience and characteristic trait (Kuhlmann 2011, 37–39; Swinton 2011, 280). In both approaches, the problem is not seen in the individual, physical, or mental situation ("deficit") of persons with disabilities but in a disabling and discriminating society, which needs cultural, social, and political change and renewal.

The influence of both of these disability studies approaches can also be seen in the aforementioned document of the World Council of Churches, for example. Highlighting the social-constructivist dimension of disability has motivated churches to become more decisive in reviewing the former interpretations, which focused on individual deficit (disability as God's punishment or test), and to work toward new, more adequate theological interpretations. This does not mean that a theological contemplation on

2 A revised version of this document is presently in work.

3 I take up here a distinction made by sociologist Andreas Kuhlmann (Kuhlmann 2011, 39). The "criticism of normalization" must be distinguished from the "principle of normalization" as a guideline for special education.

disability should or could simply adopt the ideas of disability studies without further thought. In addition, there are several theological concepts of disability that do not rely on disability studies and their assumptions.[4] However, changed social consciousness and practice in relation to disability urge theology to return to biblical texts and central beliefs of Christianity (creation, incarnation, Christian love and hope) in order to provide a more sensitive theological elaboration of the concept of disability as well as of the empowering, inclusive, and supportive potentials of Christian faith in connection with persons with disabilities. This is associated with a desire and hope to enrich – or, if necessary, adjust – the modern discussion of disability. This chapter is an attempt to take a closer look at such an endeavor, with a particular focus on the concept of justice.

3. Theological efforts at rethinking disability: Three examples

For the sake of systematic generalization, theological concepts of disability – even though they are sometimes overlapping – can be classified on the basis of three points of emphasis: (1) disability as sinful discrimination, (2) disability as a normal and positive situation of God's creation, and (3) disability as a negative situation of creation, not contingent on the human being. In the following, I will elaborate on these three approaches using as examples the discussions of disability by Nancy Eiesland, Deborah Beth Creamer and Stanley Hauerwas, and Günter Thomas. The attention is on the question of how these concepts can be associated with the modern language of rights and equality and of the role of care and love in them.

3.1 Disability: Sinful sociopolitical discrimination

Nancy Eiesland's influential book *The Disabled God* was published in 1994 and has become one of the classic texts dealing with disability from a theological perspective. Eiesland's goal was to establish a productive link between the experiences and ideas of the disability rights movement and theological thought, thereby creating preconditions for changing the situation of disabled persons in the church as well. She relies on the minority group/civil rights model of disability, seeing disability primarily as a sociopolitical situation, a result of social injustice and discrimination (Eiesland 1994, 62). Persons with disabilities are not brought together by some essentialist definition of disability but rather through a shared, emancipatory fight for liberation, equal rights, and recognition.

As mentioned earlier, Eiesland believes that such a fight is needed in the church as well. She writes, "Rather than being a structure for empowerment, the church has more often supported the societal structures and attitudes that have treated people with disabilities as objects of pity and paternalism" (20). According to Eiesland, this situation can be changed through reconceptualization of the main religious symbols of Christianity. The symbols that have facilitated discriminating beliefs and practices ("disabling theology")

4 Particularly in German theology, the breakthrough associated with disability studies has not yet occurred or is still in progress (Eurich 2008, 238).

must be replaced with empowering and liberating symbols. In its most central aspect, this pertains to the symbolic depiction of God, which in Christianity is crucially associated with Jesus Christ. In Eiesland's interpretation, the God incarnate in Jesus Christ is the disabled God. This idea is based on her personal epiphany of the "disabled God" in a meeting with a disabled person but also on the testimony in the Gospel of Luke, in which resurrected Jesus shows disciples his hands and feet, injured in crucifixion:

> Here is the resurrected Christ making good on the incarnational proclamation that God would be with us, embodied as we are, incorporating the fullness of human contingency and ordinary life into God. In presenting his impaired hands and feet to his startled friends, the resurrected Jesus is revealed as the disabled God. (100)

According to Eiesland, the idea of the disabled God entails a revolutionary understanding that our unconventional, impaired bodies are indeed the symbols of new integrity and perfection. Disability reflects our being in the image of God: "Our bodies participate in the imago Dei, not in spite of our impairments and contingencies, but through them" (101). As a consequence, this leads to a criticism of all forms of theology, which view disability through notions of individual defect or limitation, including the aforementioned approaches, associating disability with sin and punishment or divine test and virtuous suffering.

For Eiesland, the empowering symbol of disabled God and the resulting new model of integrity also means fundamental criticism of the charity approach. In her opinion, many churches continue to view disability from the perspective of benevolence and goodwill instead of justice and equality (67), thereby injecting self-pity in persons with disabilities, supporting the stereotypes of weakness and helplessness associated with disability, and sanctioning "dependency as an appropriate Christian virtue" (93). While Eiesland's criticism of the paternalistic malformations of charity and care is accurate, it also highlights one of the problems of her liberation theological concept: her focus on liberation, independence, self-representation and civil rights, and equal and full participation in society loses sight of those persons with disabilities who can never participate in such goals and experiences. For instance, it is questionable if the emphasis on independence, rights, and equality, or approaching disability as a minority group issue, can include persons with profound intellectual disabilities. In this connection, John Swinton aptly points out, "What if we *are* weak, dependent, vulnerable and helpless?" (Swinton 2011, 286); italic in original. Would we in this situation not need, in addition to the notion of rights, also – rightly understood, nonpatronizing – notions of care, friendship, and love?

3.2 Disability: Neutral or even good variability of a limited and dependent creation

A different approach to countering theologically problematic interpretations, such as divine punishment or test – while also attempting to overcome certain experiential narrowness of the medical and minority models – can be found in theological concepts, which regard disability as something essentially linked with universal and fundamental limitedness and dependence of human existence. However, limitedness and dependency should not be understood as a deficit or tragedy but as a natural – even good – situation of God's creation. For example, Deborah Creamer writes, "When understood as part of what it means to be human, limits are no longer something to be overcome in search of perfection or something which is experienced as punishment for sins" (Creamer 2009, 33). She also sees a problem in the binary logic (disabled/not disabled) of the medical and minority model and tries to take into account the fluidity of the experience of disability and the naturalness and variability of human limitedness. Limits are an "unsurprising aspect" (111) of being human, and disability is nothing extraordinary; in fact, it is "more normal than any other state of embodiment" (32).

Similarly, Stanley Hauerwas emphasizes that persons with disabilities – even, for instance, those with a profound intellectual disability – are nothing abnormal or extraordinary. Instead, they are a reflection of our own true nature:

> As Christians we know we have not been created to be "our own authors", to be autonomous. We are creatures. Dependency, not autonomy, is one of the ontological characteristics of our lives. That we are creatures, moreover is but a reminder that we are created with and for one another. . . . We are not created to be alone. . . . That the mentally handicapped are constituted by narratives they have not chosen simply reveals the character of our lives.
>
> (Hauerwas 2004a, 16)

Creamer and Hauerwas do not see limitedness and dependency as a deficit but as expressions of the diversity and goodness of God's creation. In contrast to the "tyranny of normalcy," which dominates the modern period and is defined through independence, power, and rationality, we should be able to appreciate and accept "the gift of difference" (Hauerwas 2004b, 40). The differences associated with boundaries are "gifts" that are essential for the existence of a good and healthy community.[5]

According to Creamer and Hauerwas, limitations and dependency are not only characteristics of human createdness but also aspects of God. Christian faith does not see God as a transcendent "self-sufficient power" but as perfection, which is defined through dependency, giving and receiving, loving neediness, and relatedness. Hauerwas can, in this context, also use the metaphor of the "disabled God" because God is dependency and love. However – unlike Eiesland's theologically problematic approach – his notion is not based on human experience of disability but on a genuinely Christian understanding of God as trinity (Hauerwas 2004c, 104; Swinton 2011, 297).

What role is played in such a position by the modern notion of rights, and what is the significance of care and love? Creamer would like to see the minority model with its emphasis on independence and empowerment and her own limits-based approach as

5 For this reason, Creamer also uses the term "gifts" model to describe her "limits" model of disability (Creamer 2009, 95).

complementary or supplementary options, without a detailed elaboration of the relationship between the two. Hauerwas, however, is explicitly and programmatically critical about the values of modernity (independence, individuality, rationality, choice, etc.) and the liberal policy of justice and equality. Consequently, he does not focus on the participation of Christians in the promotion of and debate about social justice but instead on the church as the genuine community of mutual love and dependency. Only such a community – not a language of rights – can be actually inclusive, encompassing in a truly human manner also persons with profound intellectual disabilities.

3.3 Disability: Risky and negative side of God's good creation

While Eiesland relies on the minority model and Creamer/Hauerwas have some overlaps with the perspective of normalcy criticism in its emphasis on diversity (without committing itself to the social model of disability), Günter Thomas, professor of systematic theology at the Ruhr University of Bochum, considers primarily the medical model of disability. He agrees with Creamer and Hauerwas that God's good creation is characterized by ontological dependency and limitedness, but in his opinion, it would be incorrect to treat disability as a reality, which is good and in accordance with God's will. Disability is, rather, the risky and negative side of God's good creation. God's creation is an open, dynamic, and experimental process, which is good but not unsurpassable, requiring correction, improvement, and minimization of risks. God's creation is not fully determined; it also entails creative and open evolutionary processes, with the inevitably associated risks, threats, diseases, and disabilities.

Consequently, it would be incorrect to regard the negative side of disability as God's punishment or test. Thomas emphasizes that the healing acts of Jesus are a symbolic revelation of God's "aversion" (*Widerwille*) to inherent risks of creation, including disability (Thomas 2014, 82–85).[6] These acts express the hope of God's "new creation," which also means a transformation of natural living conditions. Even God suffers because of the risks and limitations, which are harmful for life, and for that reason, they become the place of God's special care, loving, and comforting presence. God is not "disabled," but in caring "aversion" to disability, God "is siding with life to the utmost degree" (85).[7]

What is the relationship between the language of rights and the language of love according to Thomas? Whereas Eiesland only operated with rights and Hauerwas only with love in his critical rejection of modernity, Thomas believes that both are important for his concept of disability. However, for Thomas as well, the fundamental framework is provided by Christian love. Christians are called to participate in the compassionate, loving care of God (87). A loving orientation toward persons with disabilities can be expressed both in personal closeness and in care and support as well as in efforts to change natural and cultural/social processes of life. The latter also means, for instance,

6 This naturally also applies to any discriminating sociocultural conditions associated with disability.
7 Cf. critically against Eiesland's "disabled God" ibid, note 40.

improvement of medical, social, and legal conditions. Consequently, Thomas believes that it is important for us to be consistent in translating the language of love into the language of rights to accomplish a "transformation of compassion into justice" (90).

However, the same perspective also provides grounds for being critical about the language of rights, especially when it is overemphasized. For instance, the language of rights can include ideological tendencies, and it must be corrected with the realism of love, which sees the actual needs of persons with disabilities. For instance, any concepts and policies of inclusion should not generate new exclusion by losing sight of persons with profound multiple or intellectual disabilities. Furthermore, legal regulations can be prone to rapid erosion if they are not supported by an ethos of compassion, which focuses on the aspect of deficit (94).

4. Theology and disability in relation to human rights and theories of justice

As can be seen from this review, there is a plurality of theological concepts of disability. Disability can be seen in the context of sinful discrimination, a natural and good diversity of God's creation, or a risky and negative side of God's creation. However, all of these approaches are united in rejecting the previous interpretations, which saw disability as God's punishment or test. Discrimination, difference, and deficiency reflect the often strenuous, or even contradictory, experiential complexity of life, which poses a major challenge for any theological conceptualization of disability. In order to meet this challenge, we need a critical dialogue with biblical texts and nontheological approaches to disability (disability studies, bioethics, philosophical anthropology, etc.).

A similar diversity can be seen among the ideas about the relationship between rights and love in connection with theological concepts of disability. Obviously, this is to a greater or lesser extent linked to the underlying concept of disability. Inspired by the disability rights movement and the minority model, some approaches focus exclusively on the language of rights (Eiesland). There are other approaches, which are characterized by a dynamic similar to the feminist care ethics:[8] they assume fundamental dependency, limitedness, and vulnerability of the human being and focus on such asymmetric relations as love, compassion, and selfless care (Hauerwas). Similarly, Thomas's deficit-oriented model also emphasizes the primacy and importance of love and compassion but assumes an inseparable and critically constructive co-dynamic of love and rights.[9] Some might argue in this context that the perspective, which considers the aspect of deficit – and not the emphasis on the difference and gift (see Creamer and Hauerwas) – seems to be best equipped for mobilizing loving care and justifying any legal regulations required for ensuring special assistance (cf. Kuhlmann 2011, 42–43).

A sensitive and productive combination of the language of rights and the language of love seems indeed a correct and adequate path to take. Love has primacy from the

8 Cf., for example, the works of Eva Feder Kittay, especially Kittay (1999).

9 Such inseparable co-dynamics of love and rights also characterize the position of J. Swinton, who does not operate with the experience of deficiency but combines the perspectives of discrimination (Eiesland) and dependency/gift (Hauerwas); cf. Swinton (2011).

theological perspective: the fundamental starting point is realization of the divine love – ἀγάπη – in the world, both in direct personal interaction and in social arrangements. However, direct realization of love in social arrangements is not possible; it can only be accomplished through social and legal development of society. Consequently, the language of love needs to be translated into the language of rights. A just society should ensure realization of love to a maximum extent possible. Love has at least five important functions in relation to the language of rights: (1) protect and promote human rights, (2) participate in social debate on justice, (3) contribute to the creation of legal regulations, (4) serve continuously as a corrective force in relation to the language of rights, and (5) act as an emotional/cultural foundation of the language of rights. In the following, I will briefly discuss the first two functions. However, as we saw earlier, we can find in disability theology fundamental criticism of the charity concept of disability, pointing to the discriminating and patronizing effects of love and compassion on people with disabilities. In a last step, I will therefore focus specifically on this issue.

4.1 Theology, disability, and human rights

As was the case with disability, Christianity has a complex and ambivalent history with human rights. On the one hand, human rights are rooted in Christianity, in the ideas of human beings being created in the image of God and of Christian freedom. However, in addition to the influence of Christianity, the genesis of human rights was affected by many other factors, especially the natural law traditions of Hellenistic and Roman stoicism. While the church's response to human rights was positive in America due to the influence of Christian humanism, the churches were opposed to human rights in Europe due to the sharply anti-Christian spirit of the French Revolution. Human rights were seen as emancipation from God, immoral individualism. This attitude was finally broken only as a result of the experience with twentieth-century totalitarian regimes and World War II. Today, churches and inter-church organizations and fellowships are important global defenders and promoters of human rights. This breakthrough reflects an understanding that love requires clear human rights principles and agreements in order to be realized in society. They help to ensure the protection of human dignity in a sinful world where love is always bound to be only a fragile and fragmented reality. The goal should be legal codification of the moral postulates or pre-legal norms of human rights to a maximum extent possible.

A defense of human rights on the basis of love also includes disability-related human rights. For instance, despite being critical about potential exclusive tendencies of the pursuit of empowerment,[10] Thomas observes in connection with the UN Convention on the Rights of Persons with Disabilities (CRPD),

> The idea of inclusion, which supersedes integration, undoubtedly increases sensibility towards questionable distancing and separation strategies in connection with

10 Cf. similar criticism by Eurich (2008, 264): "In the shadow of the successes of the *empowerment* movement, one also needs to consider the situation of the non-empowered people with disabilities" (trans. by A. Helstein; italic in original).

> disabled persons and provocatively opens up new moral horizons. The transposition of the UN Convention in German law marks an important next step in transforming the ethos of compassion into justice.
>
> (Thomas 2014, 90; trans. by A. Helstein)

While the CRPD is characterized by an emancipatory orientation to autonomy and self-determination, one of its key concepts is the idea of *assisted* autonomy, which entails a social dimension and provides a relevant – non-autarchic, non-individualistic – interpretation of the notion of autonomy as a whole.[11] The previous critical opinions of the churches about human rights were abandoned partially also because of the fact that, in addition to individual negative rights, modern human rights include positive rights (economic, social, and cultural rights), which set the focus on facilitating the necessary conditions of good life. The main ideas of human rights – liberty, equality, and participation – should be seen in a mutual and constructive relationship. Consequently, despite some critical questions, Christian love can regard the CRPD as a realization of its expectation that society should ensure equal treatment, in particular, of those who need special assistance and care.

4.2 Theology, disability, and theories of justice

The practical consequences of the main concepts of human rights and the CRPD (such as dignity, freedom, inclusion) for particular social and ethical issues and situations are not immediately clear. A theory of justice is required in order to make well-considered and justifiable decisions. The situation is similar with Christian love. It provides the guiding idea for justice – the well-being of others – but does not say more precisely what the specific regulations of a just society should look like. Therefore, by protecting and promoting human rights, Christian love needs to work on a theory of justice. This can be done adequately only in a critical and productive dialogue with nontheological theories of justice. For instance, theological ethics has been in active dialogue with various theories of justice from Aristotle to Rawls. A notable recent trend is that alongside Rawls (cf. Andersen 1996, 2010; Bedford-Strohm 1993; Huber 1996) there has emerged the increasingly popular capabilities approach, associated in particular with Martha Nussbaum, which also deals specifically with disability issues (cf. Dabrock 2012; Eurich 2008).

The reason for this popularity seems to be an understanding that relying on the capabilities approach is more productive in translating love into justice than Rawls's theory of justice as fairness and its principle of difference. Rawls focuses on equal

11 Cf. Bielefeld (2011) and especially Graumann (2011). The CRPD is certainly an outstanding achievement of the empowerment movement and its ideals. One can therefore question whether this socially, or intersubjectively, oriented interpretation of the CRPD really does harmonize with the ideals of the activists and initiators behind the CRPD text. However, the possibility of this kind of productive reading of the CRPD, not centered on individual autonomy, of course makes it more sympathetic and accessible to those who are skeptical about the ideals and values of the empowerment movement.

distribution of "primary goods" but disregards different needs and capabilities of different persons, which are necessary for using the benefits and for good and dignified human life. This perspective is particularly relevant in connection with persons with disabilities. Nussbaum is generally critical of Rawls's contractualism, which operates with "normal and fully cooperating" citizens (Nussbaum 2007, 98, 111).[12] She emphasizes – as does, for instance, MacIntyre in his book *Dependent Rational Animal* (1999) and many proponents of feminist ethics – the asymmetric nature of human relations and the fundamental dependency, neediness, and vulnerability of human beings. Persons with disabilities are represented here also as paradigmatic models, and the recognition of their humanity and dignity is a test case for a sound theory of justice and for a just society.

These and some other elements – for instance, combining human dignity, care, and a list of capabilities – resonate strongly with intentionality of love, which is oriented toward a particular person with his or her specific situation, needs, and capabilities. Compassionate love steps up with particular intensity for those who are vulnerable and dependent in society. This includes especially those persons with disabilities, whose lives are fundamentally characterized by asymmetric relations. Due to this convergence, the capabilities approach seems suitable for theological reformulation as a theory of justice, the substantial rationality of which is based on love.

4.3 *Which starting point is better: Love or justice?*

As noted in the previous discussion, we can meet in disability theology a fundamental criticism of love as being patronizing and (re)producing discrimination and social segregation, irrespective of its undeniable benefits (personal care, medical and financial help provided by charitable institutions). This criticism is especially powerful because it reflects a social and cultural change that may be called a paradigm shift from "disability policy of charity to a policy of human rights,"[13] crystallized and culminating exactly in the CRPD. From the perspective of many activists and promoters of this shift, the concept of charity prevailing until recently understands people with disabilities as "objects" of care, pity, and compassion, not as "subjects" with full and equal rights. It regards people with disabilities as passive receivers of voluntary help and care, who are expected to be grateful and subordinate and to accept all (patronizing) decisions that pedagogical or medical experts consider as beneficial for their well-being (Graumann 2011, 8). Human rights policy, in contrast, sees people with disabilities as not dependent on voluntary care and goodwill. It addresses the need for special assistance in the framework of antidiscrimination and equal rights, emphasizing the autonomous choice and self-determination of people with disabilities. The influence and effect of this paradigm

12 "It is clear, however, that such theories must handle severe mental impairments and related disabilities as an afterthought, after the basic institutions of society are already designed. Thus, in effect, people with mental impairments are not among those for whom and in reciprocity with whom society's basic institutions are structured" (Nussbaum 2007, 98).

13 From the title of Graumann (2011).

shift is reflected, for example, in the interim statement "A Church of All and for All" by the World Council of Churches:

> When new understandings of disabilities emerge in society, traditional theological interpretations are challenged. In some churches, this has raised awareness that people with disabilities were not seen as equal. In many churches, traditional ways of treating people with disabilities were then perceived as oppressive and discriminatory, and actions towards people with disabilities moved from "charity" to recognition of their human rights.
>
> (World Council of Churches 2003, § 17)

At the same time, for Christian ethics, the fundamental starting point is the realization of divine love in the world.[14] Why exactly love and not justice? Love is an intention that encompasses and guides the entirety of our lives, an aspiration to live for another person. Love is characterized by asymmetry – it does not seek benefit or expect favors in return. It is a heart- and eye-opening sensitivity to another person's distress and particular situation. Love tries to identify and perform actions that would support and improve a fellow human being, considering the individual situation and the actual needs. Love entails the largest possible opportunity and power "to do justice" to his humanity (Lange 2002, 459; cf. Härle 2011, 390). Danish theologian and philosopher Knud E. Løgstrup has described this special position of love as follows:

> Why does care of the other person's life require love? . . . Because love alone corresponds to the fact that something of the other person's life is delivered over to us. Only love is able to measure up to the demands of this fact. A person runs a risk in having a part of his or her life depend upon us. And because our life is temporal, if we fail him or her – that is, if instead of caring of him or her we exploit his or her dependence upon us – the damage is irreparable. Only love can hope to avert this risk.
>
> (Løgstrup 1997, 143)

Subverting the aforementioned criticism, true love is never patronizing or oppressive. Indeed, being oriented to the well-being of another, it attempts to create an opportunity for the other person to live as an independent, free, and responsible person as far as possible. Similarly, loving care is not aimed at increasing dependency or control over another human being, but instead, it tries to support and facilitate the life opportunities of the other person in any way possible, including the person's ability for independent coping and decision making.

Consequently, despite the criticism of the charity concept, Christian ethics still has every reason to take love as its starting point. However, this also means being critically

14 Accordingly, love is seen in the Bible as the greatest commandment (cf. Mark 12, 30–31: " 'You shall love the Lord your God with all your heart, and with all your soul, and with all your mind, and with all your strength.' The second is this, 'You shall love your neighbour as yourself.' There is no other commandment greater than these").

sensitive to any patronizing and objectifying malformations of love and understanding that defending another person's well-being and dignity entails, in particular, standing up for justice and rights. Indeed, persons with disabilities should not be dependent on voluntary charity and care in society (while these continue to play an important role in personal interaction and as a form of social solidarity) but should be treated fairly, which means that their rights have to be protected. The advantage of starting with love is, from the Christian perspective, the possibility to approach justice from the position of consideration for the well-being and particular needs and situations of fellow human beings. Love serves as the guiding principle and eye-opening inspiration for justice while also providing continuous incentive and motivation.

How should we, in this light, evaluate the philosophical positions that deal only with justice or arrive at love from the position of justice? In principle, it is valid to state that any efforts to promote justice are extremely important and valuable from the perspective of love. Love needs justice! The guiding principle of love does not prescribe the exact content of the rules of justice (including legal norms) in the particular complex and conflicting reality of society. Human reason should be employed for that purpose – in a common dialogue with the existing philosophical theories of justice. Modern liberal theories of justice tend to be silent about love or avoid this issue. There may be several reasons for that: love has been thought of as an irrational impulse or emotion that belongs to the private sphere and has no relevance for the debate on a just society. There have also been fears that an emphasis on love would prescribe a particular way of (good) life, which would be incompatible with such liberal ideas and premises as freedom and autonomy.[15] This does not mean that love has nothing to learn about justice from these theories. However, it could be said that love is particularly close to those theories in which it is most recognizable. Love needs justice – but justice also needs love! Being "recognizable" does not mean that the theory of justice should focus explicitly on the phenomenon of love. For instance, proponents of theological ethics have identified Rawls's theory, particularly its difference principle, as an example of a concept of justice that is in agreement with the notion of love (cf. Andersen 1996; Bedford-Strohm 1993). A strong resonance with and connection to love can also be found in the role of care as described in Nussbaum's theory of justice. Care is linked with a list of capabilities,[16] which makes it fundamentally significant for justice: "We understand the need of care in times of acute or asymmetrical dependency as among the primary needs of citizens, the fulfilment of which, up to a suitable level, will be one of the hallmarks of a decently just society" (Nussbaum 2007, 168).

Nussbaum has explicitly discussed the relevance of love for justice in her recent book *Political Emotions: Why Love Matters for Justice* (2013). Here, she emphasises the role

15 "Liberal political philosophers sensed that prescribing any particular type of emotional cultivation might easily involve limits on free speech and other steps incompatible with liberal ideas of freedom and autonomy" (Nussbaum 2013, 4).

16 According to Nussbaum, love itself is also a capability that should be taken into account in a theory of justice (Nussbaum 2007, 76–77).

of love as an emotional force that supports, motivates, and energizes justice.[17] Love is also characterized by a cognitive dimension – an "imaginative engagement" with the life and situations of other persons, which improves the ability to identify injustice.[18] In this way, Nussbaum has started with justice and ended up with love. However, it seems true that theories that start from justice can at best regard love as something indispensable but still as having only a supplementary and supporting role. Conversely, a thought process that starts from love tries to see love as the overarching guiding principle and internal rationality of justice.

5. Theology and disability: Promising future

Theology and disability have a complex and ambivalent past with intertwining negative and positive ideas, which have accordingly influenced social practices. Only a few decades ago, disability was not a genuine part of theological reflection, being at best discussed only to concretize or exemplify other subject matters. Today, disability theology has developed into a rather significant element of theological discourse. An observation of this theology reveals a plurality of concepts as well as convergences and controversies. They function in a dialogue with nontheological models, human rights, and theories of justice. Based on the intensity and existential involvement of theological reflection, theology and disability seem to have a promising future. This could give us hope that we no longer need to talk about *disabling theology* – like Nancy Eiesland – and instead theology will be able to see disability as part of its genuine calling to be an *enabling theology*, which is inspirational and liberating and opens up new horizons.

6. References

Andersen, Svend. 1996. "Retfærdighed." In *Verbum Dei – verba Ecclesiae: Festskrift til Erik Kyndal i Anledning af 65 års Fødselsdagen den 24. August 1995*, edited by Theodor Jørgensen and Peter Widmann, 113–127. Aarhus: Det Teologiske Fakultet.

———. 2010. *Macht aus Liebe: zur Rekonstruktion einer lutherischen Politischen Ethik*. Berlin/New York: Walter de Gruyter.

Bedford-Strohm, Heinrich. 1993. *Vorrang fur die Armen: Auf dem Weg zu einer theologischen Theorie der Gerechtigkeit*. Gütersloh: Chr. Kaiser.

Bielefeldt, Heiner. 2011. "Inklusion als Menschenrechtsprinzip: Perspektiven der UN-Behindertenkonvention." In *Inklusive Kirche*, edited by Johannes Eurich and Andreas Lob-Hüdepohl, 64–79. Stuttgart: Kohlhammer.

Brock, Brian and John Swinton. 2012. "Introduction: Disability and the Quest for the Human." In *Disability in the Christian Tradition: A Reader*, edited by Brian Brock and John Swinton, 1–23. Grand Rapids, MI: Eerdmans.

17 "The idea is, instead, that the public culture cannot be tepid and passionless, if good principles and institutions are to survive: it must have enough episodes of inclusive love . . . that people's attitudes to one another and the nation they inhabit are not mere dead routine" (Nussbaum 2013, 320).

18 "The type of imaginative engagement society needs . . . is nourished by love. Love, then, matters for justice – especially when justice is incomplete and an aspiration (as in all real nations), but even in an achieved society of human beings, were such to exist" (Nussbaum 2013, 380).

Creamer, Deborah Beth. 2009. *Disability and Christian Theology: Embodied Limits and Constructive Possibilities.* Oxford: Oxford University Press.

Dabrock, Peter. 2012. *Befähigungsgerechtigkeit. Ein Grundkonzept konkreter Ethik in fundamentaltheologischer Perspektive.* Gütersloh: Gütersloher Verlagshaus.

Eiesland, Nancy. 1994. *The Disabled God: Toward a Liberatory Theology of Disability.* Nashville: Abingdon Press.

Eurich, Johannes. 2008. *Gerechtigkeit für Menschen mit Behinderun: Ethische Reflexionen und sozialpolitische Perspektiven.* Frankfurt/New York: Campus Verlag.

Eurich, Johann and Andreas Lob-Hüdepohl. 2011. "Vorwort der Herausgeber." In *Inklusive Kirche*, edited by Johannes Eurich and Andreas Lob-Hüdepohl, 7–8. Stuttgart: Kohlhammer.

Fischer, Johannes. 2011. "Krankheit und Sinn: Zur religiösen Wahrnehmung von Krankheit und ihren ethischen Implikationen." *Ethik in der Medizin* 23, 53–61.

Graumann, Sigrid. 2011. *Assistierte Freiheit: Von einer Behindertenpolitik der Wohltätigkeit zu einer Politik der Menschenrechte.* Frankfurt/New York: Campus Verlag.

Härle, Wilfried. 2011. *Ethik.* Berlin/New York: Walter de Gruyter.

Hauerwas, Stanley. 2004a. "Timeful Friends: Living with the Handicapped." In *Critical Reflections on Stanley Hauerwas' Theology of Disability*, edited by John Swinton, 11–25. Binghamton, NY: Haworth Press.

———. 2004b. "Community and Diversity: The Tyranny of Normality." In *Critical Reflections on Stanley Hauerwas' Theology of Disability*, edited by John Swinton, 37–43. Binghamton, NY: Haworth Press.

———. 2004c. "Suffering the Retarded: Should We Prevent Retardation?" In *Critical Reflections on Stanley Hauerwas' Theology of Disability*, edited by John Swinton, 87–106. Binghamton, NY: Haworth Press.

Huber, Wolfgang. 1996. *Gerechtigkeit und Recht: Grundlagen einer christlichen Rechtsethik.* Gütersloh: Chr. Kaiser.

Kittay, Eva Feder. 1999. *Love's Labor: Essays on Women, Equality, and Dependency.* New York: Routledge.

Kuhlmann, Andreas. 2011. "Behinderung und die Anerkennung von Differenz." In *An der Grenzen unserer Lebensform. Texte zur Bioethik und Anthropologie*, edited by Andreas Kuhlmann, 37–50. Frankfurt/New York: Campus Verlag.

Lange, Dietz. 2002. *Ethik in evangelischer Perspektive.* Göttingen: Vandenhoeck & Ruprecht.

Løgstrup, Knud Ejler. 1997. *The Ethical Demand.* Edited and translated by Alasdair MacIntyre and Hans Fink. Notre Dame/London: University of Notre Dame Press.

MacIntyre, Alasdair. 1999. *Dependent Rational Animals: Why Human Beings Need the Virtues.* London: Duckworth.

Nussbaum, Martha. 2007. *Frontiers of Justice: Disability, Nationality, Species Membership.* Cambridge, MA: Harvard University Press.

———. 2013. *Political Emotions: Why Love Matters for Justice.* Cambridge, MA: Harvard University Press.

Oeming, Manfred. 2011. "'Auge wurde ich dem Blinden, und Fuß dem Lahmen war ich!' (Hi 29,15). Zum theologischen Umgang mit Behinderung im Alten Testament." In *Inklusive Kirche*, edited by Johannes Eurich and Andreas Lob-Hüdepohl, 81–100. Stuttgart: Kohlhammer.

———. 2014. "Behinderung als Strafe? Zum biblisch fundierten seelsorgerlichen Umgang mit dem Tun-Ergehen-Zusammenhang." In *Behinderung – Profile inklusiver Theologie, Diakonie und Kirche*, edited by Johannes Eurich and Andreas Lob-Hüdepohl, 98–126. Stuttgart: Kohlhammer.

Swinton, John. 2011. "Who Is the God We Worship? Theologies of Disability; Challenges and New Possibilities." *International Journal of Practical Theology* 14, 273–307.

Thomas, Günter. 2014. "Behinderung als Teil der guten Schöpfung Gottes? Fragen und Beobachtungen im Kontext der Inklusionsdebatte." In *Behinderung – Profile inklusiver*

Theologie, Diakonie und Kirche, edited by Johannes Eurich and Andreas Lob-Hüdepohl, 67–97. Stuttgart: Kohlhammer.

United Nations. 2007. "Convention on the Rights of Persons with Disabilities." http://www.un.org/disabilities/convention/conventionfull.shtml.

World Council of Churches. 2003. "A Church of All and for All – An Interim Statement." http://www.oikoumene.org/en/resources/documents/wcc-commissions/faith-and-order commission/ix-other-study-processes/a-church-of-all-and-for-all-an-interim-statement.

This chapter is translated from Estonian by Alar Helstein.

Part II

Human development and inclusion

4 Grounding disability and human rights with the capabilities approach

Christopher A. Riddle

1. Introduction

In what follows, I will not argue that individuals have a human right to be healthy or to the absence of disabling barriers. Instead, I intend to assume this is the case, at least to a minimal degree, and instead suggest that if people do have a human right to some level of health or absence of disabling barriers, then the capabilities approach to justice is *the* conception of justice that ought to be used to support this claim.

2. The capabilities approach to justice

Nobel Prize laureate Amartya Sen first articulated the capabilities approach in his 1979 Tanner Lecture on Human Values titled "Equality of What?" In that lecture, he suggested that a focus on the possession of goods or resources was inadequate for the purpose of examinations of justice (Sen 1995, 328). Going further, he accused Rawls of "goods fetishism" – of taking goods to be the embodiment of advantage (Sen 1995, 326). Instead, what really mattered – what a conception of justice ought to focus on – was what people could do or be as a result of possessing the goods or resources Rawls and other resource theorists placed such great importance on. More pointedly, Sen stated, "The conversion of goods to capabilities varies from person to person substantially, and the equality of the former may still be far from the equality of the latter" (Sen 1995, 329).

Because it is often the case that the basic cost to live is increased for people with disabilities, any adequate or just distribution of resources should account for what people are actually capable of doing with the resources at their disposal. A focus solely on goods ignores the various conversation factors that influence what people are capable of becoming or doing.

In technical terms, the primary focus of a conception of justice ought to be individuals' capability to function. To elaborate further, the capabilities approach has two primary components. First, "functionings" are end states or things and/or activities that people have a choice between. Second, a "capability" is a functioning over which an individual has a choice. If functionings are properly regarded as various doings or beings – as end states – then capabilities ought to be regarded as the opportunities to secure those functionings. When one secures or realizes a capability, a functioning emerges. Therefore, one's capability set should be regarded as the set of opportunities one has to choose between various alternative states of being or lives.

Martha Nussbaum has suggested that "one way of thinking about the capabilities list is to think of it as embodied in a list of constitutional guarantees" (Nussbaum 2006, 155). In other words, one's capability set is the set of *substantial freedoms* available to pursue or realize.

In Nussbaum's early conceptualizations of the capabilities approach, she defended what would eventually become her list of basic capabilities through an appeal to a criterion of what it meant, in her mind, to be "truly human" (Nussbaum 1990, 219). Here, we can begin to see connections between the capabilities approach and the notion of human rights.

The capabilities approach is also premised upon an understanding of justice as one that requires people to possess a set of basic material conditions required to live a life worthy of human dignity (Nussbaum 2006, 74). Dignity is also a notion often defended by human rights scholars as being a cornerstone of basic justice.

Through questioning what is required to live a life worthy of human dignity, Nussbaum arrived at her list of ten basic capabilities:

1 *Life.* Being able to live to the end of a human life of normal length; not dying prematurely, or before one's life is so reduced as to be not worth living.
2 *Bodily Health.* Being able to have good health, including reproductive health; to be adequately nourished; to have adequate shelter.
3 *Bodily Integrity.* Being able to move freely from place to place; to be secure against violent assault, including sexual assault and domestic violence; having opportunities for sexual satisfaction and for choice in matters of reproduction.
4 *Senses, Imagination, and Thought.* Being able to use the senses, to imagine, think, and reason – and to do these things in a "truly human" way, a way informed and cultivated by an adequate education, including, but by no means limited to, literacy and basic mathematical and scientific training. Being able to use imagination and thought in connection with experiencing and producing works and events of one's own choice, religious, literary, musical, and so forth. Being able to use one's mind in ways protected by guarantees of freedom of expression with respect to both political and artistic speech, and freedom of religious exercise. Being able to have pleasurable experiences and to avoid nonbeneficial pain.
5 *Emotions.* Being able to have attachments to things and people outside ourselves; to love those who love and care for us, to grieve at their absence; in general, to love, to grieve, to experience longing, gratitude, and justified anger. Not having one's emotional development blighted by fear and anxiety. (Supporting this capability means supporting forms of human association that can be shown to be crucial in their development.)
6 *Practical Reason.* Being able to form a conception of the good and to engage in critical reflection about the planning of one's life. (This entails protection for the liberty of conscience and religious observance.)

7 *Affiliation.*

A Being able to live with and toward others, to recognize and show concern for other human beings, to engage in various forms of social interaction; to be able to imagine the situation of another. (Protecting this capability means protecting institutions that constitute and nourish such forms of affiliation, and also protecting the freedom of assembly and political speech.)

B Having the social bases of self-respect and nonhumiliation; being able to be treated as a dignified being whose worth is equal to that of others. This entails provisions of nondiscrimination on the basis of race, sex, sexual orientation, ethnicity, caste, religion, national origin.

8 *Other Species.* Being able to live with concern for and in relation to animals, plants, and the world of nature.

9 *Play.* Being able to laugh, to play, to enjoy recreational activities.

10 *Control over One's Environment.*

A *Political.* Being able to participate effectively in political choices that govern one's life; having the right of political participation, protections of free speech and association.

B *Material.* Being able to hold property (both land and movable goods), and having property rights on an equal basis with others; having the right to seek employment on an equal basis with others; having the freedom from unwarranted search and seizure. In work, being able to work as a human being, exercising practical reason and entering into meaningful relationships of mutual recognition with other workers (Nussbaum 2006, 76–78).

Some of these capabilities, or "constitutional guarantees" as Nussbaum has alternatively referred to them, or perhaps even "substantial freedoms" as Sen has described them, might look remarkably similar to some things mentioned in human rights discourse.

3. Human rights

In what follows, I suggest that human rights ought to be thought of as a subset of rights or freedoms guaranteed under a conception of justice. In other words, not all things that people are owed as a matter of justice are human rights, but all human rights are owed as a matter of justice.

This point is what muddies the water when we begin to discuss whether health or the absence of disabling barriers is a human right. Very few people would argue that people are not owed, as a matter of justice, some means to be healthy, but some people feel comfortable arguing that such means are not properly regarded as human rights.

This matter aside, if it is indeed the case that human rights exist as a subset of what is owed to people as a matter of justice, then the conception of justice endorsed must be compatible with both the types of human rights being guaranteed to individuals and the conceptualization of what and why this subset of rights is considered human rights.

Sen perhaps stated it best when he distinguished capabilities from human rights by claiming that capabilities do not necessarily have a "conceptual connection to government that human rights clearly do" (Nussbaum 2011, 64). Or in other words, human rights are rights that the government ought to guarantee, while there are other, perhaps less fundamental rights, that it may not be under the purview of the state to afford to its citizens. Sen has further distinguished capabilities from human rights, stating that capabilities are broader "because capabilities can include matters of procedure (whether one is able to engage in a certain sort of process) whereas rights are always matters of substantive opportunity (what one is actually able to have)" (Nussbaum 2011, 67). This claim seems to be consistent with the thought that human rights exist as a special kind of rights under an umbrella notion of justice.

Nussbaum also suggests that capabilities are broader than human rights because "some capabilities are trivial, and some are even bad" (Nussbaum 2011, 67). She asserts that the capabilities approach "supplements the standard human rights model" (Nussbaum 2011, 65).

To call something supplementary seems to, at first glance, relegate it to a less important role, but this need not be the case. I interpret her claim to be that it simultaneously supplements and encompasses the human rights model – it includes all that is within such a model and expands upon it. This too seems consistent with my claim. We typically do not view human rights to be trivial rights. Nonetheless, we can feel that something of a trivial nature might be owed to someone as a matter of justice. This suggests that human rights are not only a subset of justice-based obligations but also rights that are of special import.

Grace Kao articulates what she means by human rights by claiming she is following convention when she states that human rights are

> the set of entitlements and justified claims that every human being has simply by virtue of being human, independent of anything else that might follow as a result of national citizenship, social status or differentiation, individual accomplishments or lack thereof, or specific speech acts and transactions with others. So understood, we should regard human rights as a special class of moral rights that would ideally be recognized in, and protected by, the law and other institutions. Like other kinds of rights, we should also conceive of human rights as having prima facie priority over social goals or collectivist ends.
>
> (Kao 2011, 9)

In short, there appears to be support to suggest that a reasonable interpretation of rights considers human rights to be a special class of justice-based obligations. Therefore, we have to formulate a conception of justice that corresponds with the human rights we wish to guarantee to individuals. As such, I take the capabilities approach, as articulated earlier, to be the approach to justice we ought to endorse to support the claim that health and disability are human rights issues.

From this observation, a question emerges: What does a conception of justice have to do to support a human rights framework for health and disability? I take it to be the case that any conception of justice that is to serve as a foundation for human rights claims needs to promote at least three values: (1) equality, (2) dignity, and (3) autonomy. I derive this understanding of human rights and justice from a brief, almost passing remark, made in the World Health Organization's 2011 *World Report on Disability*. The authors mention an argument made by Gerard Quinn that suggests that disability is a human rights issue because:

- People with disabilities experience inequalities – for example, when they are denied equal access to health care, employment, education, or political participation because of their disability.
- People with disabilities are subject to violations of dignity – for example, when they are subjected to violence, abuse, prejudice, or disrespect because of their disability.
- Some people with disability are denied autonomy – for example, when they are subjected to involuntary sterilization, or when they are confined in institutions against their will, or when they are regarded as legally incompetent because of their disability.[1]

If this is why disability is a human rights issue, then our foundational conception of justice must be capable of promoting (1) equality, (2) human dignity, and (3) autonomy. I take the capabilities approach to be the best conception of justice to do so.

4. Equality

Perhaps obviously, at the heart of the capabilities approach sits the concept of equality. After all, Sen's famous lecture mentioned at the outset of this chapter is titled "The Equality of What?" It is a fantastic question: Yes, "equality," indeed, but what do we aim to equalize? Sen (as well as many others) asserts that not all forms of equality equalize as effectively as others. The capabilities approach, I suggest, promotes equality to a much greater extent than other leading forms of egalitarian justice.

The equalizing of resources has been a prime candidate as an alternate answer to the question "Equality of what?" for some time. There are, of course, more or less robust conceptions of resource egalitarianism. Of those conceptions of "The Equality of Resources" at our disposal, there is consensus that John Rawls's work in *A Theory of Justice* is perhaps the most influential resource theory from which all contemporary egalitarian debates are derived. The main thrust of Rawls's resourcism begins with a thought experiment designed "to rule out those principles that it would be rational to propose for acceptance, however little the chance of success, only if one knew certain things that are irrelevant from the standpoint of justice" (Rawls 1971, 18). As an example, Rawls believed that if a man knew he was wealthy, then self-interest might influence the sorts of decisions he might make when attempting to formulate principles of justice to benefit upper-class individuals such as himself. Rawls's thought experiment,

1 World Health Organization, *World Report on Disability* (Geneva: World Health Organization 2011), 9.

however, places an individual in a hypothetical position, deprived of most information about oneself so as to prevent partiality. Rawls attempts to have individuals "define principles of justice as those which rational persons concerned to advance their interests would consent to as equals when none are known to be advantaged or disadvantaged by social and natural contingencies" (Rawls 1971, 19).

The most interesting fundamental principles that emerge from such a position are, at least for our present purposes, principles concerning the distribution of, and emphasis on, all-purpose means and resources.

Sen was concerned with such an emphasis on resources because he viewed such conceptions of justice as guilty of taking "little note of the diversity of human beings" (Sen 1995, 325). Ultimately, Sen believed that resource theories may very well promote justice if people were relatively similar. However, Sen stresses just how different individuals are and suggests that several factors contribute to the differences among individuals in society as well as, and perhaps most importantly, the varying needs associated with those differences: "health, climate conditions, location, work conditions, temperament, and even body size (affecting food and clothing requirements)" (Sen 1995, 325). It is because of this failure to take seriously the differences among individuals that resource-based theories of justice fail to account for the variety of ways in which disadvantage is experienced by people with disabilities.

Sen's accusation that Rawls and other resource-based theorists are guilty of fetishizing goods is a striking attack motivated by this observation. He accuses Rawls of taking "primary goods as the embodiment of advantage, rather than taking advantage to be a relationship between persons and goods" (Sen 1995, 326). Sen suggests that

> primary goods suffers from a fetishistic handicap in being concerned with goods, and even though the list of goods is specified in a broad and inclusive way, encompassing rights, liberties, opportunities, income, wealth, and the social basis of self-respect, it still is concerned with good things rather than with what these good things *do* to human beings.
>
> (Sen 1995, 328)

More pointedly, Sen suggests that our conception of justice needs to shift focus away from the goods or resources that resource theorists tend to fetishize and instead focus on what resources do to human beings or what human beings can do with these goods.

Thus, if the presence of inequality in the lives of the disabled serves as a justification for disability to be considered a human rights issue, then our foundational conception of justice needs to promote the most robust notion of equality possible. If we acknowledge the claim that inequality exists in the lives of people with disabilities because they are denied access to health care, employment, education, or political participation because of their disabilities, then simply situating all persons similarly with respect to resources does little to remedy this inequality. Instead, a shift in focus to what individuals are capable of doing with the resources provided to them – a shift to asking if people with disabilities not only have equal resources but also equal opportunities with the resources they have to access health care, to have meaningful employment opportunities, to gain an enriching education, or to shape their political environment – appears to promote a far more equitable society.

5. Dignity

If we acknowledge that not only are people with disabilities experiencing inequality as a result of their disabilities but also that they are subject to violations of dignity when they are exposed to violence, abuse, prejudice, or disrespect, and that this, too, justifies viewing disability as a human rights issue, then at the heart of our conception of justice must also be a commitment to the promotion of human dignity.

"Human dignity," writes Nussbaum, "is equal in all who are agents" (Nussbaum 2011, 31). Nussbaum focuses primarily on institutional and legal denials of dignity when she argues that "the primary target of a theory of egalitarian justice ought to be the protection of freedoms so central that without them, an individual's life is not worthy of human dignity" (Nussbaum 2011, 31). She suggests that dignity and respect ought to be central in the formulation and articulation of a conception of social justice.

Foundational to the capabilities approach is a commitment to the promotion of dignity. It is indeed where the central capabilities are derived from. Nussbaum contends that without access to all central capabilities, irrespective of how well one secures all remaining capabilities, it is a failure of basic justice (Riddle 2010, 528). A failure to secure Nussbaum's minimal conception of justice constitutes an affront to one's human dignity. Nussbaum argues that, in her version of the capabilities approach, she "focuses on the protection of areas of freedom so central that their removal makes a life not worthy of human dignity" (Nussbaum 2011, 31).

There are some who suggest that the promotion of dignity is not a prime virtue of the capabilities approach and that perhaps the contrary may be true. It might be possible that the capabilities approach subjects individuals to violations of dignity. These people acknowledge the importance of dignity but suggest that the capabilities approach is not the proper means to ensure it.

Importantly, we must acknowledge that the emphasis of this critique is not on the substantive components of the capabilities approach itself but instead on the undesirable effects of the operationalization of the capabilities approach. More pointedly, the claim being made is that the capabilities approach stigmatizes individuals in "both the assessment of need, and provision of resources and accommodation, thus undermining an essential aspect of one's human dignity" (Riddle 2013, 270).

Thomas Pogge suggested that by reorienting our conception of justice toward what goods do to and for individuals and not the goods themselves, the capabilities approach introduces what he calls the vertical-inequality problem.[2]

When one aims to shape institutional arrangements in an attempt to compensate for natural inequalities in skills and endowments, Pogge concludes that capability theorists are committed to making interpersonal comparisons of individuals and are forced to

2 I have referred to this elsewhere as stigma sensitivity. See Riddle (2013, 271).

make assessments of humans beings as being better or worse than others (Pogge 2002, 204–205).

When our conception of justice forces us to assess whether individuals have less or more of a particular endowment, and to situate individuals on a vertical spectrum, Pogge claims that we become committed to viewing diversity hierarchically (Pogge 2002, 205–206).

Conversely, because resource theorists such as Rawls make no such compensatory guarantees, they are not committed to viewing diversity in hierarchical terms and are thus not committed to assigning value to difference. Pogge suggests that this allows resource theorists to value diversity and to situate difference on a horizontal spectrum (Pogge 2002, 204–205).

He claims that the capabilities theorist undermines "the shared public sense that human natural diversity *overall* is horizontal" (Pogge 2002, 205). When capability theorists affirm that institutions ought to favor a redistribution to particular people because of a lack of natural endowments, an implicit judgment is passed that suggests that the difference in natural endowment ought to be regarded not solely as a difference but as a difference that is inferior to the norm or others' differences. Furthermore, Pogge suggests that not only is the capabilities theorist committed to the view that one is worse in respect to a particular capability but also that this deficit makes that individual worse overall (Pogge 2002, 206). Pogge makes the further claim that the judgment being made about individuals is not simply one of personal preference but that it is instead a judgment made from a position of overlapping consensus – from a shared public criterion (Pogge 2002, 206).

Pogge makes a concession and suggests that while a concern for those with less natural endowments may very well be noble in intent, by returning to thinking about diversity in terms of a natural hierarchy, we are reverting to thinking about disability and diversity in a manner that constitutes a significant social loss (Pogge 2002, 206).

I have suggested elsewhere that

> in an important way, we can relate this to discussions about the proper allocation of blame for disability or inability. The argument Pogge is making suggests that blame for one's disability will be put back upon the individual under the capabilities framework, instead of on society, as social model proponents fought so hard to achieve during the early stages of the disability rights movement.
>
> (Riddle 2014, 65)

Understandably, if such a claim were true, then such a formulation of justice would be far from one that promotes dignity – the capabilities approach would fail to be an adequate conception of justice to support disability as a human rights issue.

That said, Elizabeth Anderson rejects Pogge's critical remarks and in so doing suggests that the primary difference (for our purposes) between resource theorists and capability theorists "lies rather in the degree to which their principles of justice are sensitive to internal individual differences, and environmental features and social norms that interact with these differences" (Anderson 2010, 87).

In other words, resourcism seeks to establish an institution to provide standardized packages or bundles of goods or resources to serve all individuals in achieving desired ends.

In contrast to this, Anderson suggests that capability theorists deny the notion of a standardized package and instead call on society to alter these packages based on individual endowments to ensure that no individual is unfairly disadvantaged by requiring the input of greater resources to reach similar end states or functionings. She claims that the capabilities approach adjusts resources "to that person's individual ability to convert resources into relevant functionings, and sensitive to environmental factors and social norms that also affect individuals' conversion abilities" (Anderson 2010, 87). She suggests that for any conception of justice to be regarded as one that promotes dignity, it must have "sensitivity to variations in the abilities of individuals to convert resources into functionings, which may be affected by internal variations, environmental features, and prevailing social norms" (Anderson 2010, 87) – to do otherwise is to treat each individual as identical.

In highlighting the main tenets of each theory, Anderson hopes that it becomes apparent that Pogge's argument relies on a mischaracterization of the capabilities approach. She claims that Pogge is in error to conclude that the capability theorist attributes "the blame for shortfalls in equal functioning to individuals' innate endowments" (Anderson 2010, 96).

Quite contrary to Pogge's inference, Anderson suggests that capability theorists view a person's capabilities in a much more holistic manner, comprised of many factors that contribute to the securing, or failure to secure, any given capability.

Anderson suggests that when we view capabilities as a "joint product of her internal endowments, her external resources, and the social and physical environment in which she lives" (Anderson 2010, 96), we can begin to acknowledge that disadvantage from difference need not reside (solely or partly) in the individual but can instead originate in social, legal, environmental, and attitudinal factors.

Capability theorists are not wed to the position that a lack of a natural endowment is either in itself grounds to warrant compensation or reason to devalue an individual. Instead, the idea of a capability and the various conversion factors that influence its realization (or ability to be realized)[3] involves a complex assessment of how that lack of natural endowment manifests itself in society.

Therefore, unlike Pogge's claim, capability theorists are not committed to a vertical viewing of natural endowments, and thus, the promotion of dignity that sits at the heart of the capabilities approach is not compromised.

6. Autonomy

Finally, if people with disabilities are denied autonomy, and this denial is part of what prompts us to view disability as a human rights issue, then our conception of justice ought to promote autonomy. Perhaps obviously, many conceptions of justice can be

3 For more on how conversion factors relate to capabilities, see Robeyns (2005, 99).

said to value freedom. A Nozickian notion of justice, for example, values freedom and autonomy, but I would argue, fails drastically in the other realms.

It is important not to lose sight of the fact that dignity and autonomy are closely related. George Kateb suggests that the promotion of human dignity is linked to autonomy because so much of the value of dignity derives itself from how it relates to uniqueness and how humans value unique experiences (Kateb 2011, 17–18).

Nussbaum is insistent that part of what it means to live a life worthy of human dignity involves autonomy. It involves the capabilities approach being resolutely pluralistic about value (Nussbaum 2011, 18). Standing steadfast, Nussbaum denies that functionings should be the proper target of our justice-based concerns – that we should be concerned with the ends people achieve. Instead, she stands firm in her claim that what matters for justice is the opportunity to secure that valuable end. She addresses health explicitly and states that some political views deny her claim and "hold that the right thing for government to do is to make people lead healthy lives, do worthwhile activities, exercise religion, and so on" (Nussbaum 2011, 25). In other words, while she may be a philosophical perfectionist, she is a state neutralist.

Nussbaum claims that "capabilities, not functionings, are the appropriate political goals, because room is thereby left for the exercise of human freedom" (Nussbaum 2011, 25). She argues that there is a "huge moral difference between a policy that promotes health and one that promotes health capabilities – the latter, not the former, honors the person's lifestyle choices" (Nussbaum 2011, 26).

In fact, the only concession Nussbaum grants to this assertion is that people cannot make choices in one realm. Government should "not give people an option to be treated with respect and nonhumiliation" (Nussbaum 2011, 26) – to be treated with dignity.

7. Concluding remarks

What I have done here has been modest. I have not argued that disability is a human rights issue. I have instead assumed this to be the case. I have made a modest attempt to suggest that, when properly viewed, human rights should be regarded as a subset of justice-based obligations, and as such, we need a foundational conception of justice that corresponds to our arguments concerning human rights, disability, and health. I explored why we should answer the question "What conception of justice would be best suited to address the claim that disability is a human rights issue?" by focusing on the capabilities approach and exploring how it can endorse the values of equality, dignity, and autonomy. Ultimately, I concluded that the capabilities approach was the best conception of justice to support claims that disability is a human rights issue.

8. References

Anderson, Elizabeth. 2010. "Justifying the Capabilities Approach to Justice." In *Measuring Justice: Primary Goods and Capabilities*, edited by Harry Brighouse and Ingrid Robeyns, 81–100. Cambridge: Cambridge University Press.

Kao, Grace Y. 2011. *Grounding Human Rights in a Pluralistic World.* Washington, DC: Georgetown University Press.

Kateb, George. 2011. *Human Dignity.* Cambridge, MA: Harvard University Press.

Nussbaum, Martha. 1990. "Aristotelian Social Democracy." In *Liberalism and the Good*, edited by R. Bruce Douglas, Gerald M. Mara, and Henry S. Richardson, 203–252. New York: Routledge.

———. 2006. *Frontiers of Justice: Disability, Nationality and Species Membership.* Cambridge, MA: Harvard University Press.

———. 2011. *Creating Capabilities: The Human Development Approach.* Cambridge, MA: Harvard University Press.

Pogge, Thomas. 2002. "Can the Capability Approach be Justified?" *Philosophical Topics* 30(2), 167–228.

Rawls, John. 1971. *A Theory of Justice.* Cambridge, MA: Harvard University Press.

Riddle, Christopher A. 2010. "Indexing, Capabilities, and Disability." *The Journal of Social Philosophy* 41(4), 527–537.

———. 2013. "Natural Diversity and Justice for People with Disabilities." In *Disability and the Good Human Life*, edited by Jerome Bickenbach, Franziska Felder, and Barbara Schmitz, 271–299. Cambridge: Cambridge University Press.

———. 2014. *Disability and Justice: The Capabilities Approach in Practice.* Lanham, MD: Lexington Books.

Robeyns, Ingrid. 2005. "The Capability Approach: A Theoretical Survey." *Journal of Human Development* 6(1), 93–117.

Sen, Amartya. 1995. "Equality of What?" In *Equal Freedom: Selected Tanner Lectures on Human Values*, edited by Stephen Darwall, 195–220. Ann Arbor: University of Michigan Press.

World Health Organization. 2011. *World Report on Disability.* Geneva: World Health Organization.

5 Human rights and persons with intellectual and developmental disabilities

An elusive but emerging paradigm

Donato Tarulli, Dorothy Griffiths, and Frances Owen

> Each and every life is equally sacred; each one of us is of infinite worth. To regard the life of a person with a mental or physical handicap as being less valuable than the life of a normal human being is to violate the fundamental notion of equality.
>
> (Stratford 1991, 11)

1. Historical context and rationale for a rights agenda

The history of persons with intellectual and developmental disabilities is expressed predominantly through the voices of others – the voices of professionals or family members or policymakers who have not experienced the reality of life with a stigmatizing label. In his presidential address to the American Association on Intellectual and Developmental Disabilities, Hank Bersani (2007, 400) reflected on this reality of two worlds: the world of persons who are defined by disability and the world of those doing the defining. He emphasized this divide by examining the negative power of a label, which creates "narrow lives by people defined by it – lives devoid of any of the facets that we find lend our lives dignity, afford us respect, and make our lives comfortable." Bersani's speech was given at a time when nomenclature was changing and the old term of *mental retardation* was being removed from the lexicon; however, it seems that each time the language has changed, the prejudices have not. As Bersani points out, "The fact of stigma is that the status of the lives of these individuals transfers in society to the label" (Bersani 2007, 403). It is this stark reality, and thousands of years of perpetuation of the "othering" of persons identified as having what we now refer to as intellectual and developmental disabilities, that has fueled the quest for an authentic commitment to human rights. The ever-burgeoning disability rights movement is an effort to ensure that persons with intellectual and developmental disabilities are seen as persons who have the same rights as any other citizen and that these rights, while having rhetorical power, are not just empty rhetoric but meaningfully enacted in a way that includes a commitment to persons with disabilities speaking in their own authentic voices.

Notions of human rights, and especially rights of persons regarded as having disabilities, have varied considerably over the course of human history. In his comprehensive history of what was formerly known as mental retardation, Scheerenberger (1983) describes the range of attitudes toward persons with disabilities over the centuries. The picture is not monochromatic. There is archeological evidence, for example, of members of a Neanderthal community providing some protections for a person with disabilities; the suggestion of ancient Egyptian protections for persons with disabilities being provided under the auspices of the god Osiris; and in Palestine, evidence of Hebrew laws in the Ten Commandments and the Pentateuch specifying protections of persons with disabilities and those who were poor. However, these protections were not consistent across the ancient world; for example, infanticide was practiced in Greece and Sparta (Scheerenberger 1983).

In the ancient world and into the Middle Ages, the perceived social value of persons with intellectual and developmental disabilities was mitigated by the need for people to undertake menial jobs, such as working in the fields and building canals. There was also a continuous need for warriors. There was some awareness of the need for care, as evidenced by the Masur Hospital in Cairo that provided intensive supports. Still, persons with intellectual and developmental disabilities were abused and enslaved. With the increased focus on science and philosophy in the seventeenth and eighteenth centuries, Europe saw a growing focus on understanding the cause of medical conditions and systematic approaches to their study. Nevertheless, persons with disabilities who were not cared for in their homes or in residences continued to struggle for survival (Scheerenberger 1983).

The nineteenth-century industrial period brought a new surge in the need for labor but also increased knowledge about the nature of intellectual and developmental disabilities. There was a growing interest in the development of institutional educational programs that spread to the United Sates, but these gradually shifted from a focus on training to lifelong institutionalization. This reorientation was fueled by the eugenics movement, an interpretation of social Darwinism that saw persons with disabilities as a threat to the gene pool (Scheerenberger 1983; Trent 1994). Commitment to this belief was the foundation for such rights restrictions as the legal prohibition of marriage that existed in thirty-nine US states by the early twentieth century. Between 1907 and 1958, thirty US states engaged in forced sterilization of persons with intellectual and developmental disabilities (Scheerenberger 1983). Samuel Gridley Howe, who, among other accomplishments, established the Massachusetts School for Idiotic and Feeble-Minded Youth in 1855, focused his work on the education of persons with disabilities; however, he saw his concept shift in ways that concerned him gravely. He argued against the congregation of persons with intellectual and developmental disabilities away from the larger community, saying "it is unwise to organize establishments for teaching and training idiotic children, upon such principles as will tend to make them become asylums for life. . . . *Even idiots have rights* which should be carefully considered!" (quoted in Scheerenberger 1983, 128). This tension between institutionalization and the rights of persons with intellectual and developmental disabilities persists, in some jurisdictions, to this day.

Evidence of public acknowledgment of the rights of persons with intellectual and developmental disabilities in the United States was seen in the second decade of the twentieth century with the emergence of a focus on the need for the development of comprehensive services. Walter Fernald, the first resident superintendent of the

Massachusetts School for Idiotic and Feeble-Minded Youth, proposed a wide range of educational, health, and outreach services that suggested a recognition of rights, such as the availability of local "mental retardation" specialists, as "every mentally retarded person is entitled to health and mental examinations and care" and "mentally retarded children were entitled 'even more than a normal child' to education according to [their] needs and capabilities" (quoted in Scheerenberger 1983, 173). By the early 1920s, Fernald's advocacy contributed to Massachusetts committing to early identification of children's needs; to the right to education of persons with intellectual and developmental disabilities; to the development of clinics, special education, and job training; and to a focus on placement in the community. In 1929, US President Herbert Hoover called for a conference on the health and well-being of children that included a subcommittee on persons with "mental deficiencies." The committee's report proposed the first Bill of Rights for the Handicapped Child that covered rights related to health, education, support by sympathetic people, a positive quality of life, and freedom from ridicule (Scheerenberger 1983).

The emerging focus on rights has grown since this first Bill of Rights, but the progress has been far from linear. By the 1950s, US schools began to acknowledge a responsibility to educate students identified as "trainable mentally retarded." In 1953, the Association for Retarded Citizens adopted an "Education Bill of Rights for the Retarded Child" (Scheerenberger 1983, 234). By the same decade, there was a growing focus on the need to reform US institutions, although a clear commitment to deinstitutionalization would not emerge until the 1970s. The 1960 election of President John F. Kennedy, whose sister had an intellectual disability, gave momentum to a twenty-year legislative agenda that focused on services and rights promotion for persons with intellectual disabilities and their families. Kennedy's charge to his 1961 President's Panel on Mental Retardation included the direction that "we as a nation have too long postponed an intensive search for solutions to the problems of the mentally retarded. That failure should be corrected" (quoted in Scheerenberger 1983, 247). The panel responded, and included in its report was a commitment to act "to bestow the full benefits of our society on those who suffer from mental disabilities" (quoted in Scheerenberger 1983, 248). Scheerenberger (1983) attributes a growing focus on rights to Kennedy's incentive and cites the particular significance of the Declaration of General and Special Rights of the Mentally Retarded developed in 1968 by the International League of Societies for the Mentally Retarded and subsequently adopted, in 1971, by the UN General Assembly.

The United Nations began to focus on the rights of persons who have disabilities in the period between 1945 and 1955. At that time, the major focus was on those with physical disabilities, deafness, and blindness. In 1969, the UN General Assembly adopted the Declaration on Social Progress and Development, which included "the provision of health, social security, and social welfare services for all persons, aiming at the rehabilitation of the mentally and physically disabled so as to facilitate their integration into society" (UN Enable 2004, chapter II). As described earlier, the passage of the Declaration on the Rights of Mentally Retarded Persons was a seminal event in the United Nations' role in promoting the rights of persons with intellectual and developmental disabilities. In December 1975, it was followed by the adoption of the Declaration on the Rights of Disabled Persons. This document specified that persons with disabilities "have the inherent right to respect for their human dignity" (paragraph 2) and "the same civil and political rights as other human beings" (paragraph 4). However, paragraph 4 refers to the caveat in paragraph 7 of the Declaration on the Rights of Mentally Retarded Persons (United Nations 1971) that allows for limitations of the individual's exercise of these rights dependent on an expert evaluation of their social capability. Application of this limitation was subject to review and protection from abuse. Despite this potential for restriction, the Declaration on the Rights of Disabled Persons focused on provision of the means to enable persons with disabilities to become self-reliant and to have access to treatment, rehabilitation, education, training, and services to optimize their "social integration or reintegration" (paragraph 6) without discrimination "on the basis of race, colour, sex, language, religion, political or other opinions, national or social origin, state of wealth, birth or any other situation applying either to the disabled person himself or herself or to his or her family" (paragraph 2).

An important inclusion in this 1975 declaration is paragraph 12, which states that "organizations of disabled persons may be usefully consulted in all matters regarding the rights of disabled persons" (United Nations 1975). Through twenty-first century eyes, this provision seems at best constrained, but nevertheless it represents a step toward facilitating the inclusion, or at least consultation with, those whose voice is authentic. Furthering the focus on self-advocacy was the emergence in the early 1970s of groups such as People First, an organization of persons with intellectual and developmental disabilities who make their voices heard for themselves and for the well-being of others. People First now has groups in Canada, Germany, New Zealand, the United Kingdom, and the United States (People First 2015). The First Founding Congress of Disabled People's International was held in Singapore. This cross-disability organization, now based in Ottawa, Canada, is committed to the promotion of rights and the actualization of full participation, as reflected in its motto, "Nothing About Us Without Us" (Disabled People's International 2012). Lang (2009) suggests the later development of the UN Convention on the Rights of Persons with Disabilities reflected thirty-odd years of the developing relationship between the United Nations and "civil society institutions, particularly disabled people's organizations" (Lang 2009, 268).

In the years following the Declaration on the Rights of Persons with Disabilities, the United Nations proclaimed 1981 the International Year for Disabled Persons, a year to be focused on integration, research, and public awareness of the rights of persons with disabilities (UN Enable 2004, chapter III). The 1982 adoption of the World Programme of Action Concerning Disabled Persons structured disability policy in three areas: "prevention, rehabilitation and equalization of opportunities." In the same year, the United Nations proclaimed 1983–1992 to be the United Nations Decade of Disabled Persons, during which member states were encouraged to enact the World Action Programme (UN Enable 2004, chapter IV). There was also a growing focus on employment rights with the Tallinn Guidelines for Action on Human Resources Development in the Field of Disability promoting training and employment (UN Enable 2004, chapter IV). A major move toward implementation of the World Programme of

Action was established with the 1993 adoption of the Standard Rules on the Equalization of Opportunities for Persons with Disabilities, which included mechanisms for implementing and monitoring equal opportunity and equal participation for persons with disabilities (UN Enable 2004, chapter V). However, these standard rules were not legally binding. This need for a legal foundation to promote protection and to ensure the rights of persons with disabilities is found in the 2006 Convention on the Rights of Persons with Disabilities (Lee 2008).

2. The UN Convention on the Rights of Persons with Disabilities

The UN Convention on the Rights of Persons with Disabilities (CRPD) was adopted in 2006 and opened for signature in 2007. As of March 2015, there were 159 signatories. In addition to member states, signatories to this convention include regional integration organizations (UN Enable n.d.).

In the years since the 1970s conventions, awareness of the universality of human rights and the necessity for inclusion of self-advocates in rights promotion and protection has increased. From its first meeting, the Ad Hoc Committee on a Comprehensive and Integral International Convention on the Protection and Promotion of the Rights and Dignity of Persons with Disabilities, which developed the CRPD, encouraged the UN member states to "incorporate persons with disabilities and/or other experts on disability into their official delegations at meetings, as well as to consult with them at home in the preparatory process in establishing positions and priorities" (Melish 2007, 43), and virtually all did just that. Nongovernmental organizations from both rich and poor countries were involved in meetings with the Ad Hoc Committee; their participation was facilitated by the establishment of the UN Voluntary Fund on Disability, which provided support for "participation of civil society experts from the least developed countries" (Melish 2007, 43). Funding for participation was also provided by disability organizations. Nongovernmental organizations and organizations of persons with disabilities created the International Disability Caucus, which included some fifty different organizations. The purpose of the caucus was to present a "united voice" at committee meetings and when providing feedback on the language of the convention (Lang 2009, 272). The committee's commitment to an inclusive process extended to full committee discussion of each article of the new convention, rather than separate groups taking responsibility for individual articles or sections of the document, and necessitated ensuring that meetings were held in the only large wheelchair accessible room in the UN building (Melish 2007).

Just as persons with disabilities were both heard and seen in the process of developing the CRPD, so too was the convention's focus on illuminating and rectifying the gap between rights in theory and rights in practice. Tara Melish (2007), who was involved in the process of drafting the CRPD, described the importance of seeing rights from the perspective of persons who live with disabilities to put the contributions of the CRPD in a meaningful context. Persons with disabilities experience rights infringements as do those who do not have disabilities; however, they can also experience rights violations that are linked specifically to their disabilities and that some may feel are justified by those disabilities.

> The mainstream human rights community has thus tended to remain silent when persons with disabilities are forcibly institutionalized, stripped of their legal capacity, rendered immobile by barriers in the built and social environment, or denied the right to bear or rear children, marry, inherit, access insurance or loans, or own property on the basis of their disabilities. Nor has alarm been raised when persons with disabilities are segregated from the general education system, restricted to sheltered employment or income assistance due to barriers on the open labor market, or prevented from living in the community through restricted housing and service options.
> (Melish 2007, 44)

These issues are central to the CRPD, which includes mechanisms to oversee international information sharing and the enactment of the convention provisions (Articles 31–40).

The driving focus of the CRPD is a shift from exclusion to full and meaningful inclusion of persons with disabilities recognizing their abilities; it replaces a traditional "'medical-social welfare' model with a 'social-human rights' model that focuses on *capability* and *inclusion*" (Melish 2007, 37). The CRPD includes fifty articles that describe core rights related to equality and nondiscrimination (Article 5); accessibility (Article 9); right to life (Article 10); liberty of movement and nationality (Article 18); personal mobility (Article 20); freedom of expression and opinion and access to information (Article 21); and respect for privacy (Article 22). It also includes rights related to legal and safety protections, including equal recognition before the law (Article 12); access to justice (Article 13); liberty and security of the person (Article 14); freedom from torture or cruel, inhuman, or degrading treatment or punishment (Article 15); freedom from exploitation, violence, and abuse (Article 16); and situations of risk and humanitarian emergencies (Article 11). Protections of rights related to day-to-day living are central to the convention, including respect for home and family (Article 23); education (Article 24); health (Article 25); habilitation and rehabilitation (Article 26); work and employment (Article 27); adequate standard of living and social protection (Article 28); participation in political and public life (Article 29); and participation in cultural life, recreation, leisure, and sport (Article 30). Signatories are also responsible for raising awareness (Article 8), which includes promoting respect for persons with disabilities, fighting against prejudice and stereotypes, and advocating for accurate public portrayal of persons with disabilities. Specific protections are included for women (Article 6) and children with disabilities (Article 7) (United Nations 2006).

In addition to the CRPD Article 7, the rights of children with disabilities are also protected specifically in the Convention on the Rights of the Child (CRC), which encourages sharing of information about prevention, care, and treatment related to disabilities to promote growth in an international capacity. Article 2 of the CRC prohibits rights discrimination on the basis of disability. Article 23 details protections of the rights of children with disabilities to lead a decent life, to have specialized care that, when possible, is free of charge and enables children with disabilities to have access to "education training, heath care services, rehabilitation services, preparation for employment and recreation opportunities in a manner conducive to the child's achieving the fullest possible social integration and individual development" (Lee 2008, 287–288).

The protections and expectations of the CRPD, and the congruent disability-focused provisions of the CRC, are a source of hope that the abuses described by Melish (2007) will be ended. However, there remains the need to find practical and contextually meaningful ways to ensure that the convention is used as a tool to inform policy and practice. There is evidence of the emerging influence of the CRPD on national and international legislation and policy initiatives in some jurisdictions, as required in Article 35 (Reiss 2014; Umeasiegbu et al. 2013). However, as emphasized by Lang (2009), the convention is far from being a panacea. While it has raised the political profile of issues related to disability more than previous documents, the extent to which organizations of persons with disabilities are involved authentically and with broad representation in the "development and execution of disability policy and practice" varies internationally, as does the availability of the necessary administrative infrastructures (Lang 2009, 282). As Lang points out, governments can provide legislation and policy that outlaws discrimination, but enforcing nondiscrimination at an individual or even an organizational level is extremely difficult to achieve. As we will discuss later in this chapter, realization of the CRPD principles requires a fundamental policy to practice a paradigm shift in service systems.

In 2010, an international conference of some five hundred people was held in Niagara Falls, Ontario, Canada, to celebrate the new CRPD and to examine research, policy, and practice related to its implementation for persons with intellectual and developmental disabilities. In the book that was informed by that conference, Kory Earle, President of People First of Ontario, reflected on the challenges that lie ahead in ensuring the enactment of the principles associated with the convention:

> People with disabilities have fought for many years to get any kind of rights. The United Nations Convention on the Rights of Persons with Disabilities is very important now and we must move forward to ensure that everyone is treated fairly. Why do we have to fight every day? We should not have to fight for who we are. Unless we stand up and do something, things won't improve. We need to challenge ourselves to do more. We need to challenge governments to do more. It is important that we all renew our commitment to ensuring that every person with disabilities has the same rights as everyone else. When we renew the commitment, it is very important that we follow through on the many rights out there that have not been in the public eye.
> (Griffiths et al. 2012, v)

3. Making the paradigm shift

The CRPD is heralded as a paradigm shift in both attitude and practice.

> It takes to a new height the movement from viewing persons with disabilities as "objects" of charity, medical treatment, and social protection toward viewing persons with disabilities as "subjects" with rights, who are capable of claiming those

> rights and making decisions for their lives based on their free and informed consent, as well as being active members of society.
>
> (UN Enable n.d., paragraph 2)

3.1 Policy to practice

Although it can inform practice, Endicott (2009) cautions that the "full entitlement of persons who have intellectual disabilities to be treated as equals has yet to be universally achieved" (Endicott 2009, 13). The convention presents the challenge of adopting a systems-oriented view of human rights. In the context of traditional practices of service provision, this means that the facilitation of choice-making and self-determination must be seen from a broad systemic perspective (Robertson et al. 2001). Systemic change requires agencies to begin a process to question many of the philosophical suppositions on which traditional practices have been based (Tarulli et al. 2004). Endicott (2011) puts the matter more enigmatically: "With the advent of rights for people with disabilities, the world of service provision is changing. Rather than serving children in big bodies, we begin to serve adults with big expectations" (Endicott 2011, 3).

The traditional approach to service provision was highly paternalistic and hierarchical, privileging the voices and perspectives of those immediately responsible for the care and safety of service users. Decisions were staff directed, and choices about a person's accommodations, activities, and community access were determined by others, not through any sort of meaningful dialogue with the person for whom decisions were being made. Robertson et al. (2001) surveyed 281 adults with intellectual disabilities in community settings and found that major life decisions such as where and with whom to live, as well as more minor decisions such as where and what to eat, were largely not self-directed nor the subject of any joint decision making.

Currently provided systems that have operated on traditional systems-based approaches to services must begin to examine how current practice infringes on the rights of the persons they support. In a study to explore human rights infringements that occur in the community, Griffiths et al. (2003) developed an eighty-question survey for administration to individuals supported by agencies in the community and their staff. The survey's purpose was to allow agencies to review their current practices in order to provide information on which to begin a dialogue about rights restrictions and to make policy changes. The survey questions fell into four distinctive categories: (1) access and autonomy, (2) relationships and community supports, (3) safety, security, and privacy, and (4) control and decision making. The survey was able to identify that individuals supported by the agency expressed concerns with regard to rights restrictions in all four categories (i.e. not able to choose where they live, not able to get married or have children if they want, not able to have private time with a boyfriend or girlfriend or fear of property being stolen, not able to make changes or do what they want). Staff, however, identified concerns with the access and autonomy and control and decision making categories; none of the staff prioritized rights restrictions related to relationships or community supports. In addition, individuals who were supported in different types of settings (i.e. group home, family home, independent living) reported different rights concerns. The survey findings illustrate the importance of evaluating specific rights concerns not only as they relate to a system but also as they relate to the differentiated subsystems in which people live as well as at the individual level.

The individuality of rights restrictions speaks to the importance of instituting a mechanism that will allow for rights concerns to be expressed, adjudicated, and addressed, such as setting up a human rights committee within the agency. Such a committee would be able to hear human rights concerns about day-to-day issues that are raised by individuals served by the agency and its staff and to recommend resolutions for the concerns.

3.2 Person-centered planning

Emerging from what Bersani (1996) identifies as the third wave of evolution in the disability movement is self-advocacy. A guiding principle for the CRPD is a commitment to ensuring that the voices of people with an intellectual disability are heard regarding matters that relate to their lives, whether these involve deciding where to live, with whom to live, and what to do with one's day, providing informed consent for health care or habilitative/rehabilitative services, or making decisions about any other aspect of one's life. In previous waves of the disability movement, professionals and parents were responsible for making the choices for the fundamental decisions that nondisabled persons take for granted. "Under the guise of paternalistic benevolence, people with intellectual disabilities [were] denied real voice and the opportunity to speak on their own behalf" (Tarulli and Sales 2009, 108). The third wave, which saw the emergence of self-advocacy, represents a recognition of the value of and right to self-determination.

In an effort to help realize this right to self-determination, the field of service provision has begun to employ mechanisms by which this right can be enshrined in practice. Pivotal to this effort has been a shift in how services and supports are determined and planned for each individual. Again, in previous waves, planning was conducted by others, parents, or professionals, often without the inclusion or counsel of the person with a disability – monologically, if you will. The approach was based on the premise that the professionals and family members knew what was best for the individual.

One of the key elements providing the individual with the supports and services needed to reach personal goals is Person-Centered Planning (PCP). PCP is the most common name for a "family of approaches" that, collectively called Twenty-Four Hour Planning, began in 1979 through the work of Green and Kovaks (Holburn and Vietze 2002). As the approaches evolved, names changed, with labels including Personal Futures Planning, Essential Lifestyle Planning, MAPS, and PATH – these labels and the practices they described were modified by the trends that shaped services over the previous decades (Holburn and Vietze 2002). Although known by a variety of other names, Holburn and Vietze (2002) contend that these approaches have a key theme in common – namely, to "increase choice, avoid depersonalizing labels and stigmatizing procedures, honor the choices of the person and those who know the person best, build relationships, individualize supports based on high expectations for the person's development, demand that agencies adopt new forms of service and organization to provide newly conceived supports" (Holburn and Vietze 2002, 15).

A principle fundamental to the PCP approach is that planning is conducted with the individual – dialogically, if you will – for the purpose of identifying the person's stated goals and organizing the supports needed to achieve these goals. It begins as an opportunity to help the person dream beyond the services that have been traditionally offered and provides a mechanism to put into place the resources necessary to move toward or achieve that dream. Contrary to traditional planning, the PCP approach is not grounded in what *is* but in what *could be*. The person who wants to get a job, move out on his or her own, take a vacation, or develop a new relationship is encouraged to share the dream with his or her closest friends, family, and community contacts, who will, together and in dialogue with the individual, develop a strategy to move the goals forward in a shared direction for achieving that dream. In PCP, no aspiration is diminished because it currently does not exist. The dream is the stepping stone toward building a plan to achieve what the individual would like in the future.

As idealistic as this may seem, it can be applied if the support team is creative and open to providing or obtaining the type of support needed. For example, thirty years ago, who would have dreamed that individuals with physical challenges or amputations could engage in competitive sporting events? However, with creative assistive devices and the sponsorship to enable the person to participate by individuals in the person's circle of support and beyond, dreams such as these can in fact be realized. As Holburn and Vietze (2002) observe, the power of the PCP approach is that it produces a mechanism of service provision that delivers intense core consistency.

To be sure, often the dreams may take time to achieve. Just as a nondisabled person planning for a particular career path must have a strategy for achieving the goal, which might include acquiring new skills and engaging in volunteer work or practicums to develop abilities, so too the dream of the person with an intellectual disability may require preparatory steps to move the person toward his or her final goal.

The plan's accomplishment often requires mobilization of resources. Individuals in the person's social network, such as family, friends, or community members, may be enlisted to identify the role they would play in working toward the person's goal. Also, core to the team are nonpaid individuals. As this process involves the development of wide-ranging and often informal community-based relationships, it may usefully be described in terms of the cultivation of "social capital" – that is, a person's "access to relationships that provide various forms of support toward the pursuit of his or her goals; and an individual's access to the resources and services provided in the community for people with disabilities and for all members of the community" (Carey 2010a, 193).

Although person-centered approaches to planning have gained significant popularity in the field of intellectual disabilities and are consistent with the CRPD (United Nations 2006), empirical assessments of the results of the shift from traditional to person-centered planning have, with few exceptions, been largely absent from the literature. Gosse et al. (2014) implemented a controlled study that demonstrated that individualized planning, where persons with intellectual disabilities identified their own goals and the support people they wanted to assist them, led to a significant improvement in the accomplishment of personal outcomes or goals and to an increase in the supports necessary to achieve those goals when compared to traditional planning that was largely staff or family driven.

Although this study is a promising testimonial to the empowerment of persons with intellectual disabilities to direct their own choices and goals, Wehmeyer (2002) notes that PCP is not synonymous with self-determination but suggests that self-determination can only be achieved when there is training to enhance skills and capacity so that the individual is able to exercise choice and control. Our own view is that while enhancing self-determination may, as Wehmeyer (2002) claims, involve cultivating certain individual skills and capacities and a person's strategic use of resources, self-determination is at root a social, relational accomplishment – indeed, in many respects, it is an accomplishment of the entire community in which one lives (Carey 2010a). If they are to be meaningful actions or expressions of agency, then choice and control must involve the existence of meaningful options around work, housing, and daily living; the capacity to exercise choice, in other words, is dependent on the community's capacity to make relevant, meaningful choices available to its members (Carey 2010b). Accordingly, to the extent that we focus our efforts on building human capital (individual knowledge, abilities, etc.), we must do so with an appreciation of the social capital required to support individuals as they pursue their goals. Our approach to rights education, to which we turn next, was informed by this dual focus on human and social capital.

4. Rights education

> We need to ensure that those who have never had the opportunity to learn about risk, having been protected from both information and decision making, get opportunities to learn that which should have automatically been taught. It's time to prepare people to take control of their own lives.
>
> (Endicott 2011, 3)

4.1 Training for individuals with intellectual disabilities

Rights are not just abstractions; as claims, they are linguistically embodied tools that mediate human action. They are, in this regard, a resource to be used to influence one's own and others' actions and perceptions. The challenge of designing an approach to rights education has been to resist seeing the awareness and understanding of one's rights simply as an objective, mechanically deployed skill. Unlike procedural or technical knowledge – what Aristotle called *techné* – the exercise of rights has more to do with moral or ethical knowledge – with what Aristotle referred to as *phronesis*. Moral knowledge is a matter of judgment and hence requires sensitivity to the particularities of the situation at hand. Acting in a way that is consonant with self-determination may be as much about claiming a right as about deferring to others; again, context will determine the propriety of any course of action (Tarulli et al. 2004). With its emphasis on the exercise of rights in a way that is both responsive or responsible to the needs of the situation and respectful of the needs of others, the rights training project described in the following section was expressly informed by this contextualized understanding.

In 2002, the 3Rs (Rights, Respect, and Responsibility) Community University Research Alliance developed, implemented, and evaluated an agency-wide human rights training program for individuals with intellectual disabilities (Stoner et al. 2002a, 2002b). As noted earlier, the training approach focused on teaching individuals with an intellectual disability to be aware of their rights but also to understand the exercise of these rights within the context of respect and responsibility (e.g. exercise of one person's rights cannot violate those of others). The training involved twenty-two two-hour lessons offered in groups of eight to ten. The training began by teaching the core concepts of rights, respect, and responsibility using storytelling, scenario discussion, role playing, and games depicting typical situations that might occur in the training participants' daily lives, such as rights related to relationships, choices regarding food or daily activities, and so on. Within the training, the participants were taught to discriminate between rights violations and nonviolations and provided the opportunity to learn appropriate actions to address rights violations. The training was field tested across multiple agencies with encouraging results (Owen et al. 2003; Tardif-Williams et al. 2007).

4.2 Training for care providers

Training individuals with intellectual disabilities in regard to their rights and the exercise of their rights can, however, be a futile and potentially damaging exercise if the environment in which they interact responds negatively to the demonstration of their new skills. By providing training for individuals, agencies raise not only awareness of human rights among the individuals they support but also an expectation that they can now act on this new knowledge. By not ensuring that the care providers are trained to support individuals with disabilities in the exercise of their rights, care providers could inadvertently become party to increased rights violations or abuse. As we discuss more fully next, these concerns about the social responsiveness to people's efforts to exercise their rights reflect a guiding assumption of the 3Rs Community University Research Alliance – namely, that the degree to which a right can be enacted depends crucially on the setting one inhabits and on the receptiveness to one's bids, say, for autonomy or decision-making power that others in that setting show. In a slightly different register, Carey (2010a) makes a similar point in her observation that

> one's micro-setting also has a strong impact on one's ability to effectively claim and pursue rights. Some people live in settings and amongst people who strongly support the exercise of their rights, so they may never need to claim rights in an adversarial way. Other people live in settings and amongst people who deny some or perhaps all of their rights so that the exercise of rights and participation in typical activities is a constant challenge.
>
> (Carey 2010a, 220)

Perhaps especially in light of these concerns about the differential capacity of settings to accommodate people's access to rights, it is important that agencies undertaking training implement a system-wide training approach. In keeping with this systems focus, the 3Rs Community University Research Alliance also developed a human rights training program for community agency staff and managers. The training for staff and supervisors mirrored the training provided for persons with intellectual disabilities but further addressed situations where there could be potential conflicts, such as where a person might choose to make a decision that could jeopardize the rights and safety of others. Training further involved teaching others to support persons with intellectual disabilities to exercise their rights and to advocate for their rights, such as through a human rights commission, as described earlier.

4.3 Training for the community

One of the most important elements of the CRPD is its emphasis on educating those in the community with whom the person with an intellectual disability will interact. For example, Article 25, pertaining to health rights, requires "health professionals to provide care of the same quality to persons with disabilities as to others, including on the basis of free and informed consent by, inter alia, raising awareness of the human rights, dignity, autonomy and needs of persons with disabilities through training and the promulgation of ethical standards for public and private health care" (United Nations 2006). Similarly, Article 13, pertaining to justice rights, calls for the promotion of "appropriate training for those working in the field of administration of justice, including police and prison staff" (United Nations 2006). In short, the actualization of rights of people with intellectual disabilities cannot be achieved unless those who support individuals with disabilities within the community are aware that people with disabilities have equal rights of citizenship, and as such, equal rights to education, health care, justice, relationships and family, and even the right to life.

5. Relationships and rights

While we have sought to foreground the importance of cultivating a paradigm and discourse of rights to help redress the oppression and inequities experienced by people with intellectual disabilities, we remain mindful of the ongoing need to frame our approach to rights in explicitly relational terms, lest it be seen simply as a means of enhancing individual self-determination and political agency. The discourse of rights, notwithstanding its historical legacy in liberal philosophies that exalt the isolated individual, is for us ultimately allied with an ethical injunction about our need for meaningful relationships and meaningful experiences of community. Indeed, in our emphasis on cultivating a "culture of rights" that extends across the contexts and communities that people inhabit and engage in the course of their daily lives, we recognize that the existence and enshrinement of rights in and of themselves is no guarantee that justice is at hand. Successfully exercising or enacting a right requires, at a minimum, some social recognition that one is a rights-bearing subject, and in the best circumstances, a context that is hospitable to and supportive of one's agency as a bearer of rights. Any social justice we associate with rights, then, is attendant on what people are able to accomplish collectively, in supportive communities, within networks of positive, meaningful relationships.

In this assumption, we find support in Carey's (2010b) explicitly relational approach to rights. For Carey, rights are relational in that they "potentially offer a means by which to transform the place of people with intellectual disabilities within society. Rights provide a potential source of power to influence other people, and as such, they transform relational obligations and expectations, alter the way people are perceived, and affect the identities that can be claimed" (Carey 2010b, 104). In short, rights are inherently relational in that they articulate particular expectations for social relationships.

In our own work, particularly in our emphasis on rights, respect, and responsibility, we have been led by the fundamental idea that rights are inescapably "claimed in the context of relationships, and, like most forms of power, only meaningful within such a context" (Carey 2010b, 104). While rights may be encoded in formal documents, they unfold for better or worse, but never with any guarantees, within the concrete particularity – that is, in response to the vicissitudes, negotiations, and contestations – of real-world relationships. Notwithstanding the purported universality of rights, access to and the exercise of rights is not always universally supported, hence the need for social, cultural, and institutional scaffolds (real choices, meaningful opportunities, an environment that enables access to rights) to support people with intellectual disabilities in their efforts to claim and exercise rights, either formally or informally, toward the end of achieving their goals.

We situate rights in the domain of lived experiences of solidarity and in relationships in which it is sufficiently understood that people can do justice to one another (Young and Quibell 2000). This sentiment was vividly expressed in a series of narratives shared at the 2010 Human Rights and Intellectual Disabilities Conference by members of the Deohaeko Cooperative, a family-governed individualized support network in Toronto, Ontario. The conference session, titled "In Solidarity with Each Other, Rights Emerge," focused on stories lived and told by families "living good lives within their communities" and captured the ways in which solidarity and interdependence formed the foundation of everyday experiences of decision making and self-determination. What the presenters highlighted was precisely the shared, dialogical nature of the decision-making process and the importance, over and above the formal language of rights and policy, of social connections, trust, and respect. What unfolded in these accounts was an image of community and support that communicated a palpable sense of the relational emergence of rights. As one mother put it, "We have all the rights we need right now, as long as we ensure that there are people in real relationships" (Dawe et al. 2010).

In keeping with our earlier description of person-centered planning, what these narratives help to foreground is the importance of social capital to achieve one's goals. In fact, these narratives downplay the language of rights, stressing instead the language of natural relationships and community to communicate the idea that if you are part of a meaningful social network, then the entitlements and protections that we associate with rights will come into being, naturally as it were. This framework, in which community is privileged over rights, and which, in its strongest form, "formal claims to rights are largely unnecessary" (Carey 2010a, 195), certainly helps us better appreciate the limitations of the often abstract and individual-focused discourse of rights, although at the same time we feel that it erects an unnecessarily dualistic conception of rights and community. As we have suggested, a relational view of rights readily acknowledges that rights have their lived reality precisely in social relationships and in experiences of community. Indeed, the task for us has been to enhance the social supports available to people with intellectual disabilities so that, with or without the need to claim a right, they can achieve their goals.

Notwithstanding its stance on rights, however, the "community vision" to which Carey (2010a) alludes does for us highlight an enduring truth about the fundamental need for people with intellectual disabilities to be visible and participate in valued ways in their communities. Unfortunately, the empirical research shows that, for people with intellectual disabilities, experiences of solidarity and interdependence like those described by members of the Deohaeko Cooperative and proponents of the community vision remain the exception rather than the rule. In an era of deinstitutionalization and so-called community living, people with intellectual disabilities are still left out of their communities; they have fewer friends and smaller social networks than people without intellectual disabilities and, understandably in light of this pattern of social marginalization, lack a sense of belongingness and remain ever vulnerable to feelings of loneliness (e.g. Amado 1993; Barber and Hupp 1993; McVilly et al. 2006; Nunkoosing and John 1997). Moreover, at a societal level, there continues to be relatively few meaningful options for people with intellectual disabilities regarding places to live or work or in which to access social support. The unfortunate consequence of this state of affairs is that, precisely under conditions in which the sort of community integration heralded by rights is most sorely needed, many people with intellectual disabilities "may see little opportunity to exercise their rights and may prefer not to jeopardize their relationships by asserting themselves as rights bearers" (Carey 2010a, 220).

The discourse of rights, particularly as it has been appropriated by self-advocacy groups in the struggle for greater choice, decision-making power, and self-determination, will continue to play an important role in challenging these social realities. Ultimately, however, what is needed alongside the continued demand for and enforcement of rights are strategies for enhancing the experience of community at the local level. Again, notwithstanding the great strides toward deinstitutionalization and community living, people with intellectual disabilities are still left out of communities, still socially marginalized, still lack the social capital – the natural, equitable, supportive relationships – necessary to feel like valued members of the community and to achieve their goals. Whether through the discourse of rights or through less formal means, the task remains that of cultivating greater inclusion into community life and greater social capital, and through those achievements, greater access to the sorts of entitlements formally encoded in the CRPD. Although articulating the details of this task is perhaps beyond the scope of this chapter, we can for the moment say that change must be focused on enhancing a community's capacity to acknowledge all of its members as rights-bearing subjects; to offer meaningful choices; to make available adequate resources and services; and at the level of ideology, to provide opportunities for interpersonal encounters among people with and without disabilities that can challenge some of the enduring, deficit-oriented narratives surrounding intellectual opportunities (such as those suggested earlier in connection with the Deohaeko Cooperative) for people with an intellectual disability to be better understood, and consequently, better supported by their communities (Young and Quibell 2000). Community inclusion, in short, requires change at the attitudinal, institutional, and cultural levels, change that will support empowerment through access to rights and promote social justice. Once again, to cite Carey's (2010b) relational perspective: "inclusion, respect, and meaningful participation, the ultimate goals of contemporary rights movements, are necessarily relational concepts and can only be achieved through reimagining the ways in which people relate to each other within society" (Carey 2010b, 125).

6. Conclusions

In this chapter, we have tried to communicate some of the details, conceptual and practical, surrounding the emergence of a rights paradigm for understanding services and supports for people with intellectual disabilities. What has remained somewhat more implicit in our discussion, if explicit in the chapter's title, is the notion that this is in some way an elusive paradigm. In her recent exposition of disability rights in Canada, Stienstra (2012) articulates the present shortcomings of such rights precisely in terms of this elusiveness, noting how difficult it is for many Canadians with disabilities, who are economically, socially, and culturally marginalized, to live in ways that are commensurate with the ideals of well-being embodied in legislated rights: "Disability rights continue to be elusive for most people with disabilities, and many face discrimination in their daily lives" (Stienstra 2012, 7). In this chapter, the elusiveness of rights is suggested in self-advocate Kory Earle's question, "Why do we have to fight every day?" – a question that only too poignantly reminds us that the rights currently enshrined and articulated in charters like the CRPD offer no assurances that justice is at hand. The elusiveness of rights is no less adumbrated in the concerns we have raised about the often unpredictable, lived reality of rights as they are practiced (or fail to manifest) in concrete, relational settings; indeed, both as a concept and as an achievement, much of the elusiveness of rights lies precisely in their inhabiting the space between the tidy formality of codes and the messy and inescapable contingencies of social praxis.

In its effort to raise awareness about rights among individuals with disabilities, community agency staff and managers, and the community at large, our 3Rs Community University Research Alliance project has sought to bridge the often unavoidable gap between code and conduct, rights and social reality. Our discussion has further intimated that justice is perhaps less about rights as such than about *doing the right thing*, about people coming together and collectively creating the conditions, capacities, and communities in which the provisions, protections, freedoms, and entitlements we associate with rights could emerge immanently, so to speak, as forms of daily life, and as the model of the Deohaeko Cooperative shows us, through concrete experiences of solidarity, understanding, and belonging.

7. References

Amado, Angela N., ed. 1993. *Friendships and Community Connections between People with and without Developmental Disability*. Baltimore: Brookes.

Barber, Donna and Susan C. Hupp. 1993. "A Comparison of Friendship Patterns of Individuals with Developmental Disabilities." *Education and Training in Mental Retardation* 28, 13–22.

Bersani, Hank. 1996. "Leadership in Developmental Disabilities: Where We've Been, Where We Are and Where We're Going." In *New Voices: Self-Advocacy by People with Disabilities*, edited by Gunnar Dybwad and Hank Bersani, 258–269. Cambridge, MA: Brookline Books.

———. 2007. "President's Address 2007: The Past Is Prologue: 'MR,' Go Gentle into That Good Night." *Intellectual and Developmental Disabilities* 45, 399–404.

Carey, Allison C. 2010a. *On the Margins of Citizenship: Intellectual Disability and Civil Rights in Twentieth-Century America*. Philadelphia: Temple University Press.

———. 2010b. "A Relational Approach to the Development of Civil Rights for People with Intellectual Disabilities." In *Disability as a Fluid State (Research in Social Science and Disability, Volume 5)*, edited by Sharon N. Barnartt, 103–129. Bingley, UK: Emerald.

———. 2011. "The Quest for Community: Intellectual Disability and the Shifting Meaning of Community in Activism." In *Disability and Community (Research in Social Science and Disability, Volume 6)*, edited by Allison C. Carey and Richard K. Scotch, 189–213. Bingley, UK: Emerald.

Dawe, Linda, Barb Boettcher, Caroline Dionne, Helen Dionne, and Janet Klees. 2010, March. "Deohaeko Family Governed Individualized Support Network: In Solidarity with Each Other, Rights Emerge." Paper presented at the Human Rights and Persons with Intellectual Disabilities Conference, Niagara Falls, ON, Canada.

Disabled People's International. 2012. "Welcome to Disabled People's International." http://www.disabledpeoplesinternational.org.

Endicott, Orville. 2009. "Foreword." In *Challenges to the Human Rights of Persons with Intellectual Disabilities*, edited by Frances Owen and Dorothy Griffiths, 11–13. London: Jessica Kingsley.

Endicott, Timothy. 2011. "Preface." In *Human Rights Agenda: An Action Plan to Advance the Rights of Persons with Intellectual Disabilities*, edited by Dorothy Griffiths, Frances Owen, and Shelley Watson, 15–26. Brock University, St. Catharines, ON: The 3Rs Community University Research Alliance.

Gosse, Leanne, Dorothy Griffiths, Frances Owen, and Maurice Feldman. "Impact of Individualized Planning Approach on Personal Outcomes and Supports for Persons with Intellectual Disabilities." *Journal of Policy and Practice in Intellectual Disabilities* [forthcoming].

Griffiths, Dorothy, Frances Owen, Leanne Gosse, Karen Stoner, Christine Tardif, Shelley Watson, Carol Sales, and Barbara Vyrostko. 2003. "Human Rights and Persons with Intellectual Disabilities: An Action-Research Approach to Community-Based Organizational Self-Evaluation." *Journal on Developmental Disabilities* 10, 25–42.

Griffiths, Dorothy, Frances Owen, and Shelley Watson, eds. 2012. *The Human Rights Agenda for Persons with Intellectual Disabilities*. New York: NADD Press.

Holburn, Stephen and Peter Vietze. 2002. *Person-Centred Planning: Research, Practice and Future Directions*. Baltimore: Brookes.

Lang, Raymond. 2009. "The United Nations Convention on the Right and Dignity for Persons with Disability: A Panacea for Ending Disability Discrimination?" *European Journal of Disability Research* 3, 266–285.

Lee, Yanghee. 2008. "Expanding Human Rights to Persons with Disabilities: Laying the Groundwork for a Twenty-First Century Movement." *Pacific Rim Law & Policy Journal* 18, 283–292.

McVilly, Keith R., Roger J. Stancliffe, Trevor R. Parmenter, and Rosanne Burton-Smith. 2006. "'I Get by with a Little Help from My Friends': Adults with Intellectual Disability Discuss Loneliness." *Journal of Applied Research in Intellectual Disabilities* 19, 191–203.

Melish, Tara J. 2007. "The UN Disability Convention: Historic Process, Strong Prospects, and Why the U.S. Should Ratify." *Human Rights Brief* 14(2), 43–47.

Nunkoosing, Karl and Methilda John. 1997. "Friendships, Relationships and the Management of Rejection and Loneliness by People with Learning Disabilities." *Journal of Intellectual Disabilities* 1, 10–18.

Owen, Frances, Dorothy Griffiths, Karen Stoner, Leanne Gosse, Shelley Watson, Christine Tardif, Carol Sales, and Barbara Vyrostko. 2003. "Multi-Level Human Rights Training: The First Step to Changing Systems." *Journal on Developmental Disabilities* 10, 43–64.

People First. 2015. "Welcome to Peoplefirst.org." http://www.peoplefirst.org.

Reiss, Jennifer. 2014. "Innovative Governance in a Federal Europe: Implementing the Convention on the Rights of Persons with Disabilities." *European Law Journal* 20, 107–125.

Robertson, Janet, Eric Emerson, Chris Hatton, Nicky Gregory, Sophia Kessissorglou, Angela Hallam, and Patricia Noonan Walsh. 2001. "Environmental Opportunities and Supports for Exercising Self-Determination in Community-Based Residential Settings." *Research in Developmental Disabilities* 22, 487–502.

Scheerenberger, Robert. 1983. *A History of Mental Retardation*. Baltimore: Brookes.

Stienstra, Deborah. 2012. *Disability Rights (About Canada Series)*. Halifax, NS: Fernwood.

Stoner, Karen, Leanne Gosse, Barbara Vyrostko, Dorothy Griffiths, Frances Owen, and Carol Sales. 2002a. *3Rs (Rights, Respect and Responsibility): Training for Staff in Agencies Supporting Persons Who Have Intellectual Disabilities*. Welland, ON: Community Living Welland-Pelham.

———. 2002b. *3Rs (Rights, Respect and Responsibility): Training for Individuals in Agencies Supporting Persons Who Have Intellectual Disabilities*. Welland, ON: Community Living Welland-Pelham.

Stratford, Brian. 1991. "Human Rights and Equal Opportunities for People with Mental Handicaps – with Special Reference to Down Syndrome." *International Journal of Disability, Development and Education* 38, 3–13.

Tardif-Williams, Christine, Frances Owen, Maurice Feldman, Donato Tarulli, Dorothy Griffiths, Carol Sales, Glynes McQueen-Fuentes, and Karen Stoner. 2007. "Comparison of Interactive Computer-Based and Classroom Training on Human Rights." *Education and Training in Developmental Disabilities* 42, 48–58.

Tarulli, Donato and Carol Sales. 2009. "Self-Determination and the Emerging Role of Person-Centred Planning: A Dialogical Framework." In *Challenges to the Human Rights of People with Intellectual Disabilities*, edited by Frances Owen and Dorothy Griffiths, 102–123. London: Jessica Kingsley.

Tarulli, Donato, Christine Tardif, Dorothy Griffiths, Frances Owen, Glynes McQueen-Fuentes, Maurice Feldman, Carol Sales, and Karen Stoner. 2004. "Human Rights and Persons with Intellectual Disabilities: Historical, Pedagogical, and Philosophical Considerations." *Encounters: Perspectives on Human Rights and Education* 5, 161–181.

Trent, James. 1994. *Inventing the Feeble Mind: A History of Mental Retardation in the United States*. Berkeley: University of California Press.

Umeasiegbu, Veronica, Malacy Bishop, and Alias Empofu. 2013. "The Conventional and Unconventional about Disability Conventions: A Reflective Analysis of United Nations Convention on the Rights of Persons with Disabilities." *Rehabilitation Research, Policy, and Education* 27, 58–72.

United Nations. 1971. *Declaration on the Rights of Mentally Retarded Persons: Proclaimed by General Assembly Resolution 2856 (XXVI) of 20 December 1971*. New York: United Nations.

———. 1975. *Declaration on the Rights of Disabled Persons: Proclaimed by General Assembly Resolution 3447 (XXX) of 9 December 1975*. New York: United Nations.

———. 2006. *Convention on the Rights of Persons with Disabilities*. New York: United Nations.

United Nations Enable. 2004. *The United Nations and Disabled Persons – The First Fifty Years*. http://www.un.org/esa/socdev/enable/dis50y00.htm.

———. n.d. *Convention on the Rights of Persons with Disabilities*. http://www.un.org/esa/socdev/enable/convinfopara.htm.

Wehmeyer, Michael. 2002. "The Confluence of Person-Centred Planning and Self-Determination." In *Person-Centred Planning: Research, Practice and Future Directions*, edited by Stephen Holburn and Peter Vietze, 51–69. Baltimore: Brookes.

Young, Damon and Ruth Quibell. 2000. "Why Rights Are Never Enough: Rights, Intellectual Disability, and Understanding." *Disability & Society* 5, 747–764.

6 On human rights and human duties

Is there a moral obligation to inclusion?

Holger Burckhart and Bennet Jäger

1. Introduction

Education is a human right. It is an essential prerequisite for participation in social life and must be made available to everyone. This principle is expressed in the guiding idea of "Education for All" and – at least rhetorically – the "inclusive education" that has become a global standard. But the right alone does not guarantee unimpeded and equal access for everyone to education (cf. Johnson 2013).

In almost no other developed country but Germany does[1] educational success – regardless of the intelligence and commitment of the individual – depend on social status and the cultural backgrounds and economic conditions of families (cf. Reich 2012).[2] The German education system is faced with the problem that learning opportunities for minorities or people with special needs are often inadequate, and educational institutions are poorly adapted to their individual requirements. People therefore experience indirect ostracism, and full-fledged participation in education remains denied to them (cf. Sulzer 2013).

Educational success is therefore also dependent on the extent to which the state and society are willing to compensate for this "justice gap" through structural, financial, social, and educational provisions and to ensure educational equality (cf. Reich 2012).

The prerequisite for overcoming educational inequality consists not just in considering the "social origin or sex and gender, or only the dimension of interculturality, but in that the phenomenon of diversity understood in a multi-layered manner" be taken into account for the postulate of an education for everyone (Allemann-Ghionda 2013, 13).

2. Inclusion: A human right

Human rights apply to all people. Like any human right, the right to education is also based on the principle that all people – simply by their personhood – have the same universal, indivisible, and inalienable rights. Already in the Basic Law for the Federal

1 The remarks in this chapter mainly relate to the situation in Germany. For an international perspective, see Allemann-Ghionda (2013).

2 The same applies, for example, to Austria. See Bruneforth, Herzog-Punzenberger, and Lassnigg (2012).

Republic of Germany, not only is the inviolability of human dignity (i.e. for everyone) stipulated but also the fact that "the German people . . . are admitted inviolable and inalienable human rights as the basis of every human community"[3] (Art. 1, para. 2 Basic Law) and that no one may "be discriminated against or preferred on the grounds of their gender, birth, race, language, nationality and social origin, belief, religion or political opinions."[4] Furthermore, "no one may . . . be discriminated against due to their disability"[5] (Art. 3, para. 3 Basic Law).

In the UN Convention on the Rights of Persons with Disabilities, which specifies the universal human rights for people with disabilities (cf. Randhahn 2014), the contracting states "undertake to ensure and promote the full realization of all human rights and fundamental freedoms for all persons with disabilities without discrimination of any kind on the basis of disability" (United Nations 2006, 5). To achieve this goal, "The States Parties recognize the right of persons with disabilities to education. With a view to realizing this right without discrimination and on the basis of equal opportunity, States Parties shall ensure an inclusive education system at all levels and lifelong learning" (United Nations 2006, 14).

The states shall therefore be transferred more responsibility than before, and this responsibility shall lead to more social obligations: the convention was adopted with the intention of moving the national education systems to a policy of inclusion, here in essence disabled people – that is, people who cannot or can only to a limited extent participate in the rule system of society as a result of mental or physical limitations (cf. Allemann-Ghionda 2013). Traditionally, this is the area of integration of people with disabilities.

But inclusion goes even further: it comes with claims to equality, self-determination, and participation in social life. It is utopian to believe that in our modern society all people equally participate in this. Rather, those who are perceived to be "valuable" for the common good participate in society, and those who are "valuable" are those who bring independent and distinct benefits to society (cf. Bourdieu 1992). If you can meet these requirements, then you also participate in social life. Otherwise, you will find yourself on the edge or outside society again (cf. Klaus 2009).

The implementation of inclusion is not to be understood as an expression of charity or compassion toward minorities but rather as a way to realize the human right of participation. The equal participation of everyone in the community, in the "civil, political, economic, social and cultural spheres with equal opportunities" (United Nations 2006, 3), is therefore also one of the key demands of the UN Convention on the Rights of Persons with Disabilities. However, it must be equally possible for all people.

Of course, the access to education for all people in our society is defended in principle, yet their human right to education remains normatively untouched. But the question

3 Das Deutsche Volk bekennt sich darum zu unverletzlichen und unveräußerlichen Menschenrechten als Grundlage jeder menschlichen Gemeinschaft, des Friedens und der Gerechtigkeit in der Welt.

4 Niemand darf wegen seines Geschlechtes, seiner Abstammung, seiner Rasse, seiner Sprache, seiner Heimat und Herkunft, seines Glaubens, seiner religiösen oder politischen Anschauungen benachteiligt oder bevorzugt werden.

5 Niemand darf wegen seiner Behinderung benachteiligt werden.

arises of whether the current education system and the resulting reduced participation of minorities in key aspects of social life are compatible with human rights. Human rights are violated when people cannot live sufficiently in their living environments in a manner comparable to other people due to impairments or difficulties in their activities, and the impairment is chosen as a criterion for social exclusion. Kersten Reich therefore rightly calls for the inclusion of all people, regardless of the nature of their impairments, in the education system and for the move away from "normality thinking." The needs of all must be estimated, considered, and actively supported. Failure to do so would be equivalent to the non-observance of human rights (cf. Reich 2012).

3. Inclusion as an area of responsibility in society as a whole

So that people in our society can perceive the human right to education, and inclusion can become a lived reality, we need a paradigm shift at different interacting levels.

First, a change of perspective is needed in dealing with diversity in general and specifically with disabilities in our society. Starting from the perception that society is virtually organized along dividing lines – that is, separation is seen as a socially normal condition – inclusion typically consisted of a unilateral adding, so to speak, an "entry permit" from being someone who deviates from the norm to becoming the societal norm. This was solidified under integration, which can be taken here as self-completion. Against this exaggerated image, however, it also becomes clear that ultimately the "disabled" individuals themselves were paramount in the responsibility to conform to the social norms and conditions of their environments. In terms of education, it was assumed that students attend mainstream schools and universities, and that is when they – despite their impairments – were able to cope with the conditions of the institution of learning. This means that participation was dependent on the individual's ability to adapt to the norm (cf. Burckhart and Gordon 2014) by incorporating themselves into the everyday life of normal students and being capable of social inclusion.

In contrast to the integration paradigm, inclusion is based on the idea of the uniqueness of each individual in society. Inclusion is not just the integration of people (e.g. those with a disability or migratory life) into social life but rather the adaptation of social relations in such a way that everyone can be an active part of society. It is about the adaptation of social institutions to the realities of human diversity. Inclusion "is a social claim, stating that society itself is obliged to provide services that are likely to reduce discrimination against people of any kind at all levels in order to enable the fairest chance possible for the development of all people"[6] (Reich 2012, 39). Thus, for example, the educational institutions should be adapted to the individual needs of people with disabilities, with the aim of joint education of people with and without disabilities (cf. Burckhart and Gordon 2014).

6 Inklusion . . . ist ein gesellschaftlicher Anspruch, der besagt, dass die Gesellschaft ihrerseits Leistungen erbringen muss, die geeignet sind, Diskriminierungen von Menschen jeder Art und auf allen Ebenen abzubauen, um eine möglichst chancengerechte Entwicklung aller Menschen zu ermöglichen.

Second, the transformation from integration to inclusion should not lead to certain groups being entirely replaced by the state as designers of their lives and their futures. In the current discourse, for example, people with disabilities are too often visible as "objects" and less as "subjects" with their own agendas (Burckhart and Gordon 2014). Inclusion cannot and should not mean that the state is solely responsible for the realization, but that everyone should, within their capabilities, bear joint responsibility. The state's role is to create the necessary conditions, whether they are of an administrative, medical, or social nature (cf. Randhahn 2014).

For this process to be successful, the affected people may not be patronized by a misunderstanding of care but rather must be perceived seriously as equal members of society.

On the one hand, they must get back or receive their right to self-determination (Randhahn 2014). In the process, they are to be included in the inclusion debate more strongly than ever before. It is important to talk with them and not about them; otherwise, you run the risk of having an exclusionary effect through the discourse itself.

On the other hand, the right to protection against discrimination must also not mean that all people should be treated equally. When thought of this way, inclusion would run a real risk of remaining utopian (cf. Fleischhauer 2014). This, in particular, would run counter to the principle of inclusion if individual diversity and different starting points and conditions were not considered. In addition, there will always be people who need help and who will be dependent on others. "A genuine equality of opportunity for all people in the face of social relations is therefore illusive, because also today people come into the world in very different economic, social, cultural, educational and physical conditions and develop in the world differently."[7] Of course, individual "diversity . . . cannot simply be made equal. But an increased fairness of opportunities can be ensured"[8] (Reich 2012, 31). In the implementation of inclusion, it is important in the sense of Hans Jonas's ethics of responsibility to find the balance between reasonableness and responsibility – that is, to generally perceive all people as subjects, to offer them the same assistance, and to grant them the freedom to make decisions (see Jonas 1984).

Third, inclusion must mean that people not only need access to all areas of social life but also have the feeling of being welcome. A change in mentality is required here. Members of society should not only accept the inclusion but also be involved in this development in order to enable a common growing in this process. Inclusion is subject to a principle of shared responsibility (cf. Burckhart 2000) by all members of society. The perception, recognition, and respect of inclusion as an irrevocable human right must be afforded by all community members. For human rights to achieve real

7 Eine tatsächliche Chancengleichheit aller Menschen ist angesichts der gesellschaftlichen Verhälntnisse deshalb illusorisch, weil die Menschen inder Gegenwart in sehr unterschiedlichen ökonomischen, sozialen, kulturellen, bildungsbezogenen und auch körperlichen Voraussetzungen auf die Welt kommen und sich in der Welt entwickeln.

8 Diese Unterschiedlichkeit lässt sich nicht einfach gleichmachen. Aber es kann für eine höhere Gerechtigkeit der Chancen gesorgt werden.

validity, however, requires that people also respect the rights of their fellow men. We need to break through mental barriers, to internalize diversity as a principle of human coexistence rather than to assess diversity as a dissimilarity, and to suggest through the orientation toward one subjective standard that there were two kinds of people – the "normal" and the disabled (cf. Randhahn 2014).

4. Conclusion

If inclusion is to succeed in the long term, then "mechanisms of exclusion must be perceived – and broken down" (Sulzer 2013, 16). Annika Sulzer therefore claims that "the dismantling of barriers . . . requires a coupling of awareness of diversity *and* criticism of discrimination" (Sulzer 2013, 20). Social diversity must be taken into account, and areas of exclusion must be named. Based on this characteristic, inclusion has the potential to raise awareness of exclusion (cf. Sulzer 2013, 20).

For this purpose, inclusion must be understood and internalized as a guiding principle of society as a whole that should permeate all areas of human interaction. The conditions for full participation in society that are currently being created for people with disabilities must apply to all people equally. Only then can one speak of a society where the human rights of every man, woman, and child are respected and safeguarded.

5. References

Allemann-Ghionda, Christina. 2013. *Bildung für alle, Diversität und Inklusion. Internationale Perspektiven*. Paderborn: Schöningh.

Bourdieu, Pierre. 1992. "Ökonomisches Kapital – Kulturelles Kapital – Soziales Kapital." In *Die Verborgenen Mechanismen der Macht. Schriften zu Politik und Kultur*, edited by Margareta Steinrücke, 49–80. Hamburg: VSA.

Bruneforth, Michael, Barbara Herzog-Punzenberger, and Lorenz Lassnigg. 2012. *Nationaler Bildungsbericht Österreich: Indikatoren und Themen im Überblick*. Graz: Leykam.

Bundesministerium für Arbeit und Soziales. 2011. *Übereinkommen der Vereinten Nationen über die Rechte von Menschen mit Behinderungen*. Bonn: Bundesministierum für Arbeit und Soziales.

Burckhart, Holger. 2000. "Bildung im Diskurs als Herausbildung von Mitverantwortung." In *Prinzip Mitverantwortung. Grundlage für Ethik und Pädagogik*, edited by Karl-Otto Apel and Holger Burckhart, 177–202. Würzburg: Königshausen u. Neumann.

Burckhart, Holger and John-Stewart Gordon. 2014. "Inclusion – A Moral Imperative, But Also Socially Desired? An Essay in the Ethics of Responsibility." In *Global Ethics and Moral Responsibility: Hans Jonas and His Critics*, edited by Holger Burckhart and John-Stewart Gordon, 93–101. London: Routledge.

Fleischhauer, Jan. 2014. "Übergang in eine neue Welt." http://www.spiegel.de/politik/deutschland/jan-fleischhauer-ueber-inklusion-an-schulen-a-975644.html.

Grundgesetz für die Bundesrepublik Deutschland vom 23. Mai 1949. BGBl. III, 100–1. Zuletzt geändert durch Artikel 1 des Gesetzes vom 23.12.2014 (BGBl. I S. 2438).

Johnson, Magdalena. 2013. *Schulische Inklusion in den USA – ein Lehrbeispiel für Deutschland? Eine Analyse der Vermittlung von Ansätzen der Inklusion durch die Zusammenarbeit mit einem outside Change Agent*. Bad Heilbrunn: Klinkhardt.

Jonas, Hans. 1984. *Das Prinzip Verantwortung. Versuch einer Ethik für die Technologische Zivilisation*. Frankfurt: Suhrkamp.

Klaus, Theo. 2009. "Inklusion – Ein Menschenrecht für alle." http://www.ph-heidelberg.de/fileadmin/user_upload/wp/klauss/Inklusion_Menschenrecht_Bridge.pdf.

Randhahn, Wulf. 2014. "Das soziale Menschenrecht auf Inklusion in Deutschland. Anspruch und Wirklichkeit der Rechtlichen und Tatsächlichen Umsetzung der UN-BRK." http://nbn resolving.de/urn:nbn:de:bsz:14-qucosa-134848.

Reich, Kersten. 2012. *Inklusion und Bildungsgerechtigkeit. Standards und Regeln zur Umsetzung einer Inklusiven Schule*. Weinheim: Beitz.

Sulzer, Annika. 2013. "Inklusion als Werterahmen für Bildungsgerechtigkeit." In *Handbuch Inklusion. Grundlagen Vorurteilsbewusster Bildung und Erziehung*, edited by Petra Wagner, 12–21. Freiburg, Basel, Wien: Herder.

United Nations. 2006. "Convention on the Rights of Persons with Disabilities." http://www.un.org/disabilities/convention/conventionfull.shtml.

7 The right to inclusive education

Practical implications in German schools

Petr Frantik

1. Introduction

Article 24 of the UN Convention on the Rights of Persons with Disabilities (CRPD) substantiated the right of inclusive education for persons with disabilities in May 2006. In October 2008, the German federal government passed a resolution to ratify this UN Convention. The law was approved by the Bundesrat and the Bundestag in January 2009 and came into force in March of the same year.

This ratification provoked much discussion about the proper implementation of inclusive education in Germany.[1] The changes needed to achieve inclusive education are not simply the responsibility of schools, teachers, or politicians but also must be supported by society as a whole. Thus, the discourse on inclusion takes place in schools, universities, and political bodies but also in the media and in general public settings. The different loci of discussion are interconnected and influence one another.

Currently, Germany's school system is in a difficult transitional period from the old, segregated system of regular and special needs schools to the new approaches entailed in inclusion. The implementation of inclusive concepts in regular schools is still full of challenges. On the other hand, the requisite modification and refining of old structures offers the chance to develop and realize new instructional concepts.

This chapter examines the present state of inclusive education in Germany, analyzing the reasons underlying some of the main difficulties that Germany faces in implementing inclusive education and suggesting ways to overcome them.

It is very difficult to offer a comprehensive overview of the state of inclusion in Germany because a wide range of different theories and opinions exist – in politics, in the field of education, and among teachers, parents, and students – as to how to implement inclusive education. In addition, school environments can differ considerably with regard to their socioeconomic circumstances. Therefore, I have chosen to focus on a few major aspects of the issue, drawing primarily on research findings and publications but also taking into account the personal experiences of teachers. In this way, my work contributes to the important dialogue between theory and practice.[2]

1 Gordon (2013, 760) provides a helpful summary of the arguments for and against inclusive education.

2 I myself have worked as a special needs teacher in various schools, and my current research enables me to gain further insight into daily school life, as I have the opportunity to talk with many teachers who are

To introduce the subject, section 2 of this chapter points out some of the major goals of the CRPD's Article 24 on education and provides a brief overview of the reports and recommendations of the German government, the German Institute for Human Rights, and the UN Committee on the Rights of Persons with Disabilities. The third section discusses the main difficulties surrounding the implementation of inclusive education in Germany, particularly with regard to the goals and recommendations presented in section 2. The fourth section presents some promising approaches to overcoming these difficulties and successfully implementing inclusive learning environments. A conclusion and some final remarks are offered in section 5.

2. Preliminary remarks

2.1 Major goals of Article 24

To understand the tasks and challenges involved in implementing inclusive education, it is first necessary to identify central goals of the CRPD, some of which are highlighted in the first section of Article 24 of this Convention (emphasis added):

> States Parties recognize the right of persons with disabilities to education. With a view to realizing this right *without discrimination* and on the basis of *equal opportunity*, States Parties shall ensure an inclusive educational system at all levels and lifelong learning directed to:
>
> *a* The full development of human potential and sense of dignity and self-worth, and the strengthening of respect for human rights, fundamental freedoms and human diversity;
> *b* The development by persons with disabilities of their personality, talents and creativity, as well as their mental and physical abilities, to their fullest potential;
> *c* Enabling persons with disabilities to *participate* effectively in a free society.
>
> (UN 2006)

From this section, it is possible to derive three important goals of inclusion: *preventing discrimination and stigmatization* (and thereby instilling a sense of dignity and self-worth), *equality in education* (including the possibility of developing mental and physical abilities), and *participation*. Of course, these three selected goals do not represent the entire intentions of Article 24, but they are surely crucial components of the right to inclusive education. They are also mentioned and specified in other parts of Article 24. In order to *prevent discrimination*, the article states, States Parties must develop an inclusive school system that offers individualized support to "maximize the academic and social development" (CRPD Article 24, section 2e) of each child

facing the challenges of inclusive education. Some of these personal experiences will be described here; they are often congruent with the outcomes of scientific research and provide valuable illustrations and supporting evidence.

irrespective of disability or impairment. Inclusive schools must ensure a learning environment in which all children can develop their talents, characters, and opinions in cooperation and mutual assistance with others. Therefore, children with disabilities must be protected from stigmatization or offensive language of any kind. Further, ***equality*** and ***participation*** are preconditions for "individual autonomy including the freedom to make one's own choices" (CRPD 24.3). Children shall be encouraged to develop their autonomy while respecting the rights of their classmates.[3] To ensure the development of children's "personality, talents and creativity" (24.1b), it is necessary to establish an inclusive school system that offers participation to the highest possible extent. All children should have the opportunity to develop a strong individuality by contributing their unique ideas and opinions in school life as well as to develop social skills through interaction with children of diverse personalities.

2.2 Reports and recommendations[4]

Enforcement of the CRPD in Germany lies with the Federal Ministry of Labour and Social Affairs (***Bundesministerium für Soziales und Arbeit***), which is responsible for coordinating the appropriate steps to achieve the previously mentioned goals. According to Article 35 of the Convention, all States Parties shall present reports on their measures and progress at least every four years (UN 2006). Germany's initial report was submitted in September 2011. It described the current situation of education, teacher training, and the role of special schools in Germany and listed some measures to enhance inclusive education (see UN 2013, 41–44).

The process of implementing inclusion in Germany is additionally monitored by the National Monitoring Body (NMB), established at the German Institute for Human Rights in May 2009. Its tasks include advocating for the rights of persons with disabilities, advising politicians and governments, carrying out applied research, and organizing events on CRPD issues (see German Institute for Human Rights 2015, 3). The NMB published a parallel report addressed to the UN Committee on the Rights of Persons with Disabilities in March 2015. In this document, the NMB criticized Germany's initial report, stating that "no sufficiently self-critical analysis of existing problems and deficits in the implementation of the Convention has been carried out so far. Many articles of the State Party's report simply outline the legal situation without addressing its implementation in practice" (German Institute for Human Rights 2015, 4). The parallel report noted that 72 per cent of German children with disabilities were still educated in special needs schools. Even though regular schools in Germany have become more open to children with disabilities, many federal states retain the structures of segregated education. The NMB claims that inclusion should be enforced more strongly in order to overcome this segregation in education (German Institute for Human Rights 2015, 25–27).

3 In many philosophical approaches, such as discourse ethics, the development of autonomy is strongly connected with participation in discourses (see, for example, Burckhart 2001, 181).

4 This section focuses on some main reports. For a complete list of reports, see UN (2015b).

On May 13, 2015, the UN Committee on the Rights of Persons with Disabilities responded to these reports in a document called "Concluding Observations on the Initial Report of Germany" (see UN 2015a). It named some of the major problems of inclusive education in Germany at this time:[5]

(45) The Committee is concerned that the State party has an education system where the majority of students with disabilities attend segregated special-needs schools.
(46) The Committee recommends that the State party:

(a) Immediately develop a strategy, action plan, timeline and targets to provide access to a high-quality, inclusive education system across all Länder [i.e. German states], including the required financial resources and personnel at all levels;
(b) Scale down segregated schools to facilitate inclusion and ensure that the law and policies uphold the duty that mainstream schools enroll children with disabilities with immediate effect if that is their choice;
(c) Ensure reasonable accommodation is provided at all levels of education and that the right to such accommodation is legally enforceable and justifiable before the courts;
(d) Ensure the training of all teachers in inclusive education, increased accessibility of the school environment, materials and curricula, and the provision of sign language in mainstream schools, including at the post-doctoral level.

(UN 2015a, 8)

This comment mentions important aspects of the implementation of inclusive education and details necessary changes. The main goal is to scale down segregated special needs schools and to develop a functioning inclusive school system throughout all federal states. Further, it is important to develop good teaching methods so that schools can provide appropriate education to all students according to their diverse potentials and needs. This objective can be achieved only through teacher training that recognizes the heterogeneity among students as well as teachers.

3. Current difficulties

This section examines some of the major problems and challenges involved in Germany's comprehensive transition from its former, segregated school system to the new approach of inclusive education and points out some reasons for the current difficulties. To do so, it describes the structure of the educational system in Germany, the teacher training offered at universities, and the instructional methods used in schools. It will

5 Another important comment in the UN committee report concerns Article 7 of the CRPD, "Children with Disabilities." The report states, "The Committee is concerned: (a) that children with disabilities are not systematically involved in decisions affecting their lives; (b) that the parents of children with disabilities cannot decide freely on the type of education and services provided to their children" (p. 3). These concerns underscore the role of schools in developing opportunities for children with disabilities to participate in society. School life can and should play an important role in making such participation possible.

focus on how the problems affect the three overarching goals previously discussed: preventing discrimination and achieving equality and participation.

To properly understand the challenges that inclusive education poses in German schools, it is necessary to review the structure of the German school system. The responsibility for organizing education in Germany lies primarily with the Länder (federal states), even though the German government provides a general framework. For this reason, the current state of inclusive education varies between states. For example, in Bremen 61.5 per cent of children with disabilities are educated in inclusive schools, but only 1.7 per cent in Saxony (Blum and Diegelmann 2014, 4).

The educational system in Germany is divided into regular and special needs schools, each of which contains multiple types.[6] This practice of subdivision and segregation has a long tradition in Germany and was adopted to ensure the presence of homogeneous groups of students in every school. Students are separated according to their assumed abilities, based on the presumption that the best way to teach different types of children is in different types of schools. Thus Germany continues to have one of the highest percentages anywhere in Europe of children with disabilities being educated in special needs schools (Reich 2012, 83). Conversely, the number of children with disabilities educated in regular schools is relatively small, and Germany has little experience of inclusive education.

This situation is also reflected by the translation of the CRPD into German, in which the term *inclusion* was changed to *integration*.[7] Many persons with disabilities, politicians, and scientists criticized this imprecise translation. An alternative translation using the term *inclusion* was published in 2009 by an association for human rights and the equality of persons with disability (see Netzwerk Artikel 3 2010).[8] It was argued that the term *integration* implies that each child must adapt to a fixed structure of the school system, whereas *inclusion* proposes the reverse – namely, that the educational system and school structures should adjust to students' individual capabilities. From this perspective, the school system's structure and teaching methods and the standards of society – not the students – must change in order to lay the foundations that will make inclusion work (see Hinz 2003; Reich 2012, 2014). Of course, this means a fundamental change in thinking and teaching and a huge reorganization of the school

6 The regular school system begins with *Grundschule* (primary school), which covers grades one to four (or grades one to six in Berlin and Brandenburg). After that, there are three types of secondary schools, separated according to different levels of learning: *Gymnasium* (comparable to British grammar schools or US preparatory schools and ranked highest in academic level), *Realschule* (intermediate schools ranked lower than *Gymnasium*), and *Hauptschule* (secondary general schools, ranked lowest of the three). There is also the category of *Gesamtschule* (comprehensive schools), which combines *Gymnasium, Realschule*, and *Hauptschule*. Similarly, there are different types of special needs schools, serving students with visual impairment, hearing impairment, intellectual disabilities, physical disabilities, illnesses, learning difficulties, speech defects, and behavioral problems. See European Agency (2015b).

7 The debates over these two terms, *inclusion* and *integration*, and about the costs of inclusion are very intense in Germany. An overview of this discourse is beyond the scope of this chapter. For further information see Hinz (2003, 2011); Reich (2012, 2014); Wocken (2010).

8 To compare the original English version of the CRPD with the official and the alternative German translation, see *Beauftragte der Bundesregierung für die Belange behinderter Menschen* (2015, 35–38).

system, which might also cost a lot of money. Some politicians maintain that inclusive education could be implemented on a cost-neutral basis because closing the special needs schools would save money. But this approach raises another problem, because most special needs schools would have to be closed first before the money would be available to finance inclusion adequately (see Speck 2015). Therefore, higher financial investments seem necessary to guarantee high-quality inclusive education, especially during the current, difficult transitional phase. As the Committee of the CRPD recommends, it is of utmost importance to develop a strategy to provide inclusive education "including the required financial resources and personnel at all levels" (UN 2015a, 8). A cut-rate version of inclusive education would be irresponsible toward both the students and teachers (Speck 2015).

Because Germany has traditionally maintained a segregated school system, teacher training at German universities is also divided according to the different types of schools. Therefore, most teachers of regular schools are not yet equipped to deal with the needs of children with disabilities in an appropriate and inclusive way (see Franzkowiak 2010). This is not a general reproach of the regular schoolteachers, many of whom are motivated to learn more about inclusive education (see also Humbach et al. 2014, 14). In fact, the opinions of regular teachers about inclusion are divided. In a representative survey by the Forsa Institute 49 per cent of *Gymnasium* teachers supported and 47 per cent opposed the concept of inclusive education. Furthermore, 54 per cent of the teachers in *Hauptschule*, *Realschule*, and *Gesamtschule* supported inclusive education while 43 per cent opposed it. The highest approval level came from *Grundschule* teachers, with 73 per cent in support and 26 per cent opposed (Forsa 2015, 3).[9]

This survey shows how much controversy continues to dog the topic of inclusion in Germany. Of course, some teachers might be clinging to old concepts of segregated education. In many cases, though, there is a willingness to support inclusion if the framework conditions are adequate. Often, teachers' difficulties and training needs with regard to inclusion are a consequence of their prior training and their inadequate opportunity to receive further education. In the same Forsa survey, 78 per cent of teachers in regular secondary schools described their training with respect to inclusion as *not very good* or *not good at all* (Forsa 2015, 11).[10]

Special needs teachers, on the other hand, study in great detail the learning preconditions of children with disabilities while at university. Their education is more focused on instructional methods and educational psychology and is sometimes limited to preparation for work in a specific form of special needs school (Reich 2014, 357). Interestingly, in the Forsa survey only 53 per cent of the special needs teachers supported the concept

9 The survey question was "Do you think it makes sense to teach all children with and without disabilities together?" The possible answers were "Yes" and "No, it makes more sense to teach children with disabilities in special schools" (Forsa 2015, 3; translation from German by the author).

10 The survey question was "How do you judge the quality of further training opportunities regarding inclusive education?" The three possible answers were "very good," "not very good," and "not good at all" (Forsa 2015, 11; translation from German by the author).

of inclusion, with 45 per cent opposed (Forsa 2015, 3). Also, the opportunities for further training in inclusive education were regarded as *not very good* or *not good at all* by 88 per cent of the special needs teachers (Forsa 2015, 11). This may indicate that special needs teachers are well educated in teaching children with a special form of disability in a segregated setting but not well prepared to deal with inclusive learning settings. A teacher trained specifically to work in a school for the blind, for example, might feel overburdened in an inclusive class with typically developing children and, perhaps, children with other disabilities.

As a function of teacher training in Germany, the lessons taught in regular schools are still often based on traditional teacher-centered methods,[11] with the teacher lecturing in front of the class while the children are mainly listening and have few opportunities to investigate the subject actively for themselves. Children's individual interests and capabilities receive relatively little attention in this method. Of course, some children cope reasonably well with this form of teaching, but this approach is very difficult to adapt to the various proficiency levels of students in a classroom. Children with special learning needs and those who are highly gifted may be poorly served by such lectures, and children who prefer more active forms of learning often have difficulty focusing on the lessons. This problem increases in an inclusive classroom with a broader heterogeneity of abilities, background knowledge, and preferred means of learning.

With the implementation of inclusive education, more and more special needs schools will be closed and children with disabilities will transfer to the regular schools. In the next two decades, 85 per cent of all German children with disabilities are to be educated in inclusive classes (Humbach et al. 2014, 14). Many teachers wonder how they will integrate children with disabilities into classrooms that use traditional teaching approaches (Humbach et al. 2014, 33). But here, inclusive education is confused with integration. The inclusion of children with disabilities in former regular schools is possible only by using various learning methods developed in cooperation between the regular schoolteachers and the newly arriving special needs teachers. Regrettably, up to the present time many special needs teachers have had limited opportunity to participate in the planning of classroom instruction. Usually they have to move between classes several times a day and are responsible only for certain children with disabilities, who are often still educated apart from their classmates. Some special needs teachers are even employed at two or three different schools, further complicating the situation (see Speck 2015). The consequence of this rotation between classes and schools is that the special needs teachers never have the opportunity to spend much time in a single classroom. They have no way to get to know the students and their daily social behaviors well. In such circumstances, it is not possible to develop appropriate support according to the highly individual learning conditions of all students. A good knowledge of a child's whole personality is very important in order to solve learning problems. For example, a problem in mathematics can be caused by social problems, or, as Martha Nussbaum notes, "Muscle therapy for children with Down syndrome can make

11 This method is called *Frontalunterricht* in German.

it possible for these children to negotiate their world in a way that promotes active learning" (Nussbaum 2006, 199). It is difficult for a special needs teacher to monitor a child's learning process in this holistic way if the teacher sees the child for only a few hours a week and then sometimes only in a separate room from the rest of the class. One might say that the special needs teachers themselves should be better included in regular schools to make the inclusion of children with disabilities possible.

Also, the distribution of responsibilities between regular and special needs teachers is questionable. The approach of separating children according to their officially classified form of disability and teaching them in parallel groups – and then often in different rooms – is not appropriate. In this way, the former exclusion previously created by special needs schools simply continues within a regular school building. These strict divisions do not do justice to the complex personalities and abilities of children.[12] The problems inherent in these classifications are very well described by the following quotation:

> Such classifications may not always help the child: they can be stigmatized in their own right, and they do not always point to a useful course of treatment. Moreover, they tend to be unfair to children who have problems in school but who cannot be plausibly classified as learning disabled. One feels that all children should be helped to reach their cognitive potential; but the system promotes some children over others in a way that is more than a little arbitrary.
>
> (Nussbaum 2006, 209)

This passage, written by a US author, describes quite aptly the situation in many German schools. By means of this kind of classification and segregation, children with disabilities are often stigmatized. Already the label "child with a disability" combined with special treatment can, although often well intentioned, create social outsiders among the students. Many regular as well as special needs teachers still think in terms that accentuate a child's disability instead of his or her talents (Reich 2012, 88). Often both types of teachers intensify stereotypes by using simplifying classifications to describe the whole child and distinguish him or her from the so-called normal learners. It seems necessary to enforce a deconstruction of the dualistic categories *normality* and *disability* in favor of individual support for every child. It is well known that choices of language influence or even constitute people's perception of reality. To divide students into two groups and label one as "normal learners" and the other as "disabled learners" results in stigmatization and is not sensitive to the children's individual personalities. The categorizations are often oriented by reference to a single deficit possessed by the children and ignore their capabilities and potentials (Humbach et al. 2014, 37; Reich 2014, 78). Of course, it is often necessary to diagnose and name a given pupil's learning difficulties

12 I am critical of making a general and permanent distinction between impaired and nonimpaired children. I do not generally oppose a flexible and temporary internal differentiation within a class according to learning goals, abilities, and interests. This will be further explained in the fourth section.

or impairments to offer adequate assistance, but the diagnosis should be differentiated and should consider the child's unique talents and strengths as well. To use one deficit-oriented category to describe a whole child is a reduction of complexity that does not do justice to the individual character of a growing person. In contrast, we should reflect thoughtfully and critically on this use of categories and classifications and develop a language that is more differentiated and not focussed only on deficits (Boban et al. 2014).

In the quotation presented earlier, Martha Nussbaum formulates a further problem. If children with disabilities are singled out as a separate group and given special support, then stigmatization could be accompanied by jealousy from other children and their parents (Nussbaum 2006, 209). In fact, when the special needs teacher cares exclusively for one child in a class all the time, the other children sometimes start to make offensive remarks. A female learning assistant reported recently that classmates began making comments about the child for whom she is responsible, calling him the "child who is always with his aunt." At first glance, this example does not seem very insulting, but it shows that even slight details can lead to problems. If one is not careful, then a child can quickly be regarded as fundamentally different and become a victim of insults or bullying. That becomes a serious emotional issue because children find it very painful to feel excluded by their peers and schoolmates (Prengel 2013, 179).

A permanent distinction of disabled children during the learning process seems artificial and preserves their social exclusion. This incomplete application of inclusive education might even increase stigmatization. One common reason why children with disabilities return from inclusive schools to special institutions is low self-esteem as a consequence of stigmatization (Mays 2014). Another reason is that the learning environment in special needs schools is still experienced as more suitable for the learning needs of children with a disability. Both the teacher-centered form of instruction and the frequent stigmatization make it difficult to involve children with disabilities comprehensively in regular schools.

As I mentioned previously, inclusive education has been a topic of intense and sometimes emotional discussion in Germany. Often, these debates are mainly about the *implementation* of inclusive education and are thereby helpful to refine its realization. Sometimes, though, teachers, parents, and scientists oppose the whole *idea* of inclusive education because they have experienced problems such as those previously described. This opposition could threaten the future of inclusive education throughout German society. In addition, some parents worry that their children could suffer disadvantages from the implementation of inclusive education because the level of learning might be lowered by the participation of children with disabilities.[13] Such concerns can increase levels of suspicion and prejudice. A modern and well-communicated conception of learning and knowledge is needed to show that *all* children in a class can benefit from inclusive education in various ways (Humbach et al. 2014, 25). It will be necessary to

13 These parents might not be as numerous as one might assume. In empirical studies, most respondents express a neutral or slightly positive attitude toward inclusion. Nevertheless, worries do exist among many parents and should be taken seriously (see Heyl et al. 2014).

establish substantive discussions within social discourse, listen carefully to the experiences and fears of the people concerned, and develop mutual understanding together. To grasp how to fulfil children's right to inclusive education most effectively, parents, teachers, and society as a whole must have the opportunity to gain a profound knowledge about the idea and methods of inclusion and to engage in open discussion of their problems, fears, and misunderstandings.

In conclusion, it appears that discrimination, inequality in education, and lack of participation could all be *increased* if the complicated transition from the old system of separate special needs schools to the new form of inclusive education is not properly implemented and well communicated. It could happen that the good idea of inclusion will fail and become discredited because the implementation of inclusive education in regular schools is badly organized and inadequately financed. It is necessary to build up an appropriate inclusive education program at regular schools. Then and only then will students with disabilities and their parents have a real opportunity to choose inclusive education without fearing educational disadvantage or social marginalization. That is a precondition to facilitate inclusion and the scaling down of segregated schools (see Speck 2015). Preventing discrimination and stigmatization and encouraging participation and individualized learning are necessary steps to make meaningful inclusion possible.

4. Promising approaches

Having focused on the problems and challenges involved in implementing inclusive education in Germany, I will now present some promising approaches to overcome these difficulties and point out important elements for the successful realization of inclusion in German schools.

The German Rectors Conference (*Hochschulrektorenkonferenz* or HRK) and the Standing Conference of Ministers of Education and Cultural Affairs of the Länder in the Federal Republic in Germany (*Kultusministerkonferenz* or KMK) have underscored the importance of adapting teacher training at universities so as to advance inclusive education. Regular teachers need increased coursework to learn important skills in inclusive teaching (HRK 2015). German universities have begun to set up additional learning modules in which all student teachers acquire, for example, knowledge about educational diagnostics or differentiated teaching methods (see Moser and Demmer-Dieckmann 2013, 161). It will still also be necessary to train special needs teachers in certain forms of disability, so that there will be various kinds of experts available who can contribute their knowledge (HRK 2015). One important element of teacher education will be to improve and encourage co-teaching, collaboration, and teamwork. Teachers will need to support each other in order to manage the various demands of inclusive education (see Smith 2010, 205).

Up to this point, many German teachers have not been accustomed to team-teaching or cooperating with other professions. That is also a consequence of the former school system where regular teachers were first of all responsible for teaching their subject and not very involved in developing their students' social skills. In inclusive schools, however, all teachers must contribute their special competencies, knowledge, and interests in complementary fashion as part of a multidisciplinary team (see Humbach et al. 2014, 20). Effective inclusive education requires teachers to have regular interaction with psychologists, specially trained mediators, sport coaches, employees of afternoon childcare programs, and other professionals. In addition, an interdisciplinary team could include not only social service professionals such as educators and psychologists but others as well – for example, the school custodian (Reich 2014, 91). These professionals are also part of the school system and can offer valuable opinions and support. Most of all, children and parents should be part of the team as well and should share responsibility for the learning process and the organization of school life.

There are already some fine examples of cooperative teaching teams who develop well-organized learning concepts according to their students' individual needs. One important element in this regard is the application of various learning methods such as think-pair-share, collaborative learning groups, student debates, learning cells, learning by teaching, and others. These should be carefully chosen according to the students' needs and learning goals (see Humbach et al. 2014, 34). It is important to connect and interlock all methods in a complementary way. For example, children can help one another in learning partnerships while doing research at the school library and, at the same time, preparing posters that depict stages of a manufacturing process. In this way, the different methods are not applied in isolation but, rather, provide interactive working and learning possibilities that enable children to follow their interests and improve their individual skills. It is important that effective "individualized support measures are provided in environments that maximize academic and social development, consistent with the goal of inclusion" (CRPD 24.2e). To make this possible, the classroom should be arranged as an open learning environment with different learning materials, methods, and spaces. Such learning environments can offer the children many opportunities to choose the content, mode, and pace of their learning process throughout the day. For instance, children could be given the opportunity to choose whether to work alone, in a group, or in a learning partnership. They can be introduced to various educational tools, located throughout the classroom, that permit them to engage in different forms of learning.

In many inclusive schools, there is an additional room for every class so that some students can learn separately from the others. As described in the previous section, this room is often used to split the class into one group of children with disabilities and one group of so-called normal learners, a practice that might exacerbate discrimination (Humbach et al. 2014, 34). But the division of the class into learning groups can be done in a more differentiated way, and the additional room can be used with greater variety and sensitivity (Humbach et al. 2014, 37). During certain, limited learning stages, the class can be divided variably into learning groups according to the interests, learning goals, and abilities of every child – not according to their classified disabilities, which (as we have already noted) often do not do justice to the complex individuality and abilities of a child. Every child, with or without a disability, has a wide and unique range of talents and difficulties. There are children with dyscalculia who can speak three languages fluently! In a flexible formation of learning groups, those children could participate in a group of strong language learners, while a student without a disability could join the learning group with the specialized teacher in mathematics if necessary. There must be a more differentiated evaluation of the strengths and learning difficulties of every child. Then, the special needs teachers are not limited to a certain group of classified "children with disabilities" but instead have the opportunity to help every child to overcome problems and to develop individual strengths (Humbach et al. 2014, 37).[14] In addition, when children experience receiving needed support in the same way as others, they feel equally accepted and respected in their individuality and personality as everyone else.

To make independent and autonomous learning possible, children should learn step by step how to work in different settings and with different methods. An interesting approach is using *learning by teaching methods*. This means encouraging children to learn, to a large extent, from one another how to study in inclusive environments. I will illustrate with an example. Currently, many inclusive classes are heterogeneous not only by ability but also with regard to age (see Schley 2014). In a class of first- through fourth-grade students, the children range in age from six to ten years.[15] It is difficult to teach a class of such high heterogeneity by using only the teacher-centered instruction method. Of course, often it is necessary for the teacher to give direct instruction, such as to introduce new learning methods and materials. But an effective learning organization cannot rely on one modality only. In order to handle a diversity of learners within an inclusive learning concept, it is important to enable the students to also learn from one another. In this situation, the first graders who have just started their school careers could learn basic learning methods and classroom rules from older students. The older children, having experienced the learning environment for several years, can introduce the younger ones to different forms of learning. One suitable method could be to construct learning partnerships consisting of a first grader and a fourth grader. Every year, the students' positions and duties would change because new first graders come into the class while the oldest students leave. Along the way, every child learns numerous social and pedagogical skills (see Schley 2014). In this system, everybody benefits in many ways. The older children learn about responsibility and the ability to support others by respecting their individuality. The younger children are introduced to active learning and also learn how to seek assistance from people who have various specialities. They learn to respect the unique aspects of each classmate and to cooperate with different kinds of personalities (Reich 2014, 371).

As mentioned in section 3, many parents fear that their child might be disadvantaged due to inclusive education, especially when their classmates might be younger or have learning disabilities. Let us consider additional examples of how all children

14 Also, the European Agency (2015a, 7) recommends the implementation in regular schools of teaching methods developed in special needs schools, so that they may benefit all children.

15 This is a common situation because elementary schools in Germany generally enroll children from first through fourth grade. Usually, the students are divided by ages in order to create homogeneous learning groups. But increasingly, schools are introducing instructional methods that involve teaching different age groups together, especially in schools supporting inclusive education.

might benefit from helping one another in inclusive settings through *learning by teaching* methods. Suppose that a child has to explain mathematics to a classmate (who is younger or has learning difficulties). In this situation, the "teaching" child has to understand the exercises very well and has to develop precise language skills in order to express the concepts. He or she learns to listen to the questions and feedback received from the "learning" classmate and to respond properly. In this way, the "teaching" child develops important skills and becomes a learner himself or herself.

Alternatively, children could be involved in preparing learning materials for students with special needs. Here they might learn how to visualize complex contents for deaf children (e.g., by using new technologies). In such examples of outcome-based education, the children could expand their knowledge and skills (see Humbach et al. 2014, 40). Parental concerns might be allayed if such learning processes are well communicated. In this context, it is interesting that even most economists today stress the need for companies to develop their employees' flexibility, social skills, tolerance, and capacity for teamwork so that they are prepared for our globalized world. Children should not only be educated in core subjects such as math or physics but, in addition, should have the opportunity to develop the ability to work in teams. They must learn to function in working groups where each member contributes his or her individual ideas and strengths. And where else could a child learn this better than in an inclusive classroom where he or she is trained to overcome difficulties in cooperation with children who have very different abilities? In a well-designed inclusive learning concept, the nonimpaired children benefit too.[16]

In a well-designed learning environment where diversity is encouraged, children have the opportunity to develop and represent their own opinions in discussions with other children. In order to support this opportunity, it is important to implement forms of democratic participation within the class.[17] There should be an organized way to negotiate compromises between the children in a discourse. Children greatly appreciate having their opinions respected and valued. Even at a young age, they have the capability and empathy to understand other viewpoints and are willing to make compromises when the decision-making process is transparent and regarded as fair. In this way, children learn to assume responsibility, articulate their personal opinions, and cooperate with others. In addition to the discourse within their classroom, students should be involved as much as possible in the conceptual development of the whole school on a regular basis and should have an influence on overall guidelines and general values (see Lahne-Kuhlmann 2014). The school system has the duty not only to prepare its students for the job market but also to impart social values such as respect

16 For an overview of some empirical studies on the effects of inclusive education on the learning outcomes and social development of children, see Klemm and Preuss-Lausitz (2012).

17 The importance of democratic learning in inclusive schools is emphasized in the school program of the Inclusive University School in Cologne/Inklusive Universitätsschule Köln (see School Is Open 2014, 22–27). The Inclusive University School is a project originally initiated by students of the University of Cologne to develop, implement, and explore new forms of inclusive education.

for human dignity, tolerance, and cohesion. The goal of strengthening "respect for human rights, fundamental freedom and human diversity" (CRPD 24.1a) seems to be best accomplished in a well-established, inclusive learning environment. Living with diversity every day, accompanied by support and care from teachers, makes it possible to develop sensitivity to the relevance of human rights. Children can gain self-confidence and the experience of caring for others so that they will regard people of different types as an integral part of human society. In this context, key questions of inclusion, inclusive education, and human rights should be discussed explicitly and regularly with the students. As a contribution to human rights education, children can thereby learn to understand, discuss, question, and it is hoped, support these ideas. Participation in such discussions provides an important basis undergirding people's ability to stand up for the human rights of all. Without a doubt, fostering autonomous learning processes and building cooperation among students represents a stiff pedagogical challenge, but many schools in Germany have already shown that it is worth the effort.[18] To entrust the children with more responsibility modifies learning and teaching. After a cooperative system has been established, general learning is organized to a large extent by the children while the teachers monitor the educational process and offer targeted assistance when needed. In this setting, diversity is not a problem but a useful precondition for the personal development of the children in the classroom (see Reich 2014, 399).

One fundamental basis for such a learning environment as previously described is a highly structured, comprehensible, and fair method of organization. Children must be readily able to perceive how to learn, how to help one another, and how to get help from the teachers, including the special needs teachers. An inclusive learning environment does not mean that teachers are not responsible for the structure of the lessons or their students' learning. It does not mean the advent of a "one-size-fits-all" or even an "anything goes" approach, in which the teachers stop guiding their students' learning process and stop reacting to children's difficulties by providing individual help. On the contrary, to create inclusive learning environments requires considerable pedagogical knowledge and extensive effort in planning and implementing. Guiding students to develop realistic learning goals and gain autonomy and participation demands a range of social competencies. But with some effort, a well-designed learning setting can be implemented where *all* children can benefit from the competencies of both the regular and the special needs teachers and be educated according to their individual abilities. In such a learning environment, there need not be any dualistic categorizations or fundamental differences between children. Instead, every single child can be seen in his or her unique individuality with his or her own talents, interests, and needs. And that would be a promising way to avoid discrimination and to ensure participation and equality in education for all children.

18 For further information on how to encourage cooperation among children, see, for example, Humbach et al. (2014, 29); Reich (2014); Salzberg-Ludwig (2012).

5. Conclusion and final remarks

In this chapter I have described the major goals of Article 24 of the CRPD; summarized prominent assessments regarding the implementation of inclusive education by the German government, the German Institute of Human Rights, and the UN Committee on the CRPD; outlined some of the main reasons why Germany has struggled to implement inclusive education; and presented some promising approaches to overcome these difficulties and important elements for the practical implication of inclusion in German schools.

By first describing the problems and then offering promising approaches and solutions, I have presented two quite opposite and perhaps exaggerated scenarios. Of course, the reality of inclusive education in German schools lies mostly somewhere in between. But clearly, much effort is still needed to realize the goals of Article 24 of the CRPD in Germany. Even when there are some hopeful attempts, it will take some time and intermediate procedures to achieve the ultimate goal of a well-implemented, nationwide inclusion strategy. In this regard, I conclude with some final recommendations on how to move forward.

The ratification of the CRPD has set in motion great changes in the German educational system. The old ways of classification and segregation are no longer adequate when inclusive education is to be enforced. The former regular schools must be modified to serve the needs of children with disabilities, and special needs teachers must become integrated in regular teaching teams. Multidisciplinary teams should be established to bundle different competencies. Also, teacher training at universities must be reorganized so that every teacher learns the basics of inclusive education. Many universities have already taken initial steps in this direction by setting up new learning modules. This process is enforced and supported by the guidelines of the HRK and KMK.

It will be important to set up inclusive learning environments that enable all children to plan their learning processes according to their diverse individual interests, capabilities, and needs. This planning and learning should be carefully assisted by the teachers,[19] who must ensure that every child practices important key competencies such as writing or reading. In addition, the teachers should offer different learning options and various fields of study among which the children can choose so that they can follow their interests, acquire specific skills, and try to become experts. Furthermore, there must be opportunities for children to assume responsibility and engage in cooperation. The diversity of characters, needs, and opinions in inclusive schools entails both the necessity and the possibility of constructive discourses on how to avoid exclusion, discrimination, and stigmatization and how to build a shared coexistence in society based on universal human rights. To negotiate the rules of school life with other children on an everyday basis is an important preparation for participation in a global and diverse society. Schools with diverse students can offer an excellent opportunity for students to learn how to work together with different personalities.

19 Some educationalists recommend learning plans oriented according to competencies and goals that the students can choose on their own with advice from the teachers (e.g., Reich 2014).

They permit students to take on shared responsibility for the school community and to participate in the organization of school life. Important social skills can be practiced if the advantages of diversity on the basis of equal rights are recognized in education (see Prengel 2013, 179).

In my opinion, it is important for the future of inclusive education in Germany to encourage respectful and continuing communication between politicians, scientists, and practicing teachers. In everyday working life, it is often difficult for teachers to keep up with the newest philosophical and pedagogical concepts. On the other hand, politicians and scientists might sometimes overlook tasks, needs, and challenges that arise in everyday school life. On the basis of an encouraged, respectful, and continuous dialogue, teachers can develop new methods and instructional concepts while politicians and scientists gain a deeper insight into practical circumstances. But most important, the opinions and experiences of the children and their parents who are most directly affected by inclusive education should be heard. The principle ***nothing about us without us*** requires intentionally involving persons with disabilities, as much as possible, in the conception and realization of inclusion. Communication, cooperation, and an interdisciplinary discourse are important elements of implementing the goals of Article 24, especially with regard to preventing discrimination and achieving equality in education and participation. I believe firmly that establishing inclusive education is an important achievement. Even though much work still has to be done and much money has to be spent to implement inclusive education in Germany, it is worth the effort. To orient our lives according to the principles of humanity and solidarity is the precondition for a just society based on human rights.

6. References

Beauftrage der Bundesregierung für die Belange behinderter Menschen. "Die UN-Behinderten rechtskonvention. Übereinkommen über die Rechte von Menschen mit Behinderungen." Available at: https://www.behindertenbeauftragter.de/SharedDocs/Publikationen/DE/Broschuere_UNKonvention_KK.pdf?__blob=publicationFile.

Blum, Volker and Elmar Diegelmann. 2014. "Die Ziele der UN-Konvention für Behindertenrechte und die Schulentwicklung in Deutschland." In *So kann Inklusion an Schulen gelingen. Praxisberichte aus verschiedenen Perspektiven*, edited by Volker Blum and Elmar Diegelmann, 1–14. Kronach: Carl Link.

Boban, Ines, Andreas Hinz, Elisabeth Plate, and Peter Tiedeken. 2014. "Inklusion in Worte fassen- eine Sprache ohne Kategorisierungen?" In *Inklusion und Chancengleichheit. Diversity im Spiegel von Bildung und Didaktik*, edited by Saskia Schuppener, Norah Bernhardt, Mandy Hauser, and Frederik Poppe, 19–25. Bad Heilbrunn: Klinkhardt.

Burckhart, Holger. 2001. "Bildung im Diskurs als Herausbildung von Mitverantwortung." In *Prinzip Mitverantwortung. Grundlage für Ethik und Pädagogik*, edited by Karl-Otto Apel and Holger Burckhart, 177–202. Würzburg: Königshausen und Neumann.

European Agency for Special Needs and Inclusive Education. 2015a. "Assessment für das Lernen bei Schülerinnen und Schülern mit sonderpädagogischen Förderbedarf." Available at: https://www.european-agency.org/sites/default/files/assessment-for-learning-and-pupils-with-special-educational-needs_assessment_for_learning_de.pdf.

———. 2015b. "Germany: Special needs education within the education system." Available at: https://www.european-agency.org/country-information/germany/national-overview/special-needs-education-within-the-education-system.

Forsa. 2015. "Inklusion an Schulen aus Sicht der Lehrerinnen und Lehrer-Meinungen, Einstellungen und Erfahrungen." Available at: http://bildungsklick.de/datei-archiv/md/305/inklusion-ergebnisse-bund.pdf.

Franzkowiak, Thomas. 2010. "'Dafür bin ich doch gar nicht ausgebildet!' Was lernen zukünftige Lehrkräfte an der Hochschule über 'inklusive Pädagogik.'" In *Integration und Inklusion auf dem Weg ins Gemeinwesen*, edited by Anne-Dore Stein, Stefanie Krach and Imke Niedeck, 245–256. Bad Heilbrunn: Klinkhardt.

German Institute for Human Rights. 2015. *Parallel Report to the UN Committee on the Rights of Persons with Disabilities*. Available at: http://tbinternet.ohchr.org/Treaties/CRPD/Shared%20Documents/DEU/INT_CRPD_NHS_DEU_19761_O.pdf.

Gordon, John S. 2013. "Is Inclusive Education a Human Right?" *Journal of Law, Medicine & Ethics* 41(4): 754–767.

Heyl, Vera, Silke Trumpa, Frauke Janz, and Stefanie Seifeld. 2014. "Inklusion beginnt im Kopf? Einstellungsforschung zur Inklusion (EFI)." In *Inklusion und Chancengleichheit. Diversity im Spiegel von Bildung und Didaktik*, edited by Saskia Schuppener, Norah Bernhardt, Mandy Hauser, and Frederik Poppe, 39–47. Bad Heilbrunn: Klinkhardt.

Hinz, Andreas. 2003. "Die Debatte um Integration und Inklusion- Grundlage für aktuelle Kontroversen in Behindertenpolitik und Sonderpädagogik?" *Sonderpädagogische Förderung* 48: 330–347.

———. 2011. "Von der Integration zur Inklusion – terminologisches Spiel oder konzeptionelle Weiterentwicklung? Nachdruck des Textes von 2002." In *Evangelische Bildungsverantwortung: Inklusion. Ein Lesebuch*, edited by Annebelle Pithan and Wolfhard Schweiker, 18–28. Münster: Comenius-Institut.

Hochschulrektorenkonferenz. 2015. "Lehrerbildung für eine Schule der Vielfalt. Gemeinsame Empfehlungen von Hochschulrektorenkonferenz und Kulturministerkonferenz." Available at: http://www.hrk.de/positionen/gesamtliste-beschluesse/position/convention/lehrerbildung-fuer-eine-schule-der-vielfalt/.

Humbach, Martina, Christian Kluve, Karin Kress, Dirk Schlechter, Jost Schneider, and Rainer Wensing. 2014. *Inklusion in der Schule. Das Praxisbuch*. Donauwörth: Auer Verlag.

Klemm, Klaus, and Ulf Preuss-Lausitz. 2012. "Was ist guter inklusiver Unterricht?" In *Inklusion-praxisorientiert*, edited by Klaus Metzger and Erich Weigel, 49–63. Berlin: Cornelsen.

Lahne-Kuhlmann, Ulrike. 2014. "Der Klassenrat als Keimzelle der Partizipation." In *Inklusion an Schulen*, edited by Daniel Bognar and Bianca Maring, 304–322. Cologne: Carl Link.

Mays, Daniel. 2014. "Inklusion? Auf den Selbstwert der Kinder kommt es an." *Grundschule*, 46(10): 30–31.

Moser, Vera, and Irene Demmer-Dieckmann. 2013. "Professionalisierung und Ausbildung von Lehrkräften für inklusive Schulen." In *Die Inklusive Schule. Standards für die Umsetzung*, edited by Vera Moser, 155–174. Stuttgart: Kohlhammer.

Netzwerk Artikel 3- Verein für Menschenrechte und Gleichstellung Behinderter e.V. 2010. Schattenübersetzung des Netzwerks Artikel 3. Available at: http://www.netzwerk-artikel-3.de/index.php/vereinte-nationen.

Nussbaum, Martha C. 2006. *Frontiers of Justice: Disability, Nationality, Species Membership*. Cambridge, MA: Harvard University Press.

Prengel, Annedore. 2013. "Humane entwicklungs- und leistungsförderliche Strukturen im inklusiven Unterricht." In *Die Inklusive Schule. Standards für die Umsetzung*, edited by Vera Moser, 177–185. Stuttgart: Kohlhammer.

Reich, Kersten, ed. 2012. *Inklusion und Bildungsgerechtigkeit. Standards und Regeln zur Umsetzung einer inklusiven Schule*. Weinheim und Basel: Beltz.

———. 2014. *Inklusive Didaktik. Bausteine einer inklusiven Schule*. Weinheim und Basel: Beltz.

Salzberg-Ludwig, Karin. 2012. "Teamarbeit in inklusiven Klassen." In *Inklusion-praxisorientiert*, edited by Klaus Metzger and Erich Weigel, 49–63. Berlin: Cornelsen.

Schley, Heike. 2014. "Entwicklung von Teamstrukturen und Kooperationsformen: Jahrgangsübergreifende Klassen in einer Grundschule." In *Inklusion an Schulen*, edited by Daniel Bognar and Bianca Maring, 331–334. Cologne: Carl Link.

School Is Open. 2014. *Rahmenkonzept zur Gründung einer inklusiven Praxisschule: 'Inklusive Universitätsschule Köln' – Eine Schule für alle.* Available at: http://www.schoolisopen.uni-koeln.de/wp-content/uploads/Beschlussvorlage-2014-April.pdf.

Smith, Phil. 2010. *Whatever Happened to Inclusion?* New York: Peter Lang.

Speck, Otto. 2015. "Das Schulpolitische Inklusionsdilemma in Deutschland- Die Verabschiedung des Inklusionsgesetzes im Deutschen Bundestag und deren Folgen." In *Heilpädagogische Forschung, Feb. 2015.* Available at: http://www.heilpaedagogischeforschung.de/ab1522.htm.

United Nations. 2006. *Convention on the Rights of Persons with Disabilities.* Available at: http://www.un.org/disabilities/convention/conventionfull.shtml.

———. 2013. Committee on the Rights of Persons with Disabilities. Consideration of reports submitted by States Parties under Article 35 of the Convention: Germany (DRPD/D/DEU/1). Available at: http://tbinternet.ohchr.org/_layouts/treatybodyexternal/Download.aspx?symbolno=CRPD%2fC%2fDEU%2f1&Lang=en.

———. 2015a. Committee on the Rights of Persons with Disabilities. Concluding observations on the initial report of Germany. Available at: http://daccess-dds-ny.un.org/doc/UNDOC/GEN/G15/096/31/PDF/G1509631.pdf?OpenElement.

———. 2015b. Consideration of State Reports. Available at: http://tbinternet.ohchr.org/_layouts/treatybodyexternal/SessionDetails1.aspx?SessionID=982&Lang=en.

Wocken, Hans. 2010. "Integration & Inklusion. Ein Versuch die Integration vor der Abwertung und die Inklusion vor Träumereien zu bewahren." In *Integration und Inklusion auf dem Weg ins Gemeinswesen*, edited by Anne-Dore Stein, Stefanie Krach and Imke Niedeck, 204–234. Bad Heilbrunn: Klinkhard.

Part III

Justice and legal protection

8 Disability rights, legal and moral

Hans S. Reinders

1. Introduction

In the winter of 2011, the media in the Netherlands reported the case of a young man with mild intellectual disability (ID) who had been held in detention for three years. The public outcry concerning the story was huge, which was not surprising given the fact that the young man was not a prison inmate but a resident of a home for people with ID, the aim of which is to provide care and support. Among the many questions asked, the main concern was how a resident of a service facility could be chained to the wall for three years, with only brief interruptions for physical exercise each day, and without anybody interfering. The similarities to a prison regime were just too obvious not to invoke waves of public protest.

A curious fact about the case was its resemblance to an earlier one that occurred in the Netherlands twenty-three years before and that evoked the same level of public indignation. In the fall of 1988, a national newspaper published a photograph on its front page showing a naked young woman chained to the wall. "The Netherlands in the Middle Ages" was an often-heard comment, likely because the photograph was indeed reminiscent of the practice of incarceration in previous centuries.

Both cases had several aspects worth mentioning in this connection because of their remarkable similarities. The first is the fact that, in both cases, the parents of the persons involved contacted the media with their stories, supported by pictures. The stated reason for this incisive step was their desperation about the service system not being able to get their children out of these deplorable situations and also because of their inability to listen to what these parents were telling them about their children.

Second, in both cases, the situations had been deteriorating during a longer period of time, which brought the person in a downward spiral of challenging behavior followed by a regime of restricted freedom, the result of which was more challenging behavior, more restrictions, and so on.

Third, the moment of the parents deciding to go public was identical – namely, the continuation of a deplorable situation where no initiative was taken anymore by anyone in the service system to improve the person's circumstances.

Fourth, in both cases, the justification by the service agencies for the existing situations was the same. The person was capable of extremely violent behavior toward support staff, with the possibility of serious injuries. And occasionally, self-injurious behavior had occurred. Public authorities – particularly the Inspectorate for Health-care, which is a government agency – reported in both cases that the service agencies had operated in accordance with standing regulations and procedures.

Finally, in both cases, the service providers were publicly accused of a violation of fundamental human rights. The comment was made that under no circumstance is it acceptable to restrict the freedom of human beings by chaining them to the wall without seriously violating their human dignity. It was pointed out that society does not even allow this for prisoners convicted of serious crimes, never mind that it should happen to persons with ID for whom service agencies have accepted responsibility to provide them with the care and support they need.

It is particularly in this last aspect that the similarities of both stories present us with an opportunity to discuss the relevance of human rights in relation to disability, specifically ID. At first sight, the question is by no means an obvious one to ask. Since the United Nations adopted the Convention on the Rights of Persons with Disabilities (CRPD) in 2006, the importance of human rights for people with ID has widely received a positive response. Organizations and institutions all over the world have adopted the support for the CRPD as a cornerstone of their policies and programs. In the present case human rights seem to have been blatantly violated so that the question of their relevance appears as a non-issue. Thus, the first thing to do is to clarify this chapter's goal.

The object of this chapter is to draw a distinction between two things that human rights claims can do in the public arena. First, they can be used in support of a moral cause that some people have been harmed or wronged in ways that violate their human rights. In this capacity, they can change people's hearts and minds, as well as public opinion, with regard to that particular cause. This is what I will call the moral significance of human rights. Arguments and discussions of human rights claims in this sense is the proper concern of ethics.

Second is the legal significance of human rights claims. While the moral meaning of human rights is indispensible, it is in itself insufficient to change harmful or wrongful actions or conditions and seek redress for those suffering from them. To be effective in this respect, human rights claims must be amenable to a court of law.

Furthermore, the object of this chapter is to argue that, in a practical sense, the legal significance takes precedence over the moral significance. In terms of the cases that were introduced earlier and will be discussed next, it certainly can be argued from the perspective of ethics that people with ID under no circumstances should ever be chained to the wall. But to be successful in forcing such treatment to be stopped, it must be possible to bring their cases to a court of law as a violation of their human rights.

With regard to persons with ID, there is a further concern that must be addressed. These persons can find themselves in situations where their mental competence is jeopardized to an extent that their freedom of action and/or judgment can be restricted. This may be the case, for example, when they show behavior that is either dangerous to themselves or to others. Restrictions of their freedom in such cases can certainly be argued to be thwarting their human rights. Even when such arguments are amenable to a court of law, however, it is still possible that the court decides for the lawfulness of restricting a person's freedom. While human rights are fundamental, they are not absolute.

In terms of their practical meaning, then, it is actually quite possible that the relevance of human rights claims with regard to disability are limited in one of two ways: first in the sense that they fail to be amenable to law and second in the sense that the law entails provisions to allow for legal restrictions on people's human rights.

2. Moral and legal rights

One way to demonstrate the distinction between the moral and legal significance of human rights claims is to look briefly at their historical origin. Historically speaking, the idea of human rights is at home in the tradition of natural rights (Donnelly 1982). Natural rights regard the things human persons ought to have by virtue of some conception of their human nature, whether these things are possessions, entitlements, or opportunities. One practical implication of the idea of natural rights has been that they can be claimed against positive law when it fails to respect and secure a basic concern for human dignity. However defended, natural rights were taken to reflect the moral order that was seen as grounding any decent human society (Tuck 1979).

Human rights have been discussed in similar ways. They are defended as securing the provisions that any society should make for its members. The same is true for human rights addressing disability as can be learned from the development of subsequent human rights documents in this area.

Before the CRPD was adopted, the United Nations in 1971 issued the Declaration on the Rights of Mentally Retarded Persons, followed in 1975 by the Declaration on the Rights of Disabled Persons, which was the first UN document trying to define the term *disability*.[1] It included several social and economic rights as well as civil and political rights. For each of these developmental steps, it is true that the human rights claims they introduced came alive as moral ideas. Human rights specifically aiming at persons with disabilities were mostly presented as being inherent to, as implications of, or as logical extensions of the moral vision underlying the human rights declarations that had already been accepted.

These observations are meant to indicate that human rights claims start their careers in public discourse as moral claims. Their function is to promote a particular moral cause, frequently connected with the social conditions of a particular category of human beings. As moral claims, then, human rights can be read as rights claims looking for public recognition.

In the language of ethics, the typical way to defend and promote moral rights claims is to argue for them on the basis of social justice. Social justice in any case – as in all domains of justice – is about equations. Are people in the possession of what they should

1 Langenbach (2003). This document provides a useful overview of the international instruments for the promotion and protection of human rights for people with disabilities: http://www.hrea.org/index.php?base_id=152.

have or be allowed or enabled to do? The underlying principle of answering such questions is always *suum cuique:* to each his due. Thus understood, to argue for disability rights – let us say the right to start a family – is to argue that as a matter of social justice people with disabilities should be allowed to have or do what people without disabilities are allowed to have or do, which – in the present example – is to start a family.

The way in which human rights claims are frequently supported by outcries of injustice indicates the moral force of human rights language. The fact that in this respect they are claims looking for public recognition is a strength that few other moral languages possess. Even when they are legally free to do so, authorities can often ignore them only at their own peril. Human rights claims as moral claims can therefore be used for political leverage, as a crowbar so to speak, opening up public debate in support of a particular cause by bringing it into the ambit of human rights as a fundamental moral concern of any decent society.

In contrast, the legal origin of human rights is of a very different kind. As legal rights, human rights originate from enactment, as any legal rights do. National governments enact human rights at the moment they ratify the convention in which they have been declared and adopted by the United Nations. From that moment onward, public authorities under that government can be held accountable for human rights violations. They can be tried before the courts. In this regard, the difference with human rights as moral claims cannot be clearer. Public authorities held accountable for human rights violations in a moral sense can only be tried in newspapers and in the media.

For any national government, the ratification of the CRPD is by no means a simple and straightforward act. It needs careful consideration of how the enacted rights relate to the already existing body of legal provisions. To enact human rights as part of the national legal system is not supposed to be a merely symbolic step, which means that governments must consider where enactment of such rights demand changing existing laws.

In view of these considerations, the moral issue regarding the main characters in the case introduced earlier should be clear. The question is how the human rights enshrined in the CRPD could have made a difference in the cases of both of these individuals. Having elaborated on the distinction between a legal and an ethical perspective on human rights, we will try to discover why and how both perspectives may turn out to be relevant. Even when it would be true that in the cases under consideration in this chapter a legal appeal to existing human rights instruments would have been of no avail for the persons involved, this would not preclude the possibility that a moral appeal nonetheless would retain its moral significance.

Human rights – international law in general – is a complicated subject in the sense that both aspects of morality and law are intertwined, as we will see, but they cannot be reduced to each other. No human rights instrument gets off the ground without a moral commitment to the cause of social justice it seeks to promote and protect. But without an established legal status, such instruments lack the teeth to bite. Once it has become part of the law of the land, on the other hand, the legal enforcement of human rights is relatively independent of morality.

In view of these considerations, it is possible to determine the exact nature of the issue this chapter is addressing. There are three elements in it that can and should be distinguished. One pertains to the question of being amenable to a court of law: the question of whether any human rights instrument was available to appeal to for the persons involved in the cases. Second, if so, then the question is whether the charges against the opposing party in each of these cases have a chance of being tried successfully? If not, then third, the remaining question is how moral charges of human rights violations nonetheless can be effective?

There is one final consideration on these preliminary matters. Apart from making it a human rights issue, could the service agencies involved in our two exemplary cases not have been taken to court under standing Dutch law? In other words, do we need to raise the question of a human rights violation in order to seek legal redress?

The answer can only be speculative because in actual fact there were no legal charges in either case. As noticed before in both cases, health care inspectors reported that the agencies had operated in accordance with standing regulations and procedures. The Dutch government accepted this report. In the most recent case, the Secretary of Health commented that the service provider in question had met all the standards for which they were accountable, which indicates that no legal charges were considered. Nor have parties other than public authorities brought the case before the courts.

3. Signification and ratification

The question of what a legal appeal could do for the persons involved in the two cases depends on whether the legal instrument on which the appeal is based is assumed to have the force of a binding treaty. With regard to the two cases at hand, the 1988 case, which I will refer to as the JV case – the initials of the young woman's name – could not have been tried under the existing declarations from 1971 and 1975 mentioned earlier. The reason is that both instruments were nonbinding treaties, which means that member states could not have been held accountable for implementing the provisions that both of these declarations made. No one could therefore have appealed to a Dutch court, or to any other court, to seek legal redress for a human rights violation on the basis of these declarations.

Another possibility to look at is the European Convention on the Protection of Human Rights and Fundamental Freedoms adopted in 1950. Cases that appeal to this convention are brought before the European Court of Human Rights whose decisions are legally binding. This instrument entails provisions explicitly referring to people with disabilities suggesting the possibility of taking legal action.

At this point, however, there is a restriction on admissibility upheld by the European Court that must be taken into account. Admissible cases are only those in which a *public authority* is accused of violating a human right. This can be a court, a local authority, or a national government. Cases against private enterprises or persons cannot be brought before the court, which indicates that legal redress for a human rights violation would have been impossible for the person involved in the JV case as described earlier. For the same reason, the European Court could not have tried the BI case – the initials of the young man involved in the 2011 case.

Things seem to have changed due to the adoption of the CRPD in 2006. But with regard to our two cases, we stumble on the unsettling fact that the Netherlands has signed, but ratified this convention not before the winter of 2016, so only six months ago. To explain what this means, we must look at the process of implementing a human rights document like the CRPD. The process entails several steps before it is part of the legal responsibility of member states. Once these steps have been taken, it is possible for individual citizens to report a violation to the UN Committee on the Rights of Persons with Disabilities.

First is the step of signing the convention by means of which a member state endorses its adoption by the United Nations. Second is the ratification, by means of which an individual member state declares that it will be accountable for incorporating the legal provisions the convention makes in its own laws. It is therefore obliged to submit regular reports to the committee on the processes of implementation, which are examined by the committee and followed by recommendations for the member state concerned. The third step is then the ratification of the optional protocol by which a member state declares that it allows the committee to examine individual complaints with regard to alleged violations of the convention by the states that are party to the protocol.

A further step is to incorporate a new instrument like the CRPD into an existing body of law such as, for example, the European Convention for the Protection of Human Rights and Freedoms, but only regional authorities such as the European Council can undertake this step. But again, to take the case before the European Court would mean that the same proviso becomes effective, which says that human rights violations under the CRPD are admissible only to the European Court when they are the responsibility of a public authority.

With regard to the first element of our question, whether any *binding* legal instrument was available to take the two cases by individual plaintiffs to court, the answer from these reflections is clear. They were not binding in any strictly legal sense. The legal representatives of these persons could not have accessed a court of law to claim human rights violations with the possibility of finding their claims acknowledged.

4. Promotion and protection

But this conclusion only pertains to the first element in our question. There is a further element to our question that from here on can only be discussed hypothetically. Suppose that there would be a binding legal instrument under which to try these cases. What could the courts have said?

The start of a specific UN focus on disability began with the declaration of 1971 that stated for the first time the principle of equality when it said, "The mentally retarded person has, to the maximum degree of feasibility, the same rights as other human beings." The declaration of 1975 followed with the first attempt to define the term *disability* (Langenbach 2003). It included several social and economic rights as well as civil and political rights.

The fact that both documents were nonbinding instruments indicates an important distinction within the specter of human rights concern of the United Nations – namely, the distinction between the promotion and the protection of human rights. Even when human rights cannot be protected because a legal instrument does not bind member states, it is still possible to promote the recognition of these rights within the international community. While "promotion" aims at raising public awareness of social and political responsibility for the recognition of human rights, "protection" aims at identifying accountability and the possibility of redress for violations (Mann et al. 1994, 12). In other words, effectively protecting human rights requires the kind of legal framework described earlier, without which the promotion of human rights is a primary task.

Traditionally, the United Nations has devoted much of its energy to human rights promotion, which is likely due to the fact that in their early stages the legal force of human rights was wanting. In recent times, the concept and the language of human rights has been expanding, which reflects its growing importance in the international world. In this regard, it is not by accident that the CRPD is indeed adopted as a binding treaty for member states that have ratified both the convention and the optional protocol.

In the same connection, it is remarkable to see the link the United Nations has forged between human rights and development issues. For example, in its campaign of promoting the human rights of people with disabilities, the CRPD goals have been tied to the Millennium Development Goals. This not only indicates that the United Nations considers a major objective of human rights instruments to be raising public consciousness about respect for human dignity, but it also indicates that an important role of promoting human rights has not so much to do with their implementation in legal frameworks as with an international, global appeal to the moral responsibility of public authorities. It seems that particularly the last element accounts for the fact that, in recent times, human rights language also expands in areas where no public authorities are directly involved (Mann et al. 1994, 11)

5. Liberties and claim rights

To move on to the second element in our discussion, the question is whether the charges against the service agencies in each of these cases would have had a chance of being recognized as a human rights violation. As noted earlier, this can only be a hypothetical question. On the proviso that a binding legal framework would exist, could JV and BI have a chance to have their service providers condemned? Suppose the Dutch government had already ratified the CRPD, including the optional protocol. Would it have been possible to win their cases before a court of law? Or would it have been possible to report a human rights violation to the UN Committee on the Rights of Persons with Disabilities?

To answer this question, it will be helpful to introduce a formal distinction between different "types" of rights because it will enable us to see that different types of rights imply different charges. The point is a general one and does not only apply to human rights but also to all sorts of rights, legal and moral.

Very generally speaking, rights can do one of two things for a person. First, they can establish a legal space for action – for example, the space of saying what one wants to say or the space of going where one wants to go. Rights creating legal space are called liberties, which is reflected in the notion of civil liberties. Civil liberties identify a set of activities in which citizens can freely engage without the permission of public authorities, be it a state government, court of law, or municipality. Well-known examples are the freedom of speech, freedom of print, freedom of movement, freedom of religion, and freedom of union; all of these are civil liberties.

Characteristic of rights as liberties is that they are often characterized as *negative* rights. All civil liberties are rights to non-interference. My right to freedom of movement entails that no one is allowed to stop me from going where I want. Rights of non-interference entail that other people don't have to do anything other than just let me. The freedom of movement, for example, does not entail for others an obligation to bring me where I want to go.

This consideration introduces a second type of rights. These are rights that empower persons to lay claim on other people's support. The right to adequate health care is an example. It enables me to claim treatment in case I fall ill. The right to food and shelter is another example.

Characteristic for claim rights is that they correspond to someone else's obligation. I have a positive right to treatment when I am ill that corresponds to the obligation of a doctor or a hospital to treat me if I show up at their doorsteps. Because they have an obligation to treat me, I have a right to be treated by them. The case can be stated in reverse order just as well. Because I have a right to be treated for my illness, no doctor is free to refuse me as a patient.

Similarly, when my local community is in the middle of a natural disaster, such as a tsunami, and we suffer from a short supply of water and food and our homes are destroyed, there is an obligation on the part of the international community to assist our government to do everything in its power to help us out with sufficient supplies. Again, my right corresponds to someone else's obligation.

To complicate matters further, there is a connection between liberties and claim rights. When I have the right to go where I want, nobody has a positive obligation to do anything. However, when a private person or agency is blocking my way unlawfully, this fact creates an obligation on the part of public authorities to uphold my right. In other words, someone interfering with my liberty creates a claim right for me against some public authority. When I am not allowed to enter a local space because I'm colored, say a restaurant or a theater, this creates an obligation on the part of my local government to enforce my right to freedom of movement. Similarly, when I am wheelchair bound and cannot enter a local space because it is not wheelchair accessible, this also creates an obligation for the municipality to enforce my right.

These examples already indicate the next point, which is that both kinds of rights cannot be absolute, but they are conditioned by certain restrictions. In the case of liberties, there can be good reasons to warrant interference. No one has the right to stop me from going where I want to go unless there is a sufficient reason to do so. For example, when the police are investigating a crime scene, they are allowed to stop me when I am about to enter it. When there is sufficient evidence that I am planning a serious crime, such as a terrorist attack, police officers have a right to stop me from entering an airplane. I don't have unlimited freedom of union with other people in case the goal of our coming together is for a conspiracy; I don't have an unlimited right to print – or say – what I want in case my aim is to spread hatred against a minority group. And so on.

Something similar can be true of claim rights but for different reasons. Victims of a natural disaster have the right to a sufficient supply of food and shelter, which puts their government under the obligation to provide them with these goods, but only to the extent of its ability to do so. I cannot claim a right to be treated by a doctor when there are no means to establish a health care facility. I cannot claim the right to food and shelter if public authorities are without the necessary means to provide me with such goods.

The latter circumstance indicates why some human rights have been spoken of frequently as promotional rights. They are dependent for their fulfillment on the means that public authorities can dispose of in order to enforce them. Because law enforcement is a central task of legal government, it is often the case that claims to enforce civil liberties appear to be stronger than claims to be provided with particular goods. In this connection, the rule "ought implies can" applies. When a public authority is unable to provide citizens with the goods they urgently need because of the lack of sufficient means, it cannot secure their rights to these goods for them. It cannot be charged, that is to say, with a rights violation.

6. Justifiable restrictions

In view of the cases of JV and BI against their service providers, the question to ask can now be stated with more precision. If we accept that chaining someone to the wall is an obvious violation of the person's freedom of movement, as I suggest, then the question to ask is whether the service agencies responsible for their incarcerations were justified in restricting their freedom in the way they did? Was there in both cases a sufficient reason to warrant their actions?

Obviously, in both cases, the service agencies involved argued that there was. Both JV and BI were considered to be extremely violent in their behavior toward others and therefore potentially dangerous. They had been chained to the wall because support staff were unable to control them physically. In the case of JV, she was stripped of her clothes because she would take them off and tear them apart. In times of crisis, this would happen several times a day.

Furthermore, the reason for restricting their freedom of movement was said to be the necessity of protecting other clients in their homes as well as support staff against physical assault. In this connection, it is relevant to recall in both cases that health care inspectors concluded that the service agencies had operated in accordance with standing regulations and procedures.

How do these cases appear in view of the human rights instruments that were hypothetically available to take them to court? To start with the oldest one, which is the European Convention for the Protection of Human Rights and Freedoms adopted in 1950, it is important to notice how it states the condition of ID as a possible mitigating condition.

In Article 5, the convention states, "No one shall be deprived of his liberty save in the following cases and in accordance with a procedure prescribed by law: . . . the lawful detention of persons for the prevention of the spreading of infectious diseases, of *persons of unsound mind,* alcoholics or drug addicts or vagrants" (Langenbach 2003).[2] This statement suggests that in the two cases at hand, the question would have been whether the European court would have considered both JV and BI to be persons "of unsound mind." An important fact in answering the question likely would have been the fact that both persons were diagnosed with an autism spectrum disorder in combination with ID.

The recognition of possible limitations of human rights for people with ID is not at all uncommon in UN documents. Other documents contain similar provisos that allow for legal restrictions. The Declaration on the Rights of Mentally Retarded Persons in 1971 stated in Article 1, "The mentally retarded person has, *to the maximum degree of feasibility*, the same rights as other human beings." Adding the clause "to the maximum degree of feasibility" is significant in the sense that human rights in general are subject to the restriction of feasibility without it being explicitly stated in the same way. The underlying idea appears to be that persons with ID constitute a special group that warrants special treatment. In Article 7, the recognition of the restriction of their rights is made subject to legal supervision:

> Whenever mentally retarded persons are unable, because of the severity of their handicap, to exercise all their rights in a meaningful way or it should become necessary to restrict or deny some or all of these rights, the procedure used for that restriction or denial of rights must contain proper legal safeguards against every form of abuse. This procedure must be based on an evaluation of the social capability of the mentally retarded person by qualified experts and must be subject to periodic review and to the right of appeal to higher authorities.

Again, the apparent assumption is that ID constitutes a particular condition that warrants assessing people's competence. In the same manner, the Declaration of the Rights of Disabled Persons in 1975 added a similar clause that also set apart a particular group of people. In Article 3, it states,

> Disabled persons, whatever the origin, nature and seriousness of their handicaps and disabilities, have the same fundamental rights as their fellow-citizens of the same age, which implies first and foremost the right to enjoy a decent life, *as normal and full as possible.*
>
> (United Nations 1975)[3]

Recognizing the issue of feasibility, this declaration continues to say that restrictions of the rights of persons with ID are subject to the same proviso as stated in Article 7

2 Italics added.
3 Italics added.

of the declaration from 1971. What is remarkable about these additions is the fact that the condition of feasibility holds for the human rights of all other people too, but it is only mentioned explicitly in the documents concerning the rights of people with ID. As indicated, the explanation of this fact might be that persons with ID are taken to constitute a particular class of people.

In view of these considerations, it is noticeable that the CRPD in 2006 was much more careful with regard to this assumption. For example, there is no explicit mentioning of the connection between the nature of the disability and the extent to which a "normal" life is possible. The logic of the CRPD seems to work the other way around. If a disabling condition is such that it poses more than average barriers, then this is a reason for a greater effort. In this respect, the CRPD follows an important insight from the field of disability studies. It states in the preamble, "Recognizing that disability is an evolving concept and that disability results from the interaction between persons with impairments and attitudinal and environmental barriers that hinders their full and effective participation in society on an equal basis with others" (United Nations 2006). This statement asserts that "disability" is not an inherent feature of a particular group of people but is rather the result of a particular kind of interaction. It concurs with the view that disabling conditions are not a defining characteristic of the person but are the effect of intertwining patterns of their social and cultural environments responding to their impairing conditions. In line with this view, Article 1 of the convention states, "Persons with disabilities include those who have long-term physical, mental, intellectual or sensory impairments that in interaction with various barriers may hinder their full and effective participation in society on an equal basis with others" (United Nations 2006).

The recognition of these conditions of impairment may imply that considerable effort will be needed to overcome the effects of patterns of interaction with society, which leads the CRPD to introduce in Article 2 the concept of "reasonable accommodation."

Reasonable accommodation means necessary and appropriate modification and adjustments not imposing a disproportionate or undue burden, where needed in a particular case, to ensure persons with disabilities the enjoyment or exercise on an equal basis with others of all human rights and fundamental freedoms (United Nations 2006).

This statement introduces yet again the same logic we have found in the earlier documents. Even though the CRPD is careful not to identify persons with ID as a particular category of human beings that needs to be set apart, the recognition of a "disproportionate or undue burden" takes us back to the implications of feasibility that we have seen before. It indicates the view that recognizing the human rights of these persons eventually may require more than can reasonably be expected from whoever is legally responsible for them.

Apparently, the burden placed on public authorities to ensure persons with ID the exercise of their rights can be "disproportionate," which cannot but imply that in some cases the obligation to do so is limited. This is not to deny that in principle persons with disabilities are equal in the possession of their human rights, but in actual fact the burden placed on public authorities to secure them in the exercise of their rights may exceed what can be reasonably expected.

The foregoing analysis at least indicates that, in the cases of JV and BI, it is not at all certain that a legal appeal to the CRPD, nor to any of the other human rights instruments we have been considering, would lead to the conclusion that the practice of chaining them to the walls of their rooms was a violation of their human rights to freedom of movement.

In view of this conclusion, two further considerations seem to be pertinent. It may be pointed out that in supporting persons with ID in similar circumstances, other service agencies both in the Netherlands and abroad have been successful. They have succeeded, this is to say, in avoiding situations where support staff got stuck in a negative chain of interaction with no prospect of a different kind of life for their clients. Support services can do their jobs without the need to put similar limitations on their freedoms. Could it be successfully argued, then, that in the cases of JV and BI, the requirement of providing them with reasonable accommodation would have demanded that their service providers should have transferred them to facilities that have been shown to be capable of support in ways that would avoid a violation of their rights to freedom?

Suppose the answer to this question should be affirmative. Would it follow, second, that a service provider that is approached in this connection would have an obligation to accept this client? Could service providers qualified for the task be forced to take over the responsibility for either JV or BI?

Given the hypothetical nature of the issue that we have raised in this chapter, these must remain open questions. In actual fact, both in the case of JV and of BI, the outcry of indignation once their circumstances were made known to the public led to the step of transferring them to other facilities – in the case of BI, this was indeed a facility of another service provider. This step opened the door to change that resulted in terminating the limitations of their freedoms that dominated their lives in the years before. It is therefore not unthinkable that this transfer might be regarded as a legal requirement to meet the obligation of reasonable accommodation in the CRPD.

Before moving to the moral significance of human rights claims, let us finish here with another observation within the legal domain. As the analysis of the Dutch situation does not result in strong legal possibilities to seek redress of violations of human rights through the courts, the situation in other countries can be quite different. The legal option on protecting persons with disabilities against restrictions of their freedoms such as we have been considering may not at all depend on legally binding human rights treaties. For example, the American Individuals with Disabilities Education Act enshrined the principle of the least restrictive environment in US law at least since the 1970s. The principle entails that, to the maximum extent appropriate, children with disabilities, including children in public or private institutions or other care facilities, are educated with children who are not disabled. It further demands that special classes, separate schooling, or other separations from the regular educational environment occurs only when the nature or severity of the child's disability is such that education in regular classes with the use of supplementary aids and services cannot be achieved satisfactorily.[4]

4 http://idea.ed.gov.

The principle is effectuated in the rule that no public funding will go to educational facilities that fail to provide their students with disabilities with the opportunity to be educated in the least restrictive environment. Although this is a specific example in only one area, however important, there is no reason, as a matter of principle, that this requirement of the least restrictive environment could not be made operational in other legal systems with regard to other areas as well. As noted earlier, it has been proven that the incarceration of both JV and BI was unnecessary in the sense that, once they were removed to other facilities, the inhumane restrictions of their freedoms were no longer needed. There is no reason why this fact could not be taken as a sufficient warrant to declare illegal severe restrictions of human freedom as the ones described.

7. What rights claims can do

Having laid out various reasons why the success of legal charges of human rights violations in our two cases in actual fact is doubtful, can it be argued that such charges nonetheless can be morally effective?

The question presupposes that the concept of human rights does not only have a role to play in international law but also possibly in social and political ethics. As was already noted in the introduction to this chapter, the relation between morality and law is a complicated affair. When the legal status of human rights claims is uncertain, they can still turn out to be morally significant, as argued earlier. But whether they actually are is a highly contextual matter. It all depends on the moral beliefs in the community that is addressed by such claims. When a community is seriously committed to the ethics of human rights, then charges of human rights violations, when made public, may be a powerful tool.

In fact, as pointed out earlier, this is what happened in the cases under consideration in this chapter. In both the case of JV and of BI, the media attention induced the responsible service agencies to react in a way that the restriction of their freedom to move came to an end soon after it was made known to the public.

This response indicates what human rights claims can do when appealing to a shared moral conscience. They make explicit what "we all" believe is morally wrong about the way that particular persons are treated. In the present cases, chaining a person to the wall for a longer period of time would not even be acceptable for convicted criminals, let alone for people with ID who are dependent on care and support from the agencies they have turned to.

From the perspective of ethics, a further aspect of what human rights claims can do is revealed by looking at our two cases while keeping the distinction between liberties and claim rights in mind. In terms of the former, the obligation on the part of the agencies involved is primarily one of refraining from interference with their personal freedoms. Their clients ought not to be locked away, let alone be chained to the wall, nor should they be drugged to suppress aggressive behavior. Service agency clients ought not to be restricted in these ways.

This is as far as claims to a violation of civil liberties can go. They can demand agents to abstain from limiting someone else's options, be they the option to speak up, move around, or do what they want to do. Rights can open doors – or cut chains – as the case may be. In most cases, that is sufficient to assure that the person involved can walk away freely.

However, in the context of services for persons with ID claim rights may also be involved. This is particularly the case when issues of "challenging behavior" are at stake. In those cases, it is not sufficient to simply abstain from interference. People need positive supports because without them the restoration of their freedom will hardly be beneficial. Having their civil liberties respected is coupled with the right to adequate supports, which creates a positive duty on the part of their providers.

In our exemplary cases, the support program had broken down, which can happen occasionally, of course. But what really outraged public opinion was the fact that the condition of semi-permanent incarceration of these clients was accepted by the service agencies involved as a way of providing appropriate care. The simple fact that other agencies seemed to have succeeded where they had failed indicates that alternative programs were available. Hence the conclusion that their respective service agencies were morally obliged not only to restore their freedom but also to provide them with adequate supports.

8. What disability rights cannot do

When the Dutch secretary of health concluded from the report by the Inspectorate of Healthcare in the case of BI that the service provider was not to be blamed because all of the required standard regulations and procedures had been followed, she added an interesting comment: "Even so, the result is undesirable."

The logic of this statement indicates that there were apparently two kinds of standards involved: one kind specifying legal requirements to be monitored by public authorities, the other specifying a standard of appropriate supports. Her comments implied that even when the former are met, the provided supports can nonetheless fail to meet the latter.

This distinction between what is desirable and what is legally required is very relevant with regard to what we can expect from disability rights. These expectations must be modest for several reasons. So far, we have been arguing that legal redress for human rights violations may not be very effective because adequately binding instruments are lacking, which might be called a procedural limitation. But there are at least two other kinds of limitations. First, not all values and goods that are important to people can be subject to public enforcement. The law might have been able to cut loose the chains of our two main characters, but it cannot make sure that their primary caregivers respond to them with the virtues of compassion and patience. Second, and related, rights cannot secure all that is valuable and good for human beings. In fact, they cannot even secure what many people consider the most important values and goods in their lives, such as intimacy and friendship.[5]

The first has to do with the fact that rights can only address a part of morality – namely, the part that is usually indicated by the notion of justice. Justice typically

5 See Reinders (2008).

addresses concerns about violation, discrimination, transgression, oppression, exploitation, and so on, all of which indicate an assault on human dignity. Each of these notions is about treating human beings in ways that are morally unacceptable and therefore need to be stopped. In case the perpetrators are not inclined to stop by themselves, they ought to be stopped by force.

This concern explains why the domain of justice is typically the domain of law enforcement by public authorities. Victims of injustice cannot be left in the hands of their perpetrators. The right of law enforcement does not depend on the criminal's will to comply. Perpetrators will be brought before a court of law, regardless of how they feel about it. In view of this account, the British philosopher John Lucas has aptly characterized the domain of justice as "the colder part" of morality (Lucas 1980).

As indicated, however, not all human values and goods can be secured in this way because they exceed the demands of justice. Obvious examples of such goods are love and friendship. Love and friendship are invaluable precisely because they cannot be extracted by force from other people. They are given freely and provide people with the blessing of being chosen by others as the satisfaction of their delight. Being recognized by the claims of justice can restore in people their human dignity, which is an invaluable quality of public morality. But being recognized by the claims of friendship is what makes one feel special to another person, which is what rights cannot do.

While love and friendship can be said to belong to the domain of intimacy and affection, it might be argued that this is not typically the domain we associate with professional service agencies. But on closer inspection we will see that support services are also concerned with values and goods that cannot be extracted by force. We need only ask ourselves what kind of people we prefer primary care professionals to be, and we will realize that what – or rather how – we like them to be has to do with moral virtues: human kindness, patience, attentiveness, and so on; they are character traits we usually appreciate in professionals but that cannot be enforced without losing their moral value.

This account of non-enforceable values and goods indicates at the same time why they presuppose particular kinds of moral relationships. To exercise patience, for example, one has to be a patient person; to exercise kindness, one has to be kind, and so on. This is true of many other values in the domain of human services. They are habitual, which is to say that they are expressive of what and how professional support workers want to be in relation to their clients. One cannot try to standardize, institutionalize, or enforce the expression of these moral virtues without at the same time undermining them.

9. Conclusion

Looking again at our two exemplary cases, it is clear how the force of human rights claims – legal or moral – is essential for the protection of the persons with disabilities involved in them. They call to stop treating people badly by assaulting their human dignity, as the practice of chaining both JV and BI to the wall, in my view, undoubtedly was.

Even when the legal procedures to do so are lacking, they still can break away people's chains through moral protest, which can effect change, as our cases have also shown. That is what rights can do. What they cannot do is provide people with a sense of belonging that makes them feel wanted and at home. Such valuable experiences cannot be created by force but are enjoyed because one's presence is valued and treasured by others.

10. References

Donnelly, Jack. 1982. "Human Rights as Natural Rights." *The Human Rights Quarterly* 3(4), 391–405.

Langenbach, Anna. 2003. "Human Rights of Persons with Disabilities." http://www.hrea.org/index.php?base_id=152.

Lucas, John R. 1980. *On Justice.* Oxford: Clarendon Press.

Mann, Jonathan M., Lawrence Gostin, Sofia Gruskin, Troyen Brennan, Zita Lazzarini, and Harvey V. Fineberg. 1994. "Health and Human Rights." *Health and Human Rights* 1(1), 6–23.

Reinders, Hans S. 2008. *Receiving the Gift of Friendship: Profound Disability, Theological Anthropology, and Ethics.* Grand Rapids, MI: Eerdmans.

Tuck, Richard. 1979. *Natural Rights Theories: Their Origin and Development.* Cambridge: Cambridge University Press.

United Nations. 1971. "Declaration on the Rights of Mentally Retarded Persons." http://www.hrea.org/index.php?base_id=152.

———. 1975. "Declaration on the Rights of Disabled Persons." http://www.hrea.org/index.php?base_id=152.

———. 2006. "Convention of the Rights of Persons with Disabilities." http://www.hrea.org/index.php?base_id=152.

9 From manifesto to action

Transforming the aspiration of disability human rights into accountable government action

Jerome Bickenbach

1. Introduction

In his dense but extraordinarily rich little book *Social Philosophy,* Joel Feinberg struggled with the broad notion of a *right* on his way to explicating legal rights and, ultimately, human rights (Feinberg 1973). A right is a kind of claim, he argued, but because not every claim to something is a right to it, only those claims that one justifiably or validly makes are plausible rights. When we are speaking of legal rights, validity is essentially a factual question: Is this right legally recognized? Is there a recognized and authoritative institutional mechanism (e.g. a court) to which one can appeal to enforce one's rights? Legal rights, in short, are enforceable. But what of moral rights? A person has a moral right, Feinberg asserts, when he or she has a claim, the recognition of which is justified not by legal rules but by moral principles. Human rights are the clearest examples of moral rights, as they purport to be "of a fundamentally important kind held equally by all human beings, unconditionally and unalterably" (Feinberg 1973, 68). That being said, philosophically, it remains an open question whether there are any human rights, and if so, what those rights are and whether any of them are also enforceable legal rights.

Historically, the theory that most clearly argued for human rights was the eighteenth-century account of natural rights associated with the English philosophers Thomas Hobbes and John Locke (Finnis, 2011; Tuck, 1979). As typically conceived, however, natural rights are very general and abstract, directed only against the state, and justified on theological grounds: hence the natural rights–informed US Declaration of Independence (1776) – people are "endowed by their Creator with natural rights to life, liberty, and the pursuit of happiness." As it happens, Feinberg is wholly skeptical of natural rights and makes the point that when philosophers move away from theological foundations and try instead to justify human rights in terms of the basic human needs these rights secure, in the end they can only establish a weaker sense of right – what he calls the "manifesto sense" of right:

> Such claims, based on need alone, are "permanent possibilities of rights," the natural seed from which rights grow. Manifesto writers are easily forgiven for speaking of them as if they are already actual rights, for this is but a powerful way of

> expressing the conviction that they *ought* to be recognized by states as potential rights and consequently as determinants of present aspirations and guides to present policies.
>
> (1776, 67)

But what of the human rights enshrined in the UN Universal Declaration of Human Rights in 1948 and all of the subsequent human rights treaties? Again, Feinberg is skeptical. Legal rights are logically correlated with legal duties or obligations against a specifiable individual or legal person like the state (they are, in legal terminology, claims *in personam*). But on inspection, many of the declaration's human rights are positive rights to the satisfaction of a human need for which there are no specifiable duties (hence claims *in rem*). More worrisome, UN declarations, although technically legal, do not create enforceable obligations on states because they constitute a form of consent-based governance in which sovereign states accept only those legal obligations that they consent to impose on themselves.

Here again the skeptical Feinberg thinks it is more accurate to call the provisions of the universal declaration "manifesto rights" – not because it would not be a very good thing if states guaranteed everyone work, an adequate standard of living, or an education, but because they purport to impose duties on the state that "are so difficult that they may, under widely prevalent conditions of scarcity and conflict, be impossible for *anyone* to discharge" (1776, 71). They are duties of the world at large, claims *in rem*. Although it is morally essential to continue to press for government action to meet these basic human needs, the state duties created by the universal declaration are only self-imposed, so these claims are not really human rights – in effect, they are a matter of political rhetoric about what the state *ought to do* for its citizens.

Many see the adoption of the UN Convention on the Rights of Persons with Disabilities (CRPD) in 2006 and the signature and ratification of (at the time of this writing) 153 countries of the world as the beginning of a fundamental shift in the legal and ethical foundations of disability politics around the globe. The CRPD was the culmination of more than fifty years of UN work on disability: the Declaration on the Rights of Mentally Retarded Persons (1971) and the Declaration on the Rights of Disabled Persons (1975) leading on to the 1981 International Year of Disabled Persons and the World Programme of Action the next year, which set the stage for the Standard Rules on the Equalization of Opportunities for Persons with Disabilities (1993), and, after decades of work, the creation in 2001 of an Ad Hoc Committee to consider proposals for a comprehensive convention "to protect the rights and dignity of persons with disabilities." Then, after five years of negotiations, the CRPD was drafted and adopted with much acclaim as the "first human rights document of the 21st century" (DPI 2009).

The CRPD is technically one a handful of UN "thematic" human rights declarations – such as the Convention on the Elimination of All Forms of Discrimination against Women (1979) and the Convention on the Rights of the Child (1989) – treaties that explicitly identify a group of individuals for protection. During negotiations, this meant that a case had to be made that a human rights convention for disability was needed. In the end, the United Nations was convinced that, as the basic human rights of persons with disabilities were routinely violated, even in high resource countries of the world, a specific thematic affirmation of these rights was warranted (see Quinn and Degener 2002). Moreover, the CRPD could be used to "establish universal minimum standards that should apply to everyone and . . . provide the basis for a coherent framework for action" (United Nations 2007).

The promise of the CRPD depends, as its advocates are very aware, on its implementation and more generally on its influence on the lives of persons with disabilities. That promise would be destroyed if the CRPD rights became mere manifesto rights – aspirational and rhetorical but without concrete results in the form of government action. Although the beneficial effect of political rhetoric on social change should never be underestimated, a true transformation in policy – what advocates insist on calling the paradigm shift – can only come when aspirational ideals are transformed into actions, not merely at the level of legal language but at the micro-policy level where state action directly affects the lives and opportunities of persons with disabilities. It is to be profoundly regretted that the most powerful country of the world, the United States, has not and likely will never ratify the CRPD. But it would be far more regrettable if the 150-plus countries of the world that have ratified the CRPD fail to implement it.

By the end of this chapter, I want to argue that the CRPD is uniquely positioned to be an international human rights treaty that stands a good chance of achieving a transformative effect on the lives of persons with disabilities, indeed on all people. But to build up to that conclusion, I want to prepare the groundwork by clarifying what is meant by "the human rights approach" to disability, as this phrase has dominated recent discussions of the paradigm-shifting effect of the CRPD. I then look at implementation obstacles to the CRPD and the gap between rhetoric and action. I am not interested here in the obvious and frequently identified obstacles such as lack of political will, economic forces, persistent stereotyping, and stigma, as well as what Gerald Quinn and Theresia Degener have called the "invisibility" of persons with disabilities and benign neglect (Quinn and Degener 2002). Rather, I want to identify ideological obstacles that the disability advocacy community and disability person's organizations are themselves responsible for, and which, I argue, must be addressed if the full potential of the CRPD is to be realized.

2. The "human rights approach" and the CRPD

Although frequently mentioned, there is surprisingly little said about what the "human rights approach to disability" entails. Across the UN system, however, the political and administrative significance of the human rights approach in other important domains of social policy has been actively discussed and can be summarized in the following principles (e.g. Jonsson 2003; United Nations 2003; UNAIDS 2004):

- The primary responsibility for the legal imperative to respect, protect, and fulfill human rights rests on government officials. This responsibility is a matter of legal obligation and moral duty, not charity or benevolence.

- The government must discharge its obligation to secure rights both transparently and with the full participation and collaboration of people with disabilities.
- Governments are responsible and accountable not only for outcomes (practical realization of rights) but also for the manner or process in which their decisions are made.
- Because rights are indivisible and interrelated, the implementation of one right will often entail the implementation of other rights; therefore, government responsibility is systemic across all areas of policy subject to human rights.

Embedded in these principles are responses to two traditional, and interlinked, concerns about the logical limits of the using of rights as tools for progressive social change: the "adversarial dyad" problem (so named by Yamin 2005) – the fact that only the state is the duty-bearer of these rights, although it is obvious that non-state parties, including especially the private sector, can act in ways that violated basic human rights; and – the issue that troubled Feinberg – the fact that human rights documents include both negative rights (prohibiting the state from interfering with the liberty of its citizens) and positive rights (requiring the state to perform positive actions to satisfy unmet basic needs of its citizens). Because positive rights require state resources, they raise deep, difficult, and perhaps irresolvable questions of distributive justice. Positive rights are so troubling for that and other reasons that the great liberal political thinker Isaiah Berlin refused to accept them as human rights (Berlin 1969).

Arguably, the adversarial dyad problem is a leftover from the era of Locke and Hobbes and classical political liberalism in which, in principle, only the state can violate rights by limiting individual freedom to owe and use private property (Finnis 2011). All other private arrangements, it was thought, were implicitly just, as they are based on contract and the free market (cf. Nozick 1974). Human rights doctrine has evolved since then to expand the universe of obligation, not by removing the state as the duty-bearer but by expanding its obligations to including (1) *respecting* human rights by refraining from interfering with or curtailing the enjoyment of human rights; (2) *protecting* individuals or groups against human rights abused by non-state actors; and (3) *fulfilling* human rights by taking all positive action – legislative, budgetary, judicial, and other measures – required to facilitate the enjoyment of human rights (University of Minnesota 1997; UN Development Programme 2000).

The respect-protect-fulfill framework actually arose in response to another debate involving negative and positive rights. In the human rights literature, this is a long and complex story, but it comes down to the question of whether human rights include both the classical liberal negative *political and civil rights* (rights to life and liberty, freedom from torture, freedom of expression, religion, and association, right to stand for political office and to vote) as well as positive *economic, social, and cultural rights* (rights to education, work, health, standard of life, and housing, right to cultural expression). Political and civil rights normally only require the duty to respect from the state – by not actively interfering with liberty – while far more robust and complex economic, social, and cultural rights demand more action from the state in the form of protecting and fulfilling positive rights.

The issue of whether human rights are both negative and positive was resolved, at least de facto, in 1976 with the coming into force of the *International Covenant on Economic, Social and Cultural Rights*. This was reinforced by the Vienna Declaration (Office of the High Commissioner for Human Rights 1993) that provided the language used earlier to the effect that human rights are "indivisible, interdependent, and interrelated," thereby implying that equal attention needs to be given to the implementation, promotion, and protection of both civil and political, and economic, social, and cultural rights (so stated in the Limburg Principles, 1987). The academic literature is less clear. Classical liberals (and their neo-liberal followers) firmly reject economic, social, and cultural rights, or as they are sometimes called, "second-generation human rights" (Beitz 2001; Cranston 1973), while left-leaning liberals and the consensus of the human rights community insists that economic, social, and cultural rights are essential components of a more holistic sense of human rights (e.g. Donnelly 1982, 2003; Dworkin 1977; MacNaughton and Frey 2011). It should also be mentioned that more left-leaning critics have argued that, both conceptually and practically, it might be better to limit human rights to political and civil rights and recast second-generation rights as aspects of the realm of social justice (Dean 2008; McLachlan 2005), a position that has attracted the attention of some disability advocates as well (see Jones and Marks 1999; Parker 2006).

Interestingly, neither of these traditional worries about human rights appeared to have troubled the drafters of the CRPD, nor have they been much discussed in the subsequent academic literature during or after the CRPD came into force. Gerald Quinn and Theresa Degener in their seminal report to the United Nations in 2002 successfully made the case that the linkage between civil and political rights and economic, social, and cultural rights is both obvious and "tangible" in the context of disability. This is because antidiscrimination law, the core protective legal tool of civil rights, is not enough to secure all human rights: "People with disabilities sometimes (but not always) require additional support . . . an elaborate social support structure designed to liberate people in their own lives and not to imprison them in gilded cages" (Quinn and Degener 2002, 19, 22). Michael Stein in various places has argued that disability most clearly invokes the "human right to development," a "third-generation" human right that conceptually bridges negative and positive human rights (e.g. Stein 2007; see Marks 1981; Steiner 1998).

At the end of the day, however, the essence of the human rights approach cannot be found in these academic controversies or even in the manner in which they have been finessed by the drafters of the CRPD. The core idea that animates the human rights approach comes from the fact, agreed on by all, that human rights are universal: human rights are applicable to everyone and to everyone equally, independently of every contingent difference that exists between people – be it gender, race, religion, language, culture, geographic location, or presence or extent of disability. The only eligibility criterion to be a beneficiary of human rights is to be human (see, for example, Donnelly 2003: "Human rights are, literally, the rights that one has simply because one is a human being. . . . Human rights are *equal* rights: either one is or is not a human being, and therefore has the same human rights as everyone else (or none at all)").

The universality of human rights has both a procedural and a substantive perspective. Human rights are the sorts of entitlements that are applicable to humans and reflect the inherent content of the good human life, human flourishing, and well-being – a life of dignity, freedom, relationships, real opportunity, health, and all that which makes a life go well. As these are human values, their realization in concrete circumstances requires universalistic strategies of implementation – namely, those that stand the best chance of being effective for all beneficiaries of human rights.

In the CRPD, universalism is expressed in various ways: in the preamble, the CRPD reaffirms "the universality, indivisibility, interdependence and interrelatedness of all human rights and fundamental freedoms and the need for persons with disabilities to be guaranteed their full enjoyment without discrimination." The purpose of the CRPD is said "to promote, protect and ensure the full and equal enjoyment of all human rights and fundamental freedoms by all persons with disabilities," where the expression "full and equal" carries the universalistic message. Article 4, setting out the obligations of states, requires states to "ensure and promote the full realization of all human rights and fundamental freedoms for all persons with disabilities without discrimination of any kind on the basis of disability." Article 5 insists that all of the rights in the CRPD are to be respected equally and without discrimination. And finally, the standard of comparison throughout the CRPD is "on an equal basis with others," reinforcing the fact that the CRPD guarantees not "special rights" reserved for persons with disabilities but universal human rights that everyone should enjoy.

From this common ground, I now move on to what stands in the way of implementation of human rights for persons with disabilities – once again, not the standard obstacles but those that the disability advocates themselves have created.

3. Ideological obstacles to fulfilling the promise of the CRPD

3.1 The social model fetish

The thing about political rhetoric is that, when it successfully brings about social change, advocates tend to cling to it even when it has clearly outlived its usefulness. In the area of disability scholarship, there is no better example of such a rhetorical albatross than the so-called social model of disability. Part of the problem is the sheer variety of views that go by that name. Because the theorizing about the purported shift from the medical to the social model of disability has relied on so many esoteric theories and academic disciplines, it often seems as if there are as many versions of the social model as advocates of it.

All of this confusion is unnecessary at this juncture, as there is general consensus that disability is the outcome of complex interactions between features of a person's physical and psychological condition and the physical, human-built, sociocultural, attitudinal, and political environment. To date, the only operationalized and reliable scientific tool that embodies this conception of disability, and does so in a manner directly applicable to disability classification, assessment, and measurement, is the 2001 World Health

Organization's *International Classification of Functioning, Disability and Health* (ICF). The link between the ICF person-environment interactive conception of disability and the CRPD is obvious upon inspection of the CRPD preamble clause (e) and Article 2. Still, commentators cling to the rhetoric that it is the social model that animates the convention.

More troubling is the claim that the human rights approach to disability was the essential historical consequence of the social model of disability, or more strongly, that without the social model it would have been impossible to conceptualize disability as a human rights issue (e.g. see Stein and Stein 2014). Given that one version of the social model – though admittedly one that has been soundly rejected by many disability advocates (Harpur 2012; Shakespeare 2007) – insists that disability is purely "socially constructed" and not conceptually or factually linked to features of human biology, would were it true, transform innocent rhetoric into a potential obstacle to the implementation of the convention. For if disability is entirely socially constructed, then different cultures will likely have different – even radically different – conceptions of what disability is, as indeed has been argued (Ingstad and Whyte 1995). This kind of relativism is not a very scientifically plausible view – for one thing, it is intrinsically unfalsifiable. But more to the point, it is bluntly incompatible with the notion of universal – that is, transcultural – human rights for persons with disabilities.

Nonetheless, advocates insist with compulsive regularity that recognition of human rights was made historically possible only because of the social model of disability:

> The social model is such a powerful tool because it helps illuminate the fact that the roots of disabled people's exclusion and poverty do not reside in biology, but in society. The former for most people is immutable; the latter through collective action can be transformed.
>
> (Albert and Hurst 2006)

> The social model has also provided a powerful framework for bringing disabled people together in a common struggle for equality and rights. By doing this the social model has promoted the idea that disabled people should be actors in their own lives, rather than passive recipients of care.
>
> (Albert 2004)

> The problem of disability lies in society's response to the individual and the impairment, and in the physical environment, which is mainly designed (largely by nondisabled people) to meet the needs of nondisabled people. Disability takes on a social dimension and leads to social exclusion and the denial of human rights.
>
> (Harris and Enfield 2003)

> The "medical model" of disability has frequently been contrasted in recent years with the "human rights" model. The medical model focuses on persons' medical traits such as their specific impairments. This has the effect of locating the "problem" of disability within the person. The medical model encapsulates a broader and

> deeper social attitude – a tendency to problematize the person and view him/her as an object for clinical intervention.
>
> (Quinn and Degener 2002)

> Over time, this medical model of disability is being replaced. A new model is emerging, known as the human rights model. The human rights model focuses less on the functional impairments of the individual with a disability, and more on the limitations of a society that categorizes who is normal and who is not. According to the human rights model, disability itself is a social construct.
>
> (Kanter 2003)

> In contrast to this historically prevalent medical pathology, disability rights advocates have advanced a social model of disability. This approach views the externally constructed environment, and the attitudes that drive its formation, as central in determining how "disabled" any individual will be from functioning in a given society.
>
> (Stein and Stein 2014)

Even official documents of the Office of the High Commissioner for Human Rights repeat the social model slogan:

> The development of the Convention reflects the shift that has taken place in the way disability and persons with disabilities are seen. Historically, disability has been considered to be a personal condition residing in the individual. . . . When disability is perceived in this way, society's responses are restricted to only one of two paths: individuals can be "fixed" through medicine or rehabilitation (medical approach); or they can be cared for, through charity or welfare programmes (charity approach). Over the past few decades, there has been an important change in the way disability is understood . . . disability is recognized as the consequence of the interaction of the individual with an environment that does not accommodate that individual's differences and limits or impedes the individual's participation in society. This approach is referred to as the social model of disability. The *Convention on the Rights of Persons with Disabilities* endorses this model and takes it forward by explicitly recognizing disability as a human rights issue.
>
> (Office of the High Commissioner for Human Rights 2010)

But these assertions depend on a medical approach that is an utterly fabricated, straw man position, one that denies that features of the physical, attitudinal, social, and political environment play any role in the experience of disability. Even the most thickheaded physician – one who would insist on the power of medicine to "fix" impairments and would gladly problematize the person as a "patient" – would never deny that, for a person with lower body paralysis, having access to a wheelchair makes for a less severe mobility disability than being denied a wheelchair. Is it really plausible that an adherent of the medical model would deny that stigma and irrational fear preventing a qualified person with an anxiety disorder from being hired makes the experience of disability worse? It is often suggested that only the social model sees the need for human rights for persons with disabilities because only it recognizes that stigma, discrimination, and social and economic policies that marginalize people turns the experience of having an impairment into a social disadvantage. But no one denies this. One should always be wary of a form of argument that depends on one's adversary and bête noire being utterly clueless about the world.

But fetishizing the social model and rejecting the medical approach is also profoundly ironic, as the right to health is one of the most emancipatory of all economic, social, and cultural human rights. Indeed, there are good reasons for thinking that health and human rights are "intertwined aspirations" (Grodin et al. 2013), that "the promotion and protection of human rights and promotion and protection of health are fundamentally linked" (Mann et al. 1992), and finally that, in particular, "mental health and human rights are complementary approaches to the betterment of human beings" (Gostin and Gable 2004).

Of course, one might discount such claims as professional hubris, but there is little doubt that one of the most powerful political forces for the advancement of global human rights has come out of the health and health-related professions. Moreover, recent work in social epidemiology has provided empirical support for this view (Berkman and Kawachi 2000). The vast literature on the social determinants of health perfectly mirrors the social determinants of disability as conceived by the social model and for obvious reasons: one's health state is not only an essential component of one's state of disability, but also the social and environmental factors that either worsen or lessen the influence of health on one's life are exactly those that affect one's lived experience of disability (Hunt and Backman 2008; Kawachi and Kennedy 2002; Marmot and Wilkinson 1999; World Health Organization 2008; Yamin 2008, 2009).

Arguably, the most sensible political strategy to secure human rights for persons with disabilities would be to wholly mainstream disability into health rather than demonizing the health professions and inventing the spurious medical model. Disassociating disability from health in order to cater to an ideological stance will in time be viewed by the disability community as both a conceptual and a strategic mistake. If the CRPD is to move from the domain of rhetoric to that of government action, if nothing else, then a truce must be called in the "battle of the models," a battle that has dominated disability studies for far too long.

3.2 Difference and "special rights"

Another potential ideological obstacle to implementation of the CRPD is a variant of what is often called the "dilemma of difference," originally identified and linked to disability politics by the American legal scholar Martha Minow (1990). In order to seek and achieve social equality, marginalized people are tempted to deny their socially recognizable differences ("we are just like you"); but sometimes doing so creates different barriers to achieving meaningful equality, because when the differences are genuine and require adjustments, modifications, or additional resources, to deny them is tantamount to rejecting the needed resource. In the context of our discussion, the dilemma arises under a different but potentially more disastrous guise: the possibility that the CRPD has created "special" human rights exclusively for persons with disabilities. Although vigorously rejected in official UN documents ("[The CRPD] does not recognize any new human rights of persons with disabilities" (Office of the High Commissioner for Human Rights 2007)) some disability advocates have been tempted, however cautiously, by the opposite view (Harpur 2012; Mégret 2008).

Frédéric Mégret argues that, although human rights are grounded in equality and universality, the mere fact that group-specific or thematic human rights declarations exist opens the door to the possibility of a "pluralization" of human rights – a recognition of a distinctive identity and dignity of particular groups. Exploring what about the CRPD rights might point in the direction of group specificity, he considers the level of detail, the degree of reformulation, the explicitness about the means in which the CRPD rights are to be guaranteed, and the way standard rights have been extended in scope to take disability into account. None of these drafting nuances make the rights new rights, and he understands this. The only candidate he finds is Article 12 on legal capacity, which is essentially a right to autonomy. Other human rights instruments do not include such a right because, logically, the capacity to be a bearer of rights is implicit in the very notion of a human right. Nonetheless, autonomy is precisely what is denied to those, because of mental illness or cognitive impairment, who are officially deemed to be incapable of making decisions and choices. Such practices amply warrant the inclusion of Article 12. In the end, Mégret backs away from the precipice and concludes that even Article 12 is not a right that persons with disabilities have only by virtue of being disabled.

One senses that Mégret remains very sympathetic to the prospect of group-specific human rights. Despite his caution, however, he fails to see the disaster looming. First, group-specific human rights require there to be an identifiable group; but in the case of disability, all humanity is potentially a member of this "specific group" (and if one lives long enough, one actually is a member). Thus, the specificity of disability is simply not robust enough to identify a group.

Second, and far more troubling, if there were group-specific human rights, then these would require potential rights recipients to *qualify* for these rights. But we have been here before: disability eligibility has had a long and troublesome history and is arguably responsible for much of the arbitrariness and inequity of disability policy (Bickenbach 2012). The problem is that impairments in functioning are not dichotomous but continuous – a matter of more or less rather than yes or no. How much of a problem seeing is required to qualify as having a sensory disability? How painful must the arthritis be in order to be eligible for the ranks of the mobility impaired? How much memory loss is required before one has a cognitive impairment? These questions tend to be arbitrarily decided for disability pensions and other benefits inevitably because, on a continuum of more or less, there is no non-arbitrary cut-off. In fact, decisions are made on the basis of administrative convenience, macroeconomic circumstances, political advantage, or effective lobbying. Does this mean that different countries should be allowed to determine their own eligibility requirements for human rights? Clearly, group specificity in human rights is not only conceptually pleonastic but also would undermine the very possibility of the CRPD being implemented.

Social model advocates, it is worth remarking, have an additional problem, created by a persistent ambiguity in how that model is expressed. It is rarely clear whether the influence of the social environment, from individual attitudes to laws and policies, is conceptually definitional of "disability" or factually determinative of when a person with impairments is also "disabled." If a conceptual point, then the plausibility of the model, as a theory, depends on analytic argumentation; but if a factual claim, then evidence is relevant. Thus, if the social model "views the externally constructed environment, and the attitudes that drive its formation, as central in determining how 'disabled' any individual will be from functioning in a given society" (Stein and Stein 2014 and cf. Silvers 1998, 75), then it follows that only those individuals who are, *in fact*, so limited are "disabled." This would entail that individuals with impairments who do not experience disadvantage from the social environment – a state of affairs that is the very political goal of the disability advocacy community – would not qualify for "special" disability human rights.

Despite these difficulties, the temptation of special rights is hard to resist. Even in its official documents, the Office of the High Commissioner for Human Rights hints at this. After dutifully repeating that the CRPD does not establish new rights for persons with disabilities, the authors of a 2010 report by the Office of the High Commissioner for Human Rights make a distinction not made in the CRPD itself between articles that identify "existing human rights" and those that serve to "ensure an environment conducive to the fulfilment of the rights of persons with disabilities" (24). Paul Harpur (2012) has referred to these latter as "incidental rights" and includes on the list the rights to awareness raising, accessibility, response in situations of risk and humanitarian emergencies, access to justice, personal mobility, habilitation and rehabilitation, and statistics and data collection. It is not clear whether the point being made here is that these latter are not (really) human rights but merely tools for fulfilling rights that are unique to the situation of persons with disabilities. Whatever is intended by this peculiar distinction merely adds an unnecessary and invidious ranking of the CRPD articles that can only further complicate the task of implementing the convention.

3.3 Setting the bar too high: Uncompromising interpretations

Michael Ignatieff has argued that the discourse of human rights should not become a secular religion or even a universal credo of a global society. Instead, human rights must be understood – and this is the source of their immense social value – as "the shared vocabulary from which our arguments can begin, and the bare human minimum from which different areas of flourishing can take root" (2001, 95). If the demands made by human rights are utterly novel, groundbreaking, and truly constitute a paradigm shift, then they risk being incomprehensible or falling outside our shared moral understanding of the preconditions of human flourishing. If, as moral relativists or moral skeptics are prone to believe, there is no shared moral understanding and different cultures hold radically different moral positions that are literally incommensurable with one another, then the game is over, as the entire human rights discourse becomes nonsensical. Human rights are universal moral entitlements; that is their logical character and their potential power.

Human rights advocates are thus caught in a dilemma: the moral significance of human rights lies in the fact that, as Feinberg put it, they are moral claims "of a fundamentally important kind held equally by all human beings, unconditionally and unalterably." But this characterization is only plausible of very general and basic moral claims, indeed "the bare human minimum" necessary for human flourishing to take root. The dilemma requires human rights advocates to maintain a delicate balance between asserting moral claims that are universal and unconditional yet are at the same time both culturally plausible and practically achievable around the world. This balance is only workable if the human rights one asserts are fundamental, yet the bare human minimum. Even this is a huge challenge. One would have thought that no human right could be more minimal than the right not to be tortured or subjected to cruel, inhuman, or degrading treatment or punishment, yet Amnesty International regularly reports on instances where the provisions of the UN Convention against Torture have been regularly ignored by signatories (Amnesty International 2014).

Although it would be overly fastidious to object to political rhetoric emphasizing the grand aspirations of the CRPD and the emancipatory future it will bring, one would hope that those officially mandated to interpret and monitor the implementation of the convention would be sensitive to the need to balance aspiration against realism. Keeping in mind that the CRPD, as international law, is at the end of the day a matter of consensual governance rather than legal enforcement, if the CRPD provisions are interpreted to demand radical legal and administrative change, high economic cost, or a fundamental cultural shift that moves too far beyond the anodyne moral common ground of the bare human minimum, then these demands will be rejected. The bar has been set too high.

Unfortunately, this seems to be the tactic used by the official body of independent experts mandated by the United Nations to monitor implementation of the CRPD by states – the Committee on the Rights of Persons with Disabilities. Ratifying states are required to submit regular reports to the CRPD committee on how they are responding to their (self-imposed) obligations to implement the CRPD provisions. The committee examines these reports and makes suggestions and general recommendations. The committee has also taken the initiative to prepare general comments designed to offer interpretative guidance on specific articles. In September 2013, an initial draft of the general comment on Article 12 (Equal Recognition before the Law) was released for public comment (United Nations 2013).

As already mentioned, the focus of Article 12 is on the legal procedures and practices countries regularly use to put individuals in place to make a variety of life decisions for others deemed incapable of making those decisions. These provisions often create court-appointed formal guardians or informal substitute decision makers who are obliged either to decide in the best interests of the individual, or more recently, in a way that is consistent with the individual's expressed preferences, values, and desires.

Although children before the age of majority are also subject to such practices, the individuals who Article 12 are understood to apply to are those with mental health problems or cognitive impairments of various sorts. These are the individuals who lack the capacity to decide according to some legally developed test of legal competence (such as "lacking the ability to understand or appreciate the consequences of deciding one way or the other"). Although these individuals with disabilities are the primary concern of Article 12, the same procedures and practices also apply to anyone who might temporarily or indefinitely fail the functional test of capacity – for example, people in a persistent coma after a traffic accident or someone temporarily unconscious who requires immediate medical attention.

For understandable historical reasons, and because of current practices, the value of autonomy is central to the disability movement. Practices of stripping patients in mental hospitals and other institutions of their legal capacity to make decisions has long been subject to intense criticism by human rights and disability advocates, especially in the domain of mental health (Gostin 2001, 2004). And they are obviously right to do so. Article 12 as a result has been viewed to be a core, even emblematic, disability human right in the CRPD (Quinn 2009).

Yet Article 12 does not speak in categorical language: although it reaffirms that persons with disabilities have the right to recognition everywhere as persons under the law ("on an equal basis with others"), it enjoins states parties to take "appropriate measures" to provide access to the support that persons with disabilities may require to exercise their legal capacity and to put into place "appropriate and effective safeguards" to prevent abuse and ensure that the will and preferences of the person are respected. The language of Article 12, in short, appears on its face to recognize a range of state responses, most prominently to provide appropriate support for decision making, but perhaps in special circumstances to have another person, say a best friend or close relative, make decisions consistent with the individual's will and preferences.

The general comment on Article 12 sets a very different tone. Beginning by chastising states for having "a general misunderstanding of the exact scope" of their obligations, it goes on to provide the strongest possible interpretation of the article's provisions: legal capacity is wholly unconditioned about actual decision-making mental capacity; however mental capacity or decision-making skills are assessed, these cannot ever be legitimate grounds to deny legal capacity. As a consequence, any practice or procedure that puts into place substitute decision making, of any sort, on the basis of a determination of mental capacity is discriminatory and in violation of Article 12. This means that all forms of plenary or partial guardianship, and any practice of substitute decision making, is prohibited. In its place, states must implement regimes of supported decision making, available to all, and suitable for any level of support as required for any degree of lack of mental capacity and independent of the person's mode of communication (even if nonconventional or understood by very few people).

By wholly delinking legal capacity from mental capacity, the general comment creates a legal fiction that is independent of the reality of the situation. Thus, an individual who is temporarily or permanently in a coma or in a persistent vegetative state – that is, a person who has no evidence of upper brain electrical activity – has legal capacity although he or she could not in any straightforward sense make a decision. Because the general comment does not go into details, it is not even clear whether an advance directive expressing, or highly probative evidence of, the person's will and preferences could be used as the basis for an unexpressed decision. A person in a coma cannot communicate, even nonconventionally or in a manner understood by very few people. In response, some commentators have suggested (perhaps factiously), that individuals in such a position may well require "100% support."

Comas and states of unconsciousness in emergency settings may be accommodated by some other clever use of legal language, but other situations may be harder to handle. A person with acute and severe depression may wish to commit suicide, and in clear and very conventional language, express their will and preference to do so. Because in nearly all jurisdictions of the world suicide itself is not illegal, would it constitute a violation of Article 12 to prevent the suicide in such circumstance? There certainly are those who would insist that this is a "nonconsensual psychiatric intervention" and as such a human rights violation (Dhanda 2007; Minkowitz 2007). Again, a clever use of legal language might suggest that the decision to kill oneself if depressed – given the evidence that depression quite literally undermines the capacity to be autonomous (Biegler 2010) – did not really express the individual's will and preference. It is unclear, however, whether taking that step is different from intervening in the best interests of the person.

The point that must be made here is that it is very doubtful that any ratifying state would implement Article 12 in a manner consistent with the general comment's interpretation. Setting aside the ethical issue of whether it would be right to do, a state contemplating such a move would not only have health care professionals from psychiatric social workers to physicians voicing profound objection, but also even sympathetic constituencies would balk at the practical implications of what the general comment suggests Article 12 requires. Scanning the responses to the call for comments on the general comment one finds, for example, the Swedish National Association for Persons with Intellectual Disability (2016) arguing that abolishing the "ombudsman" approach to protecting people who do not fully appreciate the consequences of their own actions or inactions would be a mistake; and the group ACT Disability, Aged and Carer Advocacy Service (2013) noted that individuals with impairments and complex needs may not, even with the best support in place, be able to fully engage the decisions that affect them.

One might argue that the general comment of the CRPD committee is strategically uncompromising, in part in order to stop the inevitable slide toward more and more minimal commitment to much-needed change in how persons with intellectual impairments and mental illnesses are treated. One expects rhetorical over-steering from advocates and academics but not official interpreters of UN conventions with legal force. It is precisely this kind of political rhetoric that, although it has had a long and admirable history of success in the disability movement (see Charlton 2000; Driedger 1989; Scotch 1984), can become an obstacle to the kind of concrete and effective government action needed to implement the CRPD. There are enough obstacles in the way of this goal as there is, and it is unfortunate that the disability advocacy community itself adds to the list. It is especially unfortunate because the CRPD, in form and content, has the potential to become a human rights success story.

4. Transforming aspiration into accountable action

The CRPD is a unique human rights document, amply justifying the accolade of being paradigm shifting. Part of its potential power has already been mentioned – namely, that it effortlessly embodies a merging of negative political and civil rights and positive economic, social, and cultural rights. Many legal scholars have noted that the revolutionary first step taken on the path to disability human rights – the passage in the United States in 1980 of the Americans with Disabilities Act – relied on an important but also importantly partial social and legal tool for achieving the social objectives of equality and full participation. This was, of course, the tool of antidiscrimination relief, most significantly under Title I forbidding discrimination of otherwise qualified persons in employment on the grounds of disability. Not only because of the somewhat disappointing performance of the act (Krieger 2003) and the subsequent need to radically amend it, but also conceptually, it has been argued that antidiscrimination relief is inadequate for achieving social equality (Bagenstos 2009; Bickenbach 2012; Satz 2008; Stein 2007).

Philosophically, the problem is that antidiscrimination is a matter of corrective justice (righting a wrong) rather than distributive justice (achieving a just distribution of social benefits and burdens). Although antidiscrimination is an essential legal tool, it must be augmented with positive government action. In the case of employment, for example, inclusion depends not only on relief from discrimination but also more importantly on positive equality measures – from the provision of vocational training, laws mandating workplace accessibility, or hiring quota and other preferences – that fundamentally alter employment practices. The CRPD, as a holistic human rights document combining antidiscrimination with positive action, is the answer, as it incorporates the fuller social agenda of human development (Stein and Stein 2014) and can address the realities of disability social exclusion. What this means in effect is that there is no tension or inconsistency between viewing disability as a social policy issue fully immersed within the context of human rights.

The second great conceptual strength of the CRPD, as I argued earlier, is that it marks the end of "special" rights for people with disabilities, the invidious notion that disability so sets one apart from the mainstream that the state, out of charity, has to provide services and benefits that make one whole and normal. Insisting that the rights of persons with disabilities are precisely the universal human rights of all persons – grounded in the same values of dignity, autonomy, equality, and solidarity (cf. Quinn and Degener 2002) – ensures that disability is not treated, either legally or socially, as an outlier condition. Rather, disability and other forms of vulnerability and dependence are what it means to be a human (Fineman 2010). The CRPD, in short, performs the ultimate mainstreaming function of transforming disability from the identifier of a minority group to a salient feature of humanity itself.

The holism and universality of the human rights in the CRPD set the conceptual stage for the implementation of the CRPD. These rights are not add-ons to social policy designed for a needy subpopulation but instead represent a full and coherent social agenda that everyone benefits from, to the extent that everyone is, potentially or as they age, inevitably a person experiencing some form of functional limitation. More practically, however, the CRPD contains some unique provisions that extend the range of legal and social policy tools that can be used for implementation. In effect, these provisions make the implementation of the CRPD itself into a human right uniquely positioned to have a transformative effect on the lives of persons with disabilities (and so, on all people).

Articles 31 and 33 of the CRPD are two provisions that are not only unique to the CRPD but also help to practically bridge aspiration and government action. Article 31 requires ratifying states parties "to collect appropriate information, including statistical and research data, to enable them to formulate and implement policies to give effect to the present Convention." The importance of having access to statistical information relevant to the domains of rights specified in the CRPD cannot be overestimated. Without these data, there is no reliable means for determining whether, and the extent to which, a government has taken steps to make policy changes, and more important, whether these changes have had a "rights-enhancing" influence on people's lives.

If the rights in the CRPD were expressed in abstract and general language, then it would be very difficult to solve the practical issue of the basic social science of matching normative claims with the actual situation on the ground. But the CRPD rights are expressed both generally in terms of basic principles (such as "Respect for inherent dignity, individual autonomy including the freedom to make one's own choices, and independence of persons" – Article 3 a.) and also in highly concrete and specific language: "States Parties shall also take appropriate measures to. . . . Develop, promulgate and monitor the implementation of minimum standards and guidelines for the accessibility of facilities and services open or provided to the public" (Article 9 2. a.). As these specifically worded provisions constitute the bulk of the human rights "attributes" set out in the CRPD, collecting relevant data is certainly feasible. Article 33 completes the picture by requiring states to designate a "focal point" within government to be responsible for developing a framework and mechanism for monitoring implementation of the convention.

Data collection is a crucial element of any monitoring framework and a major step in the standard, social scientific methodology used to monitor the influence of economic and social policy. Typically, these data are applied to indicators that have been selected as measureable proxies for the social phenomena under consideration in terms of quantitative targets or benchmarks that, when used longitudinally, make it possible to track change in, for example, employment participation rates or social benefit uptake rates over time. Much has been written on how indicators, which are standard tools in socioeconomic policy, can be adapted to monitor human rights provisions. The state of the art here is well developed, and valuable work has been done by the Office of the High Commission on Human Rights and the UN's Economic and Social Affairs in human rights indicators, especially for economic, social, and cultural rights (see United Nations 2006; UN General Assembly 2011).

While Articles 31 and 33 describe the data collection and administrative framework required for state monitoring, Article 32 mandates regional and international organizations to cooperate to promote and support these national efforts by providing technical, training, and economic support and generally facilitating capacity building at the national level. All of these efforts should actively involve the participation of organizations of persons with disabilities. Since the CRPD came into effect, the UN system has created several partnerships to concentrate and coordinate support to states in monitoring implementation. The Agency Support Group on the Convention on the Rights of Persons with Disabilities has focused on disability data collection and analysis methodologies, and the UN Partnership on the Rights of Persons with Disabilities brings together all UN entities, governments, disabled people's organizations, and the broader civil society to advance disability rights around the world.

As international human rights can only be implemented in domestic law (national law and, as the European Union is also a ratifier of the convention, transnational European law), the future of the CRPD implementation depends on what is traditionally called "domestic incorporation" (see Lord and Stein 2008). Optimally, incorporation should take place at all levels and within every process of the legal system: legislative (the passage of laws), administrative (implementation of guidelines and enforceable regulations), and judicial (authoritative interpretations of laws and regulations in judicial decisions). The process of ratification in international law further dictates that domestic law be reviewed to determine whether provisions – intentionally or inadvertently – are inconsistent with the CRPD provisions.

In addition to these traditional and purely legalistic reforms, features of the CRPD mandate other, and in some ways more radical, forms of incorporation. The CRPD, by constructive intent, is a document that mandates holistic and comprehensive actions rather than piecemeal changes. But compressive action, as authors Lord and Stein make clear (Lord and Stein 2008), will involve complex activities of socialization and potentially profound changes in the underlying legal and political cultures as they potentially undermine, or do not clearly facilitate, the implementation of specific provisions of the CRPD in particular and the paradigm shift of a reconceptualization of the experience of disability in general. This might only be accomplished by means of positive government action in education and awareness raising and, linked to and coordinated by the monitoring mechanism already mentioned, capacity building to empower organizations of persons with disabilities. The aim in all of these activities is to increase the visibility of persons with disabilities, and more importantly, to underscore the reality that disability is not the mark of some discrete and insular minority but a common characteristic shared, actually or potentially, by everyone. The universality of disability as a reconceptualization driven by the universality of human rights thus leads to the democratization of disability with the implementation of these rights.

The CRPD, both conceptually and practically, thus sets the stage for a dynamic and realistic process of transforming the aspirations, the political rhetoric, of human rights into accountable government action that can change the lives of all of us, both those currently living with disabilities and those of us who will likely experience disability in the course of our lives.

By engaging democratic processes and subtly and progressively altering entrenched attitudes and cultures of exclusion, the processes for implementing the CRPD should aim for a balance between uncompromising commitment to the inherent values in the human rights tradition and feasible and progressively realizable social change. This can be supported by harnessing the scientific power and the authority of the social sciences for the collection and analysis of relevant data and the development of appropriate indicators for monitoring implementation. In this way, the CRPD and human rights in general can successfully move beyond the domain of being merely manifesto rights and transform our world.

5. References

ACT Disability, Aged and Carer Advocacy Service. 2013. "Comments on General Comment 1 – Article 12 Equal Recognition before the Law." http://www.ohchr.org/EN/HRBodies/CRPD/Pages/DGCArticles12And9.aspx.

Albert, Bill. 2004. *Briefing Note: The Social Model of Disability, Human Rights and Development.* London: Disability KaR.

Albert, Bill and Rachel Hurst. 2006. *Disability and a Human Rights Approach to Development.* London: Disability KaR.

Amnesty International. 2014. "USA Should Use UN Hearing to Address 'Shocking Accountability Gap' on Torture." https://www.amnesty.org/en/articles/news/2014/11/usa-should-use-un-hearing-address-shocking-accountability-gap-torture/.

Bagenstos, Samuel R. 2009. *Law and the Contradictions of the Disability Rights Movement.* New Haven, CT: Yale University Press.

Beitz, Charles R. 2001. "Human Rights as a Common Concern." *American Political Science Review* 95(2), 269–282.

Berkman, Lisa F. and Ichiro Kawachi, eds. 2000. *Social Epidemiology.* Oxford: Oxford University Press.

Berlin, Isaiah. 1969. "Two Concepts of Liberty." In *Four Essays on Liberty*, edited by Isaiah Berlin, 1–32. Oxford: Oxford University Press.

Bickenbach, Jerome E. 2012. *Ethics, Law, and Policy.* Thousand Oaks, CA: Sage.

Biegler, Paul. 2010. "Autonomy and Ethical Treatment in Depression." *Bioethics* 24(4), 179–189.

Charlton, James I. 2000. *Nothing about Us Without Us: Disability Oppression and Empowerment.* Berkeley: University of California Press.

Convention on the Elimination of All Forms of Discrimination against Women. 1979. Available at: http://www.un.org/womenwatch/daw/cedaw/.

Convention on the Rights of the Child. 1989. Available at: http://www.ohchr.org/en/professional interest/pages/crc.aspx.

Cranston, Maurice. 1973. *What Are Human Rights?* New York: Taplinger.

Dean, Hartley. 2008. "Social Policy and Human Rights: Rethinking the Engagement." *Social Policy and Society* 7(1), 1–12.

Declaration on the Rights of Disabled Persons. 1975. Available at: http://www.ohchr.org/EN/ProfessionalInterest/Pages/RightsOfDisabledPersons.aspx.

Declaration on the Rights of Mentally Retarded Persons. 1971. Available at: http://www.ohchr.org/EN/ProfessionalInterest/Pages/RightsOfMentallyRetardedPersons.aspx.

Dhanda, Amita. 2007. "Legal Capacity in the Disability Rights Convention: Stranglehold of the Past or Lodestar for the Future?" *Syracuse Journal of International Law and Commerce* 34(2), 429–461.

Donnelly, Jack. 1982. "Human Rights as Natural Rights." *Human Rights Quarterly* 4(3), 391–405.

———. 2003. *Universal Human Rights in Theory and Practice.* 3rd ed. Ithaca, NY: Cornell University Press.

DPI. 2009. Available at: http://www.dpi-europe.org/past_editos/bioethics_issues_2/august_2009_time_for_partic.html.

Driedger, Diane. 1989. *The Last Civil Rights Movement*. London: Hurst.

Dworkin, Ronald. 1977. *Taking Rights Seriously*. Cambridge, MA: Harvard University Press.

Feinberg, Joel. 1973. *Social Philosophy*. New York: Prentice Hall.

Fineman, Martha A. 2010. "The Vulnerable Subject and the Responsive State." *Emory Law Journal* 60, 251–276.

Finnis, John. 2011. *Natural Law and Natural Rights*. 2nd ed. Oxford: Oxford University Press.

Gostin, Lawrence O. 2001. "Beyond Moral Claims: A Human Rights Approach in Mental Health." *Cambridge Quarterly of Healthcare Ethics* 10(3), 264–274.

———. 2004. "International Human Rights Law and Mental Disability." *Hastings Center Report* 34(2), 11–12.

Gostin, Lawrence O. and Lance Gable. 2004. "The Human Rights of Persons with Mental Disabilities: A Global Perspective on the Application of Human Rights Principles to Mental Health." *Maryland Law Review* 63(1), 20–121.

Grodin, Michael A., Daniel Tarantola, George J. Annas, and Sofia Gruskin, eds. 2013. *Health and Human Rights in a Changing World*. 3rd ed. New York: Routledge.

Harpur, Paul. 2012. "Embracing the New Disability Rights Paradigm: The Importance of the Convention on the Rights of Persons with Disabilities." *Disability & Society* 27(1), 1–14.

Harris, Alison and Sue Enfield. 2003. *Disability, Equality, and Human Rights: A Training Manual for Development and Humanitarian Organisations*. Oxford: Oxfam.

Hunt, Paul and Gunilla Backman. 2008. "Health Systems and the Right to the Highest Attainable Standard of Health." *Health and Human Rights* 10(1), 81–92.

Ignatieff, Michael. 2001. *Human Rights as Politics and Idolatory*. Princeton, NJ: Princeton University Press.

Ingstad, Benedicte and Susan Reynolds Whyte, eds. 1995. *Disability and Culture*. Berkeley: University of California Press.

Jones, Melinda and Lee Ann Basser Marks. 1999. "Law and the Social Construction of Disability." In *Disability, Divers-Ability and Legal Change*, edited by Melinda Jones and Lee Ann Basser Marks, 1–24. The Hague: Martinus Nijhoff.

Jonsson, Urban. 2003. *Human Rights Approach to Development Programming*. New York: UNICEF.

Kanter, Arlene S. 2003. "The Globalization of Disability Rights Law." *Syracuse Journal of International Law and Commerce* 30, 241–269.

Kawachi, Ichiro and Bruce P. Kennedy. 2002. *The Health of Nations: Why Inequality Is Harmful to Your Health*. New York: The New Press.

Krieger, Linda H., ed. 2003. *Backlash Against the ADA: Reinterpreting Disability Rights*. Ann Arbor: University of Michigan Press.

"The Limburg Principles on the Implementation of the International Covenant on Economic, Social and Cultural Rights." 1987. *Human Rights Quarterly* 9, 122–135.

Lord, Janet E. and Michael A. Stein. 2008. "The Domestic Incorporation of Human Rights Law and the United Nations Convention on the Rights of Persons with Disabilities." *Washington Law Review* 83, 449–479.

MacNaughton, Gillian and Diane Frey. 2011. "Decent Work for All: A Holistic Human Rights Approach." *American University International Law Review* 26, 441–485.

Mann, Jonathan M., Lawrence Gostin, Sofia Gruskin, Troyen Brennan, Zita Lazzarini, and Harvey V. Fineberg. 1992. "Health and Human Rights." *Health and Human Rights* 1(1), 6–23.

Marks, Stephen P. 1981. "Emerging Human Rights: A New Generation for the 1980's?" *Rutgers Law Review* 33(2), 435–452.

Marmot, Michael and Richard Wilkinson, eds. 1999. *Social Determinants of Health*. Oxford: Oxford University Press.

McLachlan, Hugh. 2005. *Social Justice, Human Rights and Public Policy*. Glasgow: Humming Earth.

Mégret, Frédéric. 2008. "The Disabilities Convention: Human Rights of Persons with Disabilities or Disability Rights?" *Human Rights Quarterly* 30(2), 494–516.
Minkowitz, Tina. 2007. "The United Nations Convention on the Rights of Persons with Disabilities and the Right to be Free from Nonconsensual Psychiatric Interventions." *Syracuse Journal of International Law and Commerce* 34(2), 405–428.
Minow, Martha. 1990. *Making All the Difference: Inclusion, Exclusion, and American Law*. Ithaca, NY: Cornell University Press.
Nozick, Robert. 1974. *Anarchy, State, and Utopia*. New York: Basic Books.
Office of the High Commissioner for Human Rights. 2010. *Monitoring the Convention on the Rights of Persons with Disabilities Guidance for Human Rights Monitors*. New York and Geneva: United Nations.
OHCHR, 1993. "Vienna Declaration and Programme of Action of the World Conference on Human Rights." Available at: http://www.ohchr.org/EN/ABOUTUS/Pages/ViennaWC.aspx
OHCHR. 2007. "Annual Report of the United Nations High Commissioner for Human Rights and Reports of the Office of the High Commissioner and the Secretary-General: Thematic Study by the Office of the United Nations High Commissioner for Human Rights on enhancing awareness and understanding of the Convention on the Rights of Persons with Disabilities (2009)." A/HRC/10/48, 11.
Parker, Sarah. 2006. "International Justice: The United Nations, Human Rights and Disability." *Journal of Comparative Social Welfare* 22(1), 63–78.
Quinn, Gerard. 2009. "The United Nations Convention on the Rights of Persons with Disabilities: Toward a New International Politics of Disability." *Texas Journal of Civil Liberties and Civil Rights* 15(1), 33–52.
Quinn, Gerard and Theresia Degener. 2002. *The Current Use and Future Potential of United Nations Human Rights Instruments in the Context of Disability*. New York and Geneva: United Nations.
Satz, Ani B. 2008. "Disability, Vulnerability, and the Limits of Antidiscrimination." *Washington Law Review* 83, 513–568.
Scotch, Richard K. 1984. *From Good Will to Civil Rights: Transforming Federal Disability Policy*. Philadelphia: Temple University Press.
Shakespeare, Tom. 2007. *Disability Rights and Wrongs*. London: Routledge.
Silvers, Anita. 1998. "Formal Justice." In *Disability, Difference, Discrimination: Perspectives on Justice in Bioethics and Public Policy*, edited by Anita Silvers, David Wasserman, and Mary B. Mahowald, 13–147. Lanham, MD: Rowman & Littlefield.
Standard Rules on the Equalization of Opportunities for Persons with Disabilities. 1993. Available at: http://www.un.org/esa/socdev/enable/dissre00.htm.
Stein, Michael A. 2007. "Beyond Disability Civil Rights." *Hastings Law Journal* 58, 1203–1240.
Stein, Michael A. and Penelope J. S. Stein. 2014. "Disability, Development, and Human Rights: A Mandate and Framework for International Financial Institutions." *UC Davis Law Review* 47, 1231–1278.
Steiner, Henry J. 1998. "Rights and Economic Development: Converging Discourses?" *Buffalo Human Rights Law Review* 4, 25–42.
The Swedish National Association for Persons with Intellectual Disability. 2016. "Comments from FUB to the Committee on the Rights of Persons with Disabilities Concerning the Committees General Comments on Article 12 of the Convention – Equal Recognition before the Law." http://www.ohchr.org/EN/HRBodies/CRPD/Pages/DGCArticles12And9.aspx.
Tuck, Richard. 1979. *Natural Rights Theories: Their Origin and Development*. Cambridge: Cambridge University Press.
UNAIDS. 2004. *What Constitutes a Rights-Based Approach? Definitions, Methods, and Practices*. http://data.unaids.org/Topics/Human-Rights/hrissuepaper_rbadefinitions_en.pdf.

United Nations. 2003. "The Human Rights Based Approach to Development Co-operation Towards a Common Understanding among UN Agencies." Report of the Second Interagency Workshop on Implementing a Human Rights Based Approach in the Context of UN Reform. New York, May 3–5.

———. 2006. *Report on Indicators for Monitoring Compliance with International Human Rights Instruments*. Geneva: United Nations.

———. 2007. *From Exclusion to Equality: Realizing the Rights of Persons with Disabilities*. Geneva: United Nations.

———. 2013. *General Comment on Article 12: Equal Recognition before the Law, Draft Prepared by the Committee*. Geneva: United Nations, United Nations Development Programme. 2000. *Human Development Report*. New York: Oxford University Press.

United Nations General Assembly. 2011. *Report of the United Nations High Commissioner for Human Rights*. New York: United Nations.

University of Minnesota. 1997. "Maastricht Guidelines on Violations of Economic, Social and Cultural Rights, Maastricht, January 22–26, 1997." http://www1.umn.edu/humanrts/instree/Maastrichtguidelines_.html.

U.S. Declaration of Independence. 1776. Available at: http://www.archives.gov/exhibits/charters/declaration_transcript.html

World Health Organization. 2001. *International Classification of Functioning, Disability and Health*. Geneva: World Health Organization.

———. 2008. *Closing the Gap in a Generation: Health Equity through Action on the Social Determinants of Health. Final Report of the Commission on Social Determinants of Health*. Geneva: World Health Organization.

Yamin, Alicia E. 2005. "The Future in the Mirror: Incorporating Strategies for the Defense and Promotion of Economic, Social and Cultural Rights into the Mainstream Human Rights Agenda." *Human Rights Quarterly* 27(4), 1200–1244.

———. 2008. "Will We Take Suffering Seriously? Reflections on What Applying a Human Rights Framework to Health Means and Why We Should Care." *Health and Human Rights* 10(1), 45–63.

———. 2009. "Shades of Dignity: Exploring the Demands of Equality in Applying Human Rights Frameworks to Health." *Health and Human Rights* 11(2), 1–18.

10 Human and civil models of rights

Healthy and ill disabled and access to health care

Anita Silvers and Leslie Pickering Francis

1. Introduction

The earliest accounts of protections and privileges that are due people as their right sorted humans into different social classes and ranked the groups as to their comparative worth – that is, by comparing the magnitude and fortitude of their entitlements. In contrast, human rights theory holds that all humans are basically the same, at least in the sense that all equally are owed freedom from political or state-facilitated oppression (Hannum 2006). As distinct from rights that entitle only subsets of humans who meet additional eligibility criteria to lay claims, human rights are inclusive of all members of the human species – or at least they are supposed to be.

Here, we begin by exploring the concept of human rights to learn whether it is sufficiently expansive to include people with disabilities as securely as nondisabled people. Human rights are supposed to pertain to all humans alike. But history shows that individuals' being disabled in any one of several ways has sometimes sufficed to drive doubts about the propriety of treating those individuals as fully human. Owing to their disabilities, such people are likely to have heightened needs for priority in accessing resources and for protection from constraints on freedom. Also owing to their disabilities, however, they are at risk of having any protective and prioritizing rights that are derived from the idea of humanness, and that are readily ascribed to nondisabled people, denied to them.

Next, we turn to developing an alternative account of rights, advancing a civil rights model we believe to be more appropriate for making progress toward inclusive justice for disabled people in the non-ideal world in which we reside. We contrast the justice of health care resource allocation as it may play out within human rights and civil rights frames. Then we explore whether agreement on a definition of disability, or at least adoption of a univocal explanation of disabled people's limitations, is a prerequisite for establishing disabled people's rights. Unlike human rights theory, which relies on an idealized and abstract notion of human nature on which all humans are similar at least at their cores, our approach accepts the reality that, for practical policy, humans' differences from one another make all the difference (Minow 1990).

Individuals with disabilities depart from species typicality in an enormous variety of ways. These individuals bear no more resemblance to one another than they do to the species-typical paradigm of humanness; each one in some way or other fails to match. Owing to this insight, our conclusion suggests a more nuanced than usual depiction of rights that are responsive to disability, painting a picture of rights that is far more comfortably placed in a civil rights than in a human rights frame.

2. Humanity as a basis for rights ascription

For the human rights tradition, or at least for its older branch, each human's obligation to respect and protect other humans derives from our all sharing the essential properties of human nature (Fagan 2005). This "human exceptionalism" account of rights argues that each human has a claim on recognition and respect from others because all alike seek opportunity to realize their uniquely human value in social interaction (Liao 2010). Human rights are universal rights, belonging to all persons solely by virtue of their being human (Fagan 2005, see also Finnis 1980).

If this view is not to be merely arbitrary, humans must be distinguishable from other animals in some singular objective way (Townley 2010). Human exceptionalism in its most sweeping form also denies that individuals who do not possess the essential human characteristic can be bearers of rights – it holds that all and only humans are the bearers of human rights. Rights claims pertaining to biological individuals who might resemble humans in some – indeed, in many or even most – respects are open to being dismissed on ontological grounds by reference to these individuals lacking a crucial human-making property (Silvers 2012). Questions about whether machines and animals can possess and exercise human liberty rights are intelligible and can even be practical. Nevertheless, non-human animals and other organic entities do not qualify as rights bearers owing to this deficit, according to the strong version of human exceptionalism. So should robots and other machines, however human their appearance or conduct, be denied rights.

And so, based on similar invocations of their deficits in supposedly definitive human capacities, have individuals with disabilities been excluded from recognition as persons and denied the status of rights bearers. Human rights are supposed to be universal, but the adduced essential human-making properties are not coextensive with the class of individuals who in other circumstances are taken to be humans. Contrary to human rights programs' mandate to promote equality, this strategy does not escape sorting individuals, based on nondisability or disability, into classes of higher and lower status, with the former more socially privileged and much better protected than the latter. That affirmation of full legal and moral standing to invoke rights has been so hard for disabled people to attain suggests the hazards of centering on species-definitive physical, psychological, or mental capacities in validating individuals' rights, however.

Two different components of human nature have been cited as the proper basis for recognizing human rights. One kind of property is a broadly construed psychological, intellectual, or mental property. The other is a broadly construed biological or material property (Silvers 2012).

The argument for human rights based on distinctively human psychological or mental properties usually unfolds thus: a crucial cognitive or other kind of mental capacity is asserted to differentiate humans from other species. For example, Tooley (1972) argues that "an organism possesses a serious right to life only if it possesses the concept of a self as a continuing subject of experiences and other mental states, and believes that it is itself such a continuing entity." A further step equates distinctively human psychological capacity with the capacity for self-governed rational conduct and especially for formulating aims for action through self-reflection (Wasserman et al. 2013). This singular characteristic that makes humans unique also is supposed to be the source of our fundamental value to ourselves and to one another.

Each person therefore should respect the capacity of adult humans to execute the requisite kind of rational action and to accept self-reflective responsibility for what has been done. But exercising our exceptional capacities requires being sufficiently self-directing and free from social and political subordination to self-determine the good for one's self (Silvers and Francis 2010). There are various names for this kind of process. Psychologists use the label "executive functioning." Autonomy, self-determination, and sovereignty over self are philosophical notions that, while not synonymous with executive functioning or one another, capture important aspects of this human capacity.

Thus, from a difference that purportedly makes humans exceptional has been drawn a warrant for acknowledging and attributing humans' rights. Placing rights on this basis, however, precludes the possibility that human rights can be universal in the requisite sense. Disabled people – even those whose deficits in capacity are considered to be corporeal rather than cognitive – commonly are perceived as failing to meet the standard of capacity for self-reflective, self-governing (and thereby responsible) action (Silvers 2013). Consequently, disabled people who are biologically human but are perceived as lacking the crucial degree of human capacity have been denied the usual freedom, together with its moral and legal protections, that human rights are expected to bestow.

There is, further, a history of underestimating the capacities of individuals owing to their disabilities. For centuries, for example, hearing-impaired people were mistakenly assessed as intellectually impaired just because they did not speak what they thought (Berke 2016). The centuries of denying schooling to intellectually disabled people, as well as to people with other kinds of disabilities, and then condemning them as unable to learn because they lacked reading and writing skills other people acquire through schooling also illustrates the effect of bias on accurate assessment of disabled people's capacity (Murdick, Gartin, and Crabtree 2006). In general, nonverbal individuals, and other individuals whose disabilities impede communication, remain vulnerable to misjudgment of this kind even today.

The effect of such bias is that individuals with disabilities have been regarded as not being really human or fully human persons. This pretext has regularly motivated excluding disabled people from the ranks of rights bearers. The metaphysical move of grounding rights in essential human properties thus has enabled actions of exclusion from, rather than inclusion under, rights-bearers' protections. As a result, in many legal systems, individuals with disabilities have been bereft of legal standing and thereby deprived of equal protection from the law.

Article 12 of the United Nations Convention on the Rights of People with Disabilities attempts a remedy, adjuring states parties to reaffirm the right of people with disabilities to be recognized as full legal persons and to enjoy legal capacity on an equal basis with others in all aspects of life. But the components of Article 12 that direct states parties to provide for effective safeguards to prevent abuse, coercion, exploitation, and arbitrary or excessive confinement, and of Article 13 that call for ensuring effective access to justice for persons with disabilities on an equal basis with others, indicate the enormous amount of justice system reform through which nations will have to go to achieve justice for all, including disabled people.

If having certain exceptional capacities is not the hallmark of being human, perhaps the universality of human rights lies in the other familiar articulation of human exceptionalism, which is the claim that humans are all equally products of a special and singularly successful biological evolutionary process (Kittay 2005). A non-relational version of this biological view holds that a characteristic all humans share in common is the possession of a human genome. With contemporary genetic knowledge indicating that we also share nearly all of our genome with non-human species, it has seemed increasingly arbitrary to draw a critical ethical line between humans and non-humans on this basis, especially because the genome is described in non-normative terms that do not themselves appear to carry ethical or legal implications (McMahan 1996, 2002, 2009; Singer 1993, 2009).

In reply, Eva Kittay (2005) has developed a relational view of the import of the biological evolutionary process. The idea here is that humans are naturally constructed to be concerned about ourselves and for those we believe to be our close biological kin as well. We biologically bond with kin to care for our offspring, and we naturally also ally with the smaller and larger circles of humans on whom our own welfare and our family's welfare depend.

This relational version of biological exceptionalism also lends itself to privileging some humans and marginalizing or excluding others. If kinship is supposed to be the basis of each human's duty to acknowledge human rights for others, then some individuals will enjoy a more secure status than others, depending on how broadly their family resemblances reach. Far from being an expansive basis for human rights, biological exceptionalism seems to energize a kind of tribalism that might embrace close family members who happen to have disabilities but by no means extends to most disabled people, who remain anonymous anomalous individuals distanced and treated as alien because of their disabilities.

Another reason for concern about the strength of the value of inclusiveness offered on a "family ties" basis for universal human rights emerges from the muted or absent family responses to the disappearance of their disabled relatives during the Nazi euthanasia program years (Koall 2013). Family members for many different reasons – including their own weaknesses – may be uncertain protectors of those with whom they have ties. Or family members may perceive, and therefore actively resent, their disabled relative as burdensome to such an extent that the vulnerable family member requires protection against them.

On the other side, family may be overly partial to their kin. If so, then sourcing a health care right in individuals' humanity, when this status is assigned on the basis of kinship bonds, threatens to strain the justice of the health care system. In this circumstance, the most pressing and effectively presented claims for care will come from family advocates for whom the patient is supremely human and thereby deserving of the full array of care that medicine can offer. The troubled and sometimes ruinous process whereby families of disabled children are expected to advocate extensively so as to obtain special education services should serve as a warning here. Better-educated families in more favorable economic conditions have proven more successful than less fortunate ones in obtaining services, and individuals with disabilities bereft of favorable family support may have no one advocating for them at all (Kelman and Lester 1998).

Moreover, disparities that track appearance of functional deficit but do not take into account the adaptive functionality achievable with access to effective services can create unnecessary problems in assembling an essential health care benefits package. Normal appearance or conduct is important for securing preferred status and privilege, while anomalous function or presence has the opposite result. Bias favoring species typicality places a premium on providing procedures that aim at normality rather than at adaptive functionality. Individuals are best situated to claim such rights when their appearances and conduct most resemble the species' paradigm, or else when they look and act as their family or community group expects, but rights with warrants contingent on such family ties fall short of the universality to which human rights aspire (Silvers 2013).

In sum, to invoke uniquely human properties as the basis of human rights is to place a premium on the disabled's similarity or family resemblance to species-typical or normal humans. Although some human rights theorists believe this human exceptionalist basis of rights affords dignity and therefore rights-bearer status without being defeasible due to disability (Degener 2013), there are both historical and logical reasons for being skeptical of this claim. Historically, failure to acknowledge individuals as fully human owing to their cognitive or physiological differences from most people has regularly motivated excluding disabled people from the ranks of rights bearers. Logically, the core problem is that, absent a religious source of conviction that being human means being next to God or some such faith, people's dignity usually is said to be derived from the presence of some or all of the essential attributes of being human. Such an account is circular: it proposes that individuals must be valued because human beings have dignity but also must be acknowledged as human because of their dignity.

To illustrate further, by grounding rights policy in human exceptionalism, it would seem that equitable health care entitlement packages ought in principle to cover interventions meant to make patients seem more species typical, or normal, whether or not they make the individual actually more functional. In such circumstances, we may expect a human right to health care to be invoked in demands for health care interventions. And indeed, in addition to general antidiscrimination provisions, such as equal recognition before the law (Article 12) and access to justice (Article 13), Article 25 of the Convention on the Rights of People with Disabilities assigns the right to people with disabilities to access health services of the same quality, range and, standard as those to which nondisabled people have access. Further, the text of Article 26 provides for establishment of rehabilitation support for people with functional limitations. A worry is that the language of these provisions is ambiguous, leaving open the possibility of imposing services that promote species-typical functioning, to the detriment of services that enable adaptive functioning, even if the latter are more effective in assisting disabled individuals to get what they need done.

If health care packages thus were to be designed with normality as the touchstone, likely results could be on the one hand reluctance to cover services needed to attain functionality if supposed normality cannot be fully achieved. But on the other hand, the result also might be consumption of resources and courting of risks just to gain the appearance of or to approximate normality, even if reduced functionality results from such medical treatment (Parens 2006). This recipe, called for by the standard for being treated as human that exceptionalism itself sets, appears to drive misguided, but also unnecessarily costly or downright dangerous, health care interventions.

To summarize so far, human exceptionalism is a traditional, and perhaps the prevailing, approach to grounding human rights, one with roots that predate the Enlightenment and one that remains strong today. But theories about an exceptional human psychological capacity for logical or reflective thinking, or an exceptional human biological capacity for personal attachment, both turn too easily into rationales for excluding at least some disabled humans from human rights protection by portraying them as so lacking in crucial, and exclusively human, dignity-conferring properties that they fail to qualify as rights bearers (Silvers 2013). And in regard to individuals whose disabilities do not debar them from the usual ontology of the human species or humankind, a traditional human rights approach lacks theoretical resources to respond to those who are concerned that rights will become costly demands for services that are less about functionality than about the appearance of normality.

In general, justifying rights by appeal to humanness, humanity, or membership in the human race invokes an idealized abstraction as the ground for assignment of protections and privileges in the interactions of particular individuals in the non-ideal world of actual social circumstance. We believe that such abstractions do not work in practice to protect the rights of some individuals to whom they apply. Or even worse, they may become tools to undermine anomalous individuals' protections. They are, in these respects, defective as justifications and should be treated with suspicion, especially if their failures are systematically exclusionary.

We should note at the outset that part of our view is that how rights appeals function practically is relevant to the judgments we make about justifications. Abstract justifications for any rights that do not work to protect these same rights for some to whom they apply, or that even worse undermine protection, are in that respect defective as justifications. This is especially so if their failures are systematic, failing for groups lacking privilege. This is a view of justification as it functions in a non-ideal world of actual social circumstances. On this view, justifications might falter in some contexts when they do not do so in others.

3. Collective agreement as a basis for rights justification

An alternative approach to rights rejects metaphysical beliefs about essential humanizing properties and instead understands rights as tools that both emerge from and enable the kinds of human interactions that shape our social environment. We humans are, individually as well as collectively, both creators of our own political and cultural values yet also creatures of the liberating or constricting political and cultural conditions we create. It follows that we humans possess individual and collective powers to narrow or expand who can be considered the parties included in such tacit cooperative agreements as well as to regulate the repertoire of roles made available to facilitate different people's inclusion. As Rousseau observed, our frailty is a main characteristic that we humans have in common (see also Turner 1993, 501–507). What approach to avoiding disability bias in delineation of essential health care benefits might be developed by invoking such non-metaphysical grounds for rights?

In a pragmatist view, what political morality requires is evolving and context dependent. Humans live and interact in communities, developing, shaping, testing, and reshaping norms by which to live together. As Ruth Anna Putnam (2000) points out, "Unlike other social animals, we are able to reflect on the ways in which we cooperate and on the effects of the manner of our association on ourselves and others." And as we have argued (Silvers and Francis 2005), justice is constructed through building trust relationships that are inclusive of outliers.

Thus, as we also have argued, justice should be understood always as a work in progress (Silvers and Francis 2005). We should not suppose, despite ideal justice theorizing pressing us to do so, that fully inclusive and therefore universal justice can be a *fait accompli*. Rights claims are no exceptions. Political rights are the original core of the civil rights and international rights movements (Sieghart 1985).

Made within social communities (Carreira da Silva 2013), the function of rights is to press political institutions to recognize what is necessary for each of their members to lead flourishing lives within them, hence their acknowledgement of universal aspiration. Understood pragmatically, rights are instruments for expanding equality among different kinds of individuals who happen to be interacting with one another. Thus, their expression resists schemes that appoint some individuals as more deserving of flourishing than others.

This expansive drive emerges from the nature of such rights, which is to protect individuals' interactions by promoting respect equally for the integrity of people who have occasion to engage with one another. As such, rights claims both reflect and challenge social arrangements. They both accept and question resource constraints, building on what exists in the continuing effort to create conditions under which all flourish because each can flourish.

From a practical political organizing perspective, calls for civil rights engagement are familiar inspiration for such progressive pragmatic efforts. Within this context, rights are claims on the social resources needed to meet basic interests that are critical to individuals' interactive flourishing. For what have been termed *negative* rights, rights to non-interference, these are the institutions that protect physical security, freedom from torture and slavery, liberty of thought and expression, privacy, freedom of movement, and the like (United Nations 1948, Arts. 3–19). They are the political rights of assembly and participation (United Nations 1948, Arts. 20, 21). For what have been called *positive* rights, rights to specified resources, these are means by which to meet critical human needs: food, shelter, health care, education, employment, and the like

(United Nations 1948, Arts. 22–27). Our contention here is that these rights should be understood in a pragmatic rather than a metaphysical framework, grounded explicitly in acknowledgement of people's differences rather than rooted in claims about how humans essentially are the same.

How rights are instantiated specifically in a given social context depends on the normative understandings in place at that time. These tacit understandings are not static, however; they are continually pressed to develop possibilities of flourishing for all.

Rights to health care, for example, can be understood purely as civil rights rather than as human rights in this way. Existing assumptions and resources are the start. But their inclusiveness is subject to ongoing challenge in terms of whether they allow everyone equally to lead flourishing lives in accord with their conceptions of their good.[1]

4. Health care rights in a civil rights frame

Health care provides an example of the import of a civil rights approach. We have already noted how casting the right to health care as a human right may impose normality as a functional standard or invite unjust disregard, or instead, partiality, depending on the human rights justification employed. In contrast, construing access to health care as one among other civil rights can provide a fairer and more practically reasonable approach.

When rights are understood to be absolutes, as human rights theory does, they operate as trump cards or side constraints, thereby preempting other considerations from coming into play.[2] This poses a difficulty if human rights conflict among themselves, a problem usually resolved by narrowing accounts of what these rights require. Civil rights, however, need not function as such absolutes; balances among them can be weighed and developed through adjudication. Health care allocation provides many occasions for such a solution.

One example is the supposed separation and potential conflict between health care and other social services. If health care is narrowly construed as the provision of medical services and payment for these services is restricted to contexts in which they can be delivered efficiently, then people who are seeking support for their health needs may find themselves limited in their choices of residency. If residency is seen only as a place for people who can function on their own to live, then people who require living assistance may be denied support to reside in an independent living community situation in which they can develop their talents and flourish. They may instead be confined in institutional settings that deny them access to any of the social roles citizens usually seek to occupy in the community (Gawande 2014).

Or take the question of what durable medical equipment government or private health care programs should provide or what living conditions beneficiaries must

1 We have argued elsewhere that people who are not articulate may be able to formulate conceptions of their good that require respect from others (Francis and Silvers 2007, Silvers and Francis 2010).

2 We leave aside here complications about the differences among versions of this view. Our only point here is that human rights approaches introduce an element of inflexibility that civil rights approaches do not.

meet to be eligible. Prosthetics and mobility assistive devices are cases in point. As we described earlier, if health care is seen in civil rights terms, then it will be responsive to different individuals' various modes of functioning, so as to offer solutions that are effective in regard to their personal needs instead of advancing a program that takes species-typical functioning to be the standard and the goal. To illustrate, US Medicare covers prosthetics when ordered by a physician to "replace a body part or function" (Medicare.gov 2015a), which suggests limitation to prosthetics that attempt to mimic normal functioning. Likewise, Medicare coverage for durable medical equipment extends only to equipment that is medically needed for use within the home (Medicare.gov 2015b). Thus, individuals who require different types of mobility assistive devices to ambulate beyond the home for work, school, or recreation will not be served in this regard by Medicare.

5. Group-differentiated rights and the problem of clashing models of disabilities

Individuals with diverse decrements, deficits, or other disadvantageous departures from the human species-typical biological condition have been collectivized as a separate class that is claimed to coalesce around some distinctive set of properties, at least for purposes of sociopolitical policy or programs. Extending the rights of a full citizen's role to individuals previously denied social participation on the basis of disability cannot occur, it is claimed, absent consensus about the conception or definition of disability itself (Barnes 2009, Bickenbach 2012). Unless deduced from or otherwise definitively shaped by such a basic idea, model, or definition of disability, disability rights policy is presumed to be in danger of missing its target population as well as of lacking plausible justificatory ground. Must political and social agreement upon a definitive general account of disability be attained prior to ascribing rights that effectively permit people with disabilities equitable access to good lives?

Models of disability are formulated for purposes of identifying relevant kinds of limitations disabled citizens endure and explaining why such limitations occur, as well as for repairing, reducing, or overcoming disability-associated limitations. Such models can identify the kinds of impediments to a good life disablement imposes, the reasons these impediments occur, and remedies for removing them. The main theoretical proposals, currently construed as rivals, are the divergent explanatory accounts[3] known as the medical model and the social model, which advance different strategies to remedy disability-related constraints. Meant to prompt and then guide progressive social

3 Samaha (2007) also understands the social and medical models each to convey a causal explanation rather than to constitute a normative justice theory from which disability policy directly flows. For normative grounding, however, he falls back to traditional, mutually exclusive, ideal justice theories. This chapter takes a different approach, considering whether the medical and social explanations of disability are compatible, or clash, when disability policy is prompted not by ideal justice theory but instead by social rights exercised under conditions of injustice (that is, when disability policy is informed by partial compliance theory).

reform, both of the prevailing models portray disability as a locus of difficulties that justice demands be cleared away.

These alternative accounts constitute well-known contenders for characterizing what disability is for purposes of ascribing rights. In common, the medical and social models presume disabled people are a definable class. That said, while the classes addressed by the two models may have similar, or at least significantly overlapping, extensions, they differ in their paradigms of the disabled individual and therefore also in regard to how to select the kinds of rights such individuals most need to exercise. If a generally acceptable account of disability can be found, then the accord achieved among affected actors will authorize arguments warranting disabled people's rights and thereby establish their status as rights bearers.

In theory, securing agreement about disability identity should result in a perspective within which plausible claims to productive rights for disabled people come clearly into view. If a generally acceptable account of disability could be found, then the accord achieved among affected actors would authorize arguments warranting disabled people's rights and thereby establish their status as rights bearers. If the medical and social models of disability were compatible, then group-differentiated disability rights theory could aspire to moderate robustness at least, for both models would pick out the same individuals as being disabled. If so, then the repertoire for mitigating each individual's dysfunction might be more replete than whatever either one of the models could tender alone.

6. Disability as a medical problem

The medical model explains disabled people's limitations in terms of biological pathology, treating both the natural and the built or artificially arranged environment as an invariable to which humans have no choice but to adjust. This makes medical intervention the route through which to address disabled people's limitations. If medicine can cure them of biological anomaly – make them like typical people, that is – then the physical or intellectual barriers they encounter and that limit them will be no greater than whatever constrains the majority of people and keeps everyone alike from being fully free. On this medical model, justice for disabled people – as well as where their freedom lies – is to be found by pursuing health care reform, both expanding access and improving effectiveness in remedying disabling health conditions.

Contentiousness that sometimes rises to the level of instability is inherent within the medical model itself and is especially problematic in areas where medical diagnosis and social services delivery cross paths. Yet there is another obstacle to achieving reliability in referencing disablement across different contexts. The history and nature of medical accounts of disability reveal conceptualizing processes wracked with controversy that undercut the robustness of medical theory-dependent definitions and analyses of disability.

The World Health Organization's approach to defining disability has been under construction for more than thirty years, and one of its major projects – to craft a classification system to serve health care clinicians – has been expanded in attempts to serve social service systems, and political and legal aspirations as well, resulting in a bewilderingly multivariant, multilayered scheme (Stein et al. 2014). Related bafflement about diagnosing disabling conditions may be provoked by the American Psychiatric Association's *Diagnostic and Statistical Manual of Mental Disorders*, now in a version of its fifth edition, from which it seems that some familiar illnesses have ceased to exist and some previously undiscovered ones have been detected (Kutchins and Kirk 1997).

The referent of "disability" is even less reliable, and explanatory theory built on this concept even flabbier (taking "flabby" as an antonym of "robust"), in the domain of public policy. To illustrate, the US Social Security Administration (SSA) expends enormous amounts of time and money on an administrative process that assesses and reassesses some people's claims to be work disabled, with standards changing as the political, medical, and legal scenes shift. The US Census Bureau expands on the SSA definition to include anyone unable to perform any of a long list of everyday tasks, including housework (Brault 2012). For the US Department of Housing and Urban Development, disability is an enduring physical, mental, or emotional impairment that substantially impedes independent living but can be improved by a more suitable residence (Stein et al. 2014).

Further, while some individuals with physical or mental impairments fight to be acknowledged by the SSA as being disabled, others – sometimes with identical impairments – deny that the label fits. For example, the officer who served as a model for a new monument to wounded US military personnel – a captain who lost her right arm in Iraq – stated at the dedication of the American Veterans Disabled for Life Memorial: "I don't like the term 'disabled' because I don't think of myself that way, but I get what they're trying to do" (Schneider 2014). Some groups – for example – deaf people (people who are members of deaf culture) also do not think of themselves as disabled (Kent 1997). Far from facilitating broad accord about how to sweep away disadvantage and difficulties correlated with disability, attempts to gather people together under the umbrella of a general concept of disability can precipitate fragmentizing.

Even more perplexing, the same individual may be both disabled and not disabled under current US law. The US Supreme Court declared in *Cleveland v. Policy Management Systems Corp.*[4] that being disabled for Social Security Disability Insurance purposes could be compatible with being able, with workplace accommodation, to execute the essential components of a particular job. The court eschewed proposing that such conflicts be resolved as a matter of law, supposing that neither courts nor SSA procedures had sufficient resources to take on adjudicating such discrepancies between different disability policies' definitions of disability (Stein et al. 2014). Instead, it placed the burden on Cleveland of explaining how she could meet the divergent standards. Although the court's stopgap decision may be a useful resolution for a particular practical context – individuals covered by Social Security Disability Insurance whose employers balk at offering the reasonable accommodation they need to stay productively at work – it's hard to see how group-differentiated rights theory can identify proper

4 526 U.S. 795 (1999).

disability rights bearers if individuals can be both disabled and not disabled at the same time and in regard to the same job.

Such a result contraindicates attempting to derive disabled people's rights from a definition, model, or other conceptualization of disability. Thus in practice, an unexpected disconnect between, on the one hand, devising a general disability theory built around a definitive specification of what shall count as disability and, on the other hand, making headway with rights justification that addresses the disparately disadvantageous effect of disability on justice, comes into view. Not atypically in such a circumstance, various parties contest whether an individual is sufficiently dysfunctional to qualify as disabled, while sight is lost on questions about whether the individual has been free to exercise general rights meaningfully despite disability and whether injustice to the individual based on disability has been done.

7. Disability as a social problem

A distinctive thread runs through formulations of the social model. The theme foregrounds experiences in which biological condition remains constant, but due to prohibitive social arrangements, or to disruptions of facilitative ones, dysfunction becomes magnified so that the individual is blocked from accessing, or driven out of, social participation in meaningful roles. The subtext is that, by accommodating or otherwise altering social arrangements to compensate or be a better fit for their capacities, the debilitating result of disabled peoples' incapacities can be eliminated or at least significantly reduced. When social practice adjusts to respond in ways that fit and thereby welcome them, so that they no longer must struggle against a hostile social environment, people with disabilities shall be transformed from dysfunctional to functional beings, according to the social model of disablement.

In the United States, the social model surfaced at the height of the civil rights era and struck a resounding chord among disabled people who had participated in freedom actions to end racial segregation in public transportation systems and other public facilities from which they themselves remained excluded due to their disabilities.[5] This dynamic idea of disability, aimed at inspiring disabled people themselves to pursue their own paths to social change, was labeled "the social model of disability."[6] In the United Kingdom in the early 1970s, the made-for-political-action social model disseminated by the newly organized Union of the Physically Impaired Against Segregation (UPIAS)

5 Testimony of the author, based on personal experience.

6 Tanaka, Koichiro, *The Roots of the Social Model: A Life History of Paul Hunt*. Hokusie Gakuen University, Japan. See http://disability-studies.leeds.ac.uk/files/library/Tankana-Life-history-of-Paul-Hunt1.pdf. The crucial discussions during which the social model of disability was articulated occurred between the wheelchair user Vic Finkelstein, who had migrated from South Africa after being jailed and was employed as an Open University instructor, and the wheelchair user Briton Paul Hunt who, having spent the majority of his years in institutions (including, as a child, a geriatric ward), was attempting to form an independent living movement. See also the United Kingdom's web page for the Disabled People's Council, "A Tribute to Vic Finkelstein, the First Chair of BCODP and Pioneer of the Social Model of Disability" at http://www.ukdpc.net/site/news-archive/38-vic-finkelstein.

traced the cause of disabled people's severely constricted access to societal participation to uncongenial or oppressive social arrangements rather than blaming their biological differences for their dysfunction.[7]

As with the Independent Living Movement in the United States during the same time period, a UPIAS goal was liberating disabled individuals from confinement to lives as dependent patients in residential care.[8] UPIAS organizer Paul Hunt, a Briton diagnosed initially with muscular dystrophy and later with spinal musculature atrophy, who had resided in institutions since beginning to use a wheelchair at age thirteen, articulated what was then a radical view – namely, that what most limited people with disabilities was their segregation and the resulting social isolation (Hunt 1966). Hunt attributed their social disadvantage not to their biological conditions preventing them from executing valuable social roles but instead to their being the victims of socially embedded caricaturing that branded them sick, unfortunate, and useless. In other words, he accounted for their disadvantage as being similar to that imposed on the victims of race-based and sex-based discrimination.

Hunt's idea is widely accepted as having been seminal in the development of what has become known as the social model of disability. Moreover, it aligns with other late twentieth-century movements by subordinated groups to hold a moral mirror up to politically dominant people – in this case, the nondisabled majority – as a step toward liberating themselves (Samaha 2007, Silvers 2009). Such movements were seen to have altered prevailing popular consensuses about the inferior status of various disregarded kinds of people by forging social, political, and legal agreements to expand opportunity and related access rights. Activism propelled by the social model of disability challenged repressive practices of the majority population and the state, especially those that, based on disability, deny equal access to public places and programs and protections that the state provides to everyone else.

The social model identifies being disabled as dysfunction that social action can cure if disabled people can gain the right to propel remedial social change. Such an account accorded with a common experience of people with disabilities. The explanation of disadvantageous dysfunction was especially enlightening and liberating to disabled people who had achieved integration into such ordinary societal systems as those through which employment, education, and housing are obtained only to find their functionality precipitously impaired, to the point of barring them from their dearly won social roles, by thoughtlessly changed arrangements or circumstances that had no similar deleterious effect on nondisabled people.

7 See note 2.

8 Evans, John. "We Won't Give Up on Independent Living." *The Guardian*, July 16, 2014. http://www.theguardian.com/society/2014/jul/16/independent-living-fund-closure-disabled-people-residential-care. In the late 1960s/early1970s, young UK disability leaders sought liberation from living in residential care, which they experienced as being imprisoned. For an account comparing the experiences of residents of institutions for the disabled and prisoners in correctional institutions, see also Anita Silvers, "Beyond Prison Walls: Curtailed Liberty, Custodial Responsibility, and Institutional Health Care," *American Philosophical Association Philosophy and Medicine Newsletter* 14(1), 2014.

The social model strengthens social rights for disabled people by underlining the arbitrariness of disability-based denials of role access from employment to parenting and the concomitant attenuation of their resources and liberty. Further, the social model has a ready account of why states owe disabled people more than perfunctory access to these goods: to execute the roles they have an equitable opportunity right to enjoy, meaningful access to other rights – such as entitlements to resources and guarantees of liberty – must be made available for them.[9]

At least two related sociopolitical narratives have proven well suited to leveraging the strengths of the social model. One theme is to defeat segregation by accommodating individuals' physical, mental, and intellectual limitations so as to open up access for them to natural and built sites, to information and communication, and to other components of the human environment nondisabled individuals take for granted they have a right to enjoy. The social model's initial application was to liberate some people whose disabilities resulted in their being institutionalized by providing the additional resources needed so that they could reside in the same places other people do. The second theme is to enable integration through the right to various accommodations that provide for participation in traditionally valued social roles such as working and playing.

8. Disability identity: Healthy versus ill?

Hardly had the social model gained traction in practical politics, prompting policies that called for social arrangements to be adapted so that they did not exclude disabled individuals from full access to community life, then a wave of debate about the scope of societal remedies broke over it. People whose social participation restrictions could not be ameliorated by social change – people with chronic pain or fatigue, for example, and surrogates for profoundly cognitively impaired individuals – contended that social model theory could not deliver societal compensations for physiological deficits. Thus arose a dispute that is sometimes – misleadingly, in our judgment – characterized as between healthy disabled people and disabled people who are ill.

The backlash against the social model might be read as signifying that a better account of disability – perhaps a biological model or some other medically sensitive means of identifying members of the disability group – is needed to do the job. To illustrate, rearranging the environment by requiring all restaurants to offer level entry access may greatly improve a wheelchair user's sociability. Now she can freely join her friends with dinner plans; no longer need she dissemble, pretending to have too much work to participate or to have another engagement, just because the others are set on dining at a place her wheelchair cannot go. But no similar change can reach the person whose severely incapacitating peanut allergy prevents permitting any morsel of

9 Samaha is correct in observing that, because the social model reveals a species of causal connection, normative conclusions cannot follow from it alone. But of course, social cause explanations need not stick to neutral descriptions in characterizing the causes they assert.

food or drink contaminated ever-so-slightly from peanuts from touching his mouth, for he never can be sure that restaurants workers' and diners' hands and clothing are completely peanut free. Joining friends to share a meal is an activity to which, it seems, social arrangement alteration alone cannot secure access for him. Medical intervention such as a sophisticated allergy desensitization program – action seemingly more compatible with a medical explanation of disability – appears more effective here.

The first individual will find the social model congruent with her experience of disabling constraints and will assent to the prospect that rights propelled by this theory possess power to make her free. The second individual's personal experience does not confirm the promise of liberation that the social model invites, so deriving rights from its account of disability will fail to capture his confidence and assent. For the second individual, the cure to his dysfunction is being able to claim medical intervention in the form of desensitization treatment to alter his biological condition, not his environment's social conditions. In his case, a medical explanation of the barriers to opportunity that confront him will be the more powerful one because it aligns more fully with his experience of both the source of his limitations and the way(s) he has found some relief.

Considering that by definition disabled people deviate sharply from species-typical ones, and that as a group they hardly are uniform among themselves, resting their status as rights bearers on achieving agreement about who disabled people definitively are is a highly risky strategy at best. The recent history of efforts to secure recognition of disabled people's rights does nothing to lay this suspicion to rest. In the United States, for example, during the very same decades when momentum for articulating disabled people's rights gathered force, acrimonious debate flared between cause lawyers and conservative judges, as well as among disability activists and disability scholars (to name just four of the perspectives brought by prominent combatants who have entered this fray), about the proper or propitious definition of disability (Silvers 2009).

The social model stands accused in some quarters of misrepresenting disabled people by abridging who they are, or of even more malignant distortions such as promoting values that exclude people with certain kinds of physical or cognitive limitations (Shakespeare and Watson 2001, Wendell 2001; see also Silvers 2009). These complaints are connected, in that the former criticizes the social model for suppressing rather than showcasing disabled people's differences, especially dysfunctional ones, while the latter objects to advancing an ideal of independence that some disabled people's dysfunctions make unrealizable for them.

These charges echo concerns brought by adherents of the medical model – namely, that to ignore experiences of being weak, enervated, in pain, and vulnerable in modeling disability is deceptive because these are the most salient experiences in most, or at least in many, disabled people's lives. Of course, almost all people, regardless of whether they are disabled, have occasion to learn how such experiences feel. Yet some or all of these feelings chronically pervade the lives of at least some people with disabilities to a degree so marked and therefore so different as to distinguish their embodied lives at both the sentience and societal levels.

Critics of the social model argue that distinctive marks of their limitations inscribe disabled individuals' embodied subjectivity, inducing abiding awareness of their inescapably compromised capacity. Critics argue as well that experiences of this sort, that seem to reflect deficiencies of minds or bodies (or both) so as to inflect disabled individuals' consciousness of their own minds and bodies, shape virtually all disabled people's consciousness of themselves. Such characterizations of disabled embodiment have been taken by many disability studies scholars, and by medical model-influenced scholarship as well, to be indispensable to understanding disability.

Different disabled people respond to their deficits in different ways, of course. The ones seeking to exercise their right to productive social roles may find other disabled individuals, who pursue resource rights for general sustenance due to disability-associated non-productivity, to be threatening because they equate disability with dependence – a stereotypically confining role. The social model account of disability-associated limitation may be more attractive, offering more insight and illumination into respected social role rights seekers than to people whose route to a good life places pursuit of better resources first. Concomitantly, the latter – feeling protected rather than confined by the sick role – may perceive the so-called healthy disabled (a category constructed by feminist philosopher Susan Wendell) as presenting the threat because their very existence seems to lower the urgency of allocating disability-warranted resources based on special need. That disabled people are not uniform in their priorities, however, does not discount the social dimensions of disability.

9. Regarding robustness

In their classic article "The Equal Protection of the Laws," Joseph Tussman and Jacobus tenBroek (1949) suggested that attempts at classification of subjects such as that at issue in establishing group-differentiated rights could not avoid straying into under-inclusive or over-inclusive classificatory errors. We shall make a related point about the disability category. A similar problem occurs in building a theorized definition of disability, one that is supposed to align equitably with the varied experiences of individuals with differing dysfunctions and the varied uses to which the idea of disability is put.

Attempts to construct a definitive model of disability for a policy's purposes generally commence by selecting whatever individuals best approximate the paradigmatic patient, client, citizen, or other beneficiary the policy aims to serve. But variations in programmatic purpose cannot help but influence where, for example, the line between normality and pathology most persuasively is drawn (Canguilheme 1966). Endemic to this process, therefore, is the delineation of a disability class that fits well with the motivating policy's purpose but is likely to appear parsimoniously small (that is, under-inclusive), or else profligately large (that is, over-inclusive), from other disability policies' points of view.

Instability of the reference class thus is a manifestation of the problem provoked by proceeding as if there is an all-purpose concept of disability, one that can be called upon to serve a multiplicity of programs and in very different ways. Moreover, too often to ignore, or try to explain away, attempts to build clarity and consensus about who is deserving of disability rights, undertaken in order to fashion progressive practices of ascribing disabled people's rights, have been bought up short by a culture of contesting theoretical definitions that has turned toxic and become so polemical as to be counterproductive in practice. Contrary to the direction theorizing about the rights of disabled people currently takes, therefore, definitions, so-called models, and other representations of disability should not be supposed to precede elucidation of the social rights of people with disabilities, for they are not stable enough to serve as a justificatory ground for either individual or group rights.[10]

10. Disability rights as civil rights

Justice for people with disabilities ought not become mired in dissension about who truly is disabled. The disjuncture between fashioning a definitive account of disability and gaining fair access to justice for people who are disabled appears too deep to be bridged.

Struggles about whether the social model of disability is progressive, or instead is an oppressive imposition by one kind of disabled person upon another kind, should be kept a safe distance away from the pursuit of justice for disability in legislatures and courts.

Moreover, consideration of whether the social model of disability strengthens the recognition and effectiveness of disabled people's social rights need not cast these models as attempts to be definitive. Rather than confining the account of disabled people's rights to one or the other of the contesting models of disability, or to yet another contender theory that defines disability, an attractive reconciliatory path forward exists. This is to explore the usefulness of the models within a strong and broadly acceptable general civil rights frame rather than to suppose them to be touchstones for group-differentiated disability rights.

Rights bearers with disabilities then will possess and exercise rights not because they are disabled but because everyone has these rights. To do so, we leave behind the idea of assessing the social model, and the medical model as well, in regard to their sufficiency to ground group-differentiated disability rights. The social rights that disabled people rely on should be the rights nondisabled people enjoy as well, although the heightened vulnerabilities from which disabled people typically suffer may call for the exercise of special configurations of ordinary rights.

As an illustration, such a configuration might develop and impose applications of liberty rights to provide for freedom to access every level of education provided for the general public, and of resource entitlements to achieve a level playing field that enables such educational opportunity to be meaningful. Moreover, for some individuals, the effective route for gaining access to and for expending resources may lie in therapeutic intervention, while for others, altering the social environment and allocating adaptive equipment offers a better chance of success. Further, these packages of rights may be

10 See Samaha (2007) for a somewhat similar, but not an identical, observation about the relationship between models of disability and normatively driven conclusions.

so characteristic of or closely associated with some instantiations of disability as to be mistakenly identified as special disability rights.

In his important article "Disability Human Rights," legal scholar Michael Ashley Stein downgrades the social model as self-defeating by "limiting itself to civil and political rights" and thereby disregarding the empowerment available through other kinds of rights, especially the economic, social, and cultural resources known as second-generation rights (Stein 2007, 22). Within an interdependent social rights account such as the proposal being explored here, this problem recedes because embracing a civil or political right warrants economic, social, or cultural rights that can be construed as materially necessary, and therefore instrumental, for exercising the civil or political right. Similarly, exercising an economic, social, or cultural right may in some contexts be valuable in itself, yet in that context, bringing the intrinsically valuable right to bear may materially require the instrumentality of a civil liberty right or a political role right.

But how can a right be both intrinsically and instrumentally valuable, especially when to be intrinsic value is unconditional but instrumental value is not so? Both intrinsic and instrumental rights are claims against particular actors (whether individuals or more abstract entities such as a legal system or state) as well as claims to something that is to be permitted or provided by the referenced actors. The object to be secured through a rights claim may in one situation be valuable in itself and in another be valuable only as a means. The character of a rights claim thus can shift depending on how the disadvantage it is invoked to remedy is sourced and situated.

To illustrate, contextualized to the state of medicine today, much otherwise desirable biological alteration is either infeasible or very risky with low rates of success. In this context, implementation of an intrinsically valuable right to work productively by an individual with diabetes may require the individual to exercise a liberty right for breaks from work to monitor blood sugar. In the current context of what medical science enables us to do, at present, the compelling causal explanation of the individual's employment disadvantage – what makes his diabetes a disabling condition for him rather than just a biological fact about him – is in terms of societal arrangements about work schedules.

Suppose the medical situation now changes: effective replacement pancreases now become available, although the medical costs of constructing one for a particular person, installing it, and providing maintenance to ensure it continues to work are high. Individuals with disadvantaged employment prospects, for which diabetes figures large, no longer need to monitor their blood sugar in order to exercise their role right to be employed. They still have diabetes, but working around potential dysfunction no longer calls for liberty to take regular breaks. What is most instrumental for maintaining, despite having diabetes, the intrinsic value of equitable opportunity to assume a productive worker's role despite being diabetic now depends on having an instrumental resource right to the requisite medical treatment.

Note that in this example the context indicates whether the explanatory medical or the explanatory social model of disability suits the situation best. In the scenarios depicted earlier, initially a liberty right to an adjusted work schedule, as recommended on a social model account, is centrally instrumental, but when the situation changes, a resource right to an adjusted physiological state, underwritten by the medical model, becomes centrally instrumental to being able to execute the valuable role.

To what use can the social model best be put within a strong and broadly acceptable general social rights frame? Not as a definition of disablement – that much is clear.

The social model originated as a liberating explanation of disabled people's disadvantage. And as with other heavily populated and highly complex groups of phenomena, a single explanatory theory may not suffice for the variety of ways in and degrees to which disability correlates with disadvantage. The broader the set and the more distant from each other its instances are, the more likely that broadly construed explanatory theories will lack robustness because allusions to "disability" made in different applications do not refer to the same thing. Conversely, correlating narrowly delineated instances of disadvantage with narrowly tailored homogenous examples of disablement sets the stage for formulating a narrowly focused and hence more potent explanatory theory, one capable of propelling a narrowly tailored protective or remedial configuration of rights. In sum, theories designed to account for disability's being disadvantageous can be the basis of preserving justice by predicting the comparative efficacy of various configurations of rights. But the more capacious the theory is intended to be, the less reliable and robust its references to "the disabled" and hence the more puny and problematic as support for specialized disability rights.

11. Conclusion

At present, no univocal definition of disability unites the nations of the world, or even of the European Union. A very real possibility is that an individual who can count on disability rights protection in one state could be bereft of such rights in neighboring ones because, once over the border, she or he does not count as being disabled (McTigue 2014)[11]. Despite the popularity of positing definitions (and models and other accounts) of disability, however, adopting such a strategy still will leave some people who strike us now as being disabled without disability rights, although in that case, the range of individuals protected would depend on who they are and not, as is the case currently, where they are.

A more attractive, because better grounded, jurisprudential approach appeals to a framework of underlying basic social rights that pertain to everyone and thus are less likely to be blocked at national borders. Doing so calls for developing a replete repertoire of causal theories that explain disabled people's experiences of physiological and social constraints and consequent difference-sensitive policy strategies for a range of remedies. Then medically diverse people living in different social conditions all can apply instrumental social rights effectively and, as well, avoid disadvantage through the exercise of intrinsically valuable social rights. Rights theorists aspiring to improve justice for disability should assign weight to both the intrinsic and the instrumental value

11 McTigue argues that Europe ought to adopt a univocal definition of disability based on the social model so that individuals with all kinds of disabilities will be equally shielded by the law.

of each kind of social right. Any univocal social value theory is likely to devalue some individuals with disabilities; each such theory will neglect different disability groups.

Given the present state of research into the triggers of political, social, economic, and cultural disadvantage, there is room and need for both the medical and social models as well as for other explanations of the disadvantages that disability characteristically brings. What also is needed, however, is to ratchet up the sophistication with which one from among various available explanations of disablement's disadvantage is selected as providing the most powerful, and therefore apt, explanation for each particular case.

As well, we should be alert for situation(s) where the availability of both a biological and a social explanatory theory of disability create confusion or invite conflict over how to make disabled rights bearers' exercise of a right meaningful. To illustrate, one set of circumstances frequently encountered at the level of the individual rights bearer involves deciding which rights route is preferable for a person with a disability to forge a good fit with a role. For some persons, the route may reside in being able to claim resources to alter an anomalous biological condition that now bars the individual from functioning in the role. For other disabled individuals – even for some with the same biological condition as those seeking medical intervention – circumstances may diminish the effectiveness of a medical fix, or the proposed treatment intervention may be too precarious, perilous, or otherwise problematic to be risked. For persons for whom the latter circumstances hold, low-risk alteration of the social conditions for executing the role, rather than high-risk medical alteration of the individual herself, may be a more effective route to filling the role.

Such disparities warn against supposing that any right can be categorically effective for all individuals assigned to a non-circularly defined and broadly construed disability class.[12] Variance marks this group of actors, whose members are hallmarked by their dissimilarity from one another as much as they also are marked by differences from nondisabled people. An application of the view developed here deflects policy development efforts from codifying what disability is by branding as misguided the hope that doing so will stabilize membership in the group rights ascribed to the disabled should protect. Nor will individuals with disabilities all flourish under the same explanatory umbrella or succeed similarly if supplied with only a narrowed range of rights.

12. References

Barnes, Elizabeth. 2009. "Disability, Minority and Difference." *Journal of Applied Philosophy* 26(4), 337–355.

Berke, Jamie. 2016. "Deaf, Not Retarded: When Misdiagnoses Are Made, Everyone Pays." *Very-Well*, February 23. http://deafness.about.com/cs/featurearticles/a/retarded_2.htm.

Bickenbach, Jerome. 2012. *Ethics, Law, and Policy.* Thousand Oaks, CA: Sage.

Brault, Matthew W. 2012. *Americans with Disabilities: 2010 Household Economic Studies.* http://www.census.gov/prod/2012pubs/p70-131.pdf.

12 That is, other than a rubric that defines membership in the disability class as all and only individuals for whom exercising the right is effective.

Canguilheme, Georges. 1966, tr. 1991. *The Normal and the Pathological*, trans. Carolyn R. Fawcett and Robert S. Cohen. New York: Zone Books.

Carreira da Silva, Felipe. 2013. "Outline of a Social Theory of Rights: A Neo-Pragmatist Approach." *European Journal of Social Theory* 16(4), 457–475.

Degener, Theresia. 2016. "Human Rights of Persons with Disabilities in International and EU Law." In *EUI Working Papers*, edited by Dorothy Estrada-Tanck, European University Institute, http://cadmus.eui.eu/bitstream/handle/1814/41985/WP_2016_01.pdf?sequence=1.

Fagan, Andrew. 2005. "Human Rights." *Internet Encyclopedia of Philosophy*. http://www.iep.utm.edu/hum-rts/.

Finnis, John. 1980. *Natural Law and Natural Rights*. Oxford: Clarendon Press.

Francis, Leslie P. and Anita Silvers. 2007. "Liberalism and Independently Scripted Accounts of the Good: Meeting the Challenge of Dependent Agency." *Social Theory and Practice* 33, 311–334.

———. 2008. "Debilitating Alexander v. Choate: 'Meaningful Access' to Health Care for People with Disabilities." *Fordham Urban Law Journal* 35, 447–477.

Gawande, Atul. 2014. *Being Mortal*. New York: Henry Holt.

Hannum, Hurst. 2006. "The Concept of Human Rights." In *International Human Rights: Problems of Law, Policy, and Practice*, edited by Hurst Hannum, S. James Anaya, and Dinah Shelton, 31–33. Frederick, MD: Aspen.

Hunt, Paul. 1966. "A Critical Condition." In *Stigma: The Experience of Disability*, edited by Paul Hunt. London: Geoffrey Chapman. http://disability-studies.leeds.ac.uk/archiveuk/Hunt/a%20critical%20condition.pdf.

Kelman, Mark and Gillian Lester. 1998. *Jumping the Queue: An Inquiry into the Legal Treatment of Students with Learning Disabilities*. Cambridge, MA: Harvard University Press.

Kent, Bill. 1997. "Atlantic City; Deaf, Not Disabled." *The New York Times*, October 19. http://www.nytimes.com/1997/10/19/nyregion/atlantic-city-deaf-not-disabled.html.

Kittay, Eva Feder. 2005. "At the Margins of Moral Personhood." *Ethics* 116, 100–131.

Koall, Carsten. 2013. "Historian Götz Aly: Victims of Nazi Euthanasia 'Have Been Forgotten.'" *Spiegel Online International*, April 25. http://www.spiegel.de/international/germany/historian-goetz-aly-on-nazi-euthanasia-program-and-inclusion-debate-a-896209.html.

Kutchins, Herb and Stuart A. Kirk. 1997. *Making Us Crazy: DSM: The Psychiatric Bible and the Creation of Mental Disorders*. New York: Free Press.

Liao, Matthew. 2010. "The Basis of Human Moral Status." *Journal of Moral Philosophy* 7, 159–179.

McMahan, Jeffrey. 1996. "Cognitive Disability, Misfortune, and Justice." *Philosophy and Public Affairs* 25, 3–31.

———. 2002. *The Ethics of Killing*. New York: Oxford University Press.

———. 2009. "Radical Cognitive Limitation." In *Disability and Disadvantage*, edited by Kimberly Brownlee and Adam Cureton, 240–259. New York: Oxford University Press.

McTigue, Peter. 2014. "The Disorganised Nature of European Disability: Rethinking Protection for HIV Positive Individuals." *CELLS Online Paper Series* 3(4). http://dx.doi.org/10.2139/ssrn.2483377.

Medicare.gov. 2015a. "Prosthetic Devices." https://www.medicare.gov/coverage/prosthetic-devices.html.

———. 2015b. "Durable medical equipment (DME) coverage." http://www.medicare.gov/coverage/durable-medical-equipment-coverage.html.

Minow, Martha. 1990. *Making All the Difference: Inclusion, Exclusion, and American Law*. Ithaca, NY: Cornell University Press.

Murdick, Nikki L., Barbara L. Gartin, and Terry Lee Crabtree. 2006. *Special Education Law*. 2nd ed. San Francisco: Pearson Education.

Parens, Eric, ed. 2006. *Surgically Shaping Children: Technology, Ethics, and the Pursuit of Normality*. Baltimore: Johns Hopkins University Press.

Putnam, Ruth Anna. 2000. "Neither a Beast Nor a God." *Social Theory and Practice* 26(2), 177–200.

Samaha, Adam. 2007. "What Good Is the Social Model of Disability?" *University of Chicago Law Review* 74, 1251–1308.

Schneider, Elena. 2014. "A Prominent Location to Remember Veterans Who Were Wounded." *The New York Times*, August 23. http://www.nytimes.com/2014/08/23/us/a-prominent-location-to-remember-veterans-who-were-wounded.html?_r=0.

Shakespeare, Tom and Nicholas Watson. 2001. "The Social Model of Disability: An Outdated Ideology?" In *Exploring Theories and Expanding Methodologies: Where We Are and Where We Need to Go*, edited by Sharon N. Barnartt and Barbara M. Altman, 9–28. Bingley, UK: Emerald.

Sieghart, Paul. 1985. *The Lawful Rights of Mankind: An Introduction to the International Legal Code of Human Rights*. Oxford: Oxford University Press.

Silvers, Anita. 2005. "Predicting Genetic Disability While Commodifying Health." In *Quality of Life and Human Difference*, edited by Jerome Bickenbach, Robert Wachbroit, and David Wasserman, 43–66. Cambridge: Cambridge University Press.

———. 2009. "The Social Model of Disability." In *Philosophical Reflections on Disability*, edited by Chris Ralston and Justin Ho, 19–36. New York: Springer Academic Press.

———. 2012. "Moral Status: What a Bad Idea!" *Journal of Intellectual Disability Research* 56(11), 1014–1025.

———. 2013. "Embracing Freedom for Disability: The Hardest Thing To Do." Keynote Address for Menschen Recht Inklusion: International Symposium on the Implementation of the Convention on the Rights of People with Disabilities into Practice. Evangelische Fachhochschule RWL, Bochum, Germany, June 6–8.

Silvers, Anita and Leslie P. Francis. 2005. "Justice Through Trust: Disability and the 'Outlier' Problem in Social Contract Theory." *Ethics* 116(1), 40–77.

———. 2009. "Thinking about the Good: Reconfiguring Metaphysics (or Not) for People with Cognitive Disabilities." *Metaphilosophy* 40(3–4), 475–498.

———. 2010. "Thinking about the good: reconfiguring metaphysics (or not) for people with cognitive disabilities." In *Cognitive Disability and its Challenge to Moral Philosophy*, edited by Eva Feder Kittay & Licia Carlson, Wiley-Blackwell.

Singer, Peter. 1993. *Practical Ethics*. 2nd ed. Cambridge: Cambridge University Press.

———. 2009. "Speciesism and Moral Status." *Metaphilosophy* 40(3–4), 567–581.

Stein, Michael Ashley. 2007. "Disability Human Rights." *California Law Review* 95, 75–121.

Stein, Michael Ashley, Anita Silvers, Bradley Areheart, and Leslie P. Francis. 2014. "Accommodating Every Body." *University of Chicago Law Review* 81(2), 689–757.

Tooley, Michael. 1972. "Abortion and Infanticide." *Philosophy & Public Affairs* 2(1), 37–65.

Townley, Cynthia. 2010. "Animals and Humans: Grounds for Separation?" *Journal of Social Philosophy* 41, 512–526.

Turner, Bryan S. 1993. "Outline of the Theory of Human Rights." *Sociology* 27(3), 489–512.

Tussman, Joseph and Jacobus tenBroek. 1949. "The Equal Protection of the Laws." *California Law Review* 37(3), 341–381.

United Nations. 1948. "The Universal Declaration of Human Rights." http://www.un.org/en/documents/udhr/.

Wasserman, David, Adrienne Asch, Jeffrey Blustein, and Daniel Putnam. 2013. "Cognitive Disability and Moral Status." *Stanford Encyclopedia of Philosophy*. http://plato.stanford.edu/archives/sum2013/entries/cognitive-disability/.

Wendell, Susan. 2001. "Unhealthy Disabled: Treating Chronic Illnesses as Disabilities." *Hypatia* 16(4), 17–33.

11 Agency and disability

A rights-based approach

Michael Boylan

Like snowflakes falling from the sky, each of us is unique in our place on this earth. Even identical twins are unique.[1] So what does it mean to be "unique"? It means that we are one of a kind – though not sui generis. The "kind" is Homo sapiens. But we are all singularly different. What are we to make of this difference? Is it a mere fact? Can some facts entail value? Can some values entail rights and duties? These are just a few of the central questions concerning public policy and disability.

1. Central definitions

To begin our quest, we must sort out the background conditions for comparison. This involves a journey into systematics and physiology. In systematics, various biological taxa are identified via anatomy and the corresponding physiology.[2] There is always variation within each taxon. This is the dogma of evolutionary biology that I accept.[3]

The way that anatomical organs, bones, and systems interact is physiology. This is viewed on the same scale: How can the various body parts work together so that the individual can perform the actions that he or she wants to perform? For simplicity, let us call this the successful purposive agent. From my perspective, this is a firm statement of human nature: we all desire to be able purposively to act toward ends that we believe to be good.

If we accept this characterization of human nature, then what follows from this? I contend that there is a hierarchical set of goods to which we all aspire and that can be judged according to how proximate these ends are to the possibility of purposive action. Thus, any person on earth has a positive rights claim to these in descending order (the level-one basic goods trump all other claims and so forth). I base this rights claim on what it would take to understand one's humanity as a prospective purposive

1 This is a tortured question. On the identical twin angle, see Farber (1981) and Juel-Nielsen (1980). For two more narrow analytic approaches, see Joseph (1998) and Owens (2013).

2 I discuss this issue in the context of ancient philosophy of science in two books: *Method and Practice in Aristotle's Biology* (1983) and *The Origin of Ancient Greek Science: Blood, a Philosophical Study* (2015).

3 For an excellent outline on the basic tenets of evolutionary theory in biology and what it signifies, see Gould (2002).

agent and what it would take to get there. I call this argument "The Moral Status of Basic Goods."[4]

1 All people, by nature, desire to be good – fundamental assumption
2 In order to become good, one must be able to act – fact
3 All people, by nature, desire to act – 1, 2
4 People value what is natural to them – assertion
5 What people value they wish to protect – assertion
6 All people wish to protect their ability to act – 3–5
7 Fundamental interpersonal "oughts" are expressed via our highest value systems: morality, aesthetics, and religion – assertion
8 All people must agree, upon pain of logical contradiction, that what is natural and desirable to them individually is natural and desirable to everyone collectively and individually – assertion
9 Everyone must seek personal protection for her own ability to act via morality, aesthetics, and religion – 6, 7
10 Everyone, upon pain of logical contradiction, must admit that all other humans will seek personal protection of his or her ability to act via morality, aesthetics, and religion – 8, 9
11 All people must agree, upon pain of logical contradiction, that because the attribution of the basic goods of agency are predicated generally, that it is inconsistent to assert idiosyncratic preference – fact
12 Goods that are claimed through generic predication apply equally to each agent, and everyone has a stake in their protection – 10, 11
13 Rights and duties are correlative – assertion
14 Everyone has at least a moral right to the basic goods of agency, and others in society have a duty to provide those goods to all – 12, 13

This general right to the goods of agency is proportional to the importance of the good set out for action. I have set out one hierarchy of goods based upon this principle. I call it the Table of Embeddedness. The first goods listed are the most basic for action and then they become less embedded as we go on.

Basic Goods:

Level one: most deeply embedded (that which is absolutely necessary for human action): food, water (including sanitation), clothing, shelter, protection from unwarranted bodily harm (including basic health care)

Level two: deeply embedded (that which is necessary for effective basic action within any given society)

- Literacy in the language of the country
- Basic mathematical skills

4 I have discussed these at more length elsewhere (Boylan 2004, chapter 3; Boylan 2014, chapter 6).

- Other fundamental skills necessary to be an effective agent in that country (e.g., in the United States, some computer literacy is necessary)
- Some familiarity with the culture and history of the country in which one lives
- The assurance that those you interact with are not lying to promote their own interests
- The assurance that those you interact with will recognize your human dignity (as per above) and not exploit you as a means only
- Basic human rights such as those listed in the US Bill of Rights and the UN Universal Declaration of Human Rights

Secondary Goods:

Level one: life enhancing (medium to high-medium on embeddedness)

- Basic societal respect
- Equal opportunity to compete for the prudential goods of society
- Ability to pursue a life plan according to the personal worldview imperative
- Ability to participate equally as an agent in the shared community worldview imperative

Level two: useful (medium to low-medium embeddedness)

- Ability to utilize one's real and portable property in the manner she chooses
- Ability to gain from and exploit the consequences of one's labor regardless of starting point
- Ability to pursue goods that are generally owned by most citizens (e.g., in the United States today, a telephone, television, and automobile would fit into this class)

Level three: luxurious (low embeddedness)

- Ability to pursue goods that are pleasant, even though they are far removed from action and from the expectations of most citizens within a given country (e.g., in the United States today, a European vacation would fit into this class)
- Ability to exert one's will so that she might extract a disproportionate share of society's resources for her own use

When there are impediments to some particular individual possessing these goods – basic goods (levels one and two) and secondary goods (level one) – then it is the duty of all other people to provide these goods to those without.[5] For example, take food. The United Nations has set out that the minimum calorie intake on a regular basis is five hundred (given some variation for soma type).[6] Seven hundred fifty calories is

5 Levels two and three of secondary goods are to be considered after the more embedded levels have been realized.

6 *The 2007 Human Development Report* (New York: United Nations Development Program, 2007), 27.

better, and one thousand calories is the aspirational goal. These nutritional needs allow the brain to operate in such a way that purposive action (toward that which we consider to be good) is possible.

There are many reasons why some individuals may not be successful at garnering level-one and level-two basic goods and level-one secondary goods. These generally include socioeconomic deprivation that describes one's position in the community such that one's ability to commit purposive action toward one's conception of the good is restricted. One may be born into this state or descend there due to factors both in and not within one's power. This chapter will understand the word *disability* to refer to just such a state in which one does not have the positive liberty (or faces a negative liberty roadblock) to be able effectively to seek after these goods.

Positive liberty will be taken to be the power one possesses to be able to effect purposive action that leads toward the ends that one believes are good (both prudentially and morally). The power is demonstrated in the activity of the agent as she seeks to move in the direction of realizing the desired end.[7]

Negative liberty will be taken to refer to barriers from either within the agent or without that prevents the agent from fulfilling what he desires to do. Examples of "within the agent" include physiological impairments (either mental, emotional, or in the operation of one's muscular/skeletal system and its support systems[8]). Examples of "without" include environmental restraints either natural or social/political. For example, if one were born with the ability to concentrate for a long period of time before acting, then this might be an advantage if one were born into a hunting society where one had to have the patience to wait for game before making his move. However, if one were a Wall Street broker, then that same characteristic would mean that you would be always short on the one critical trade for your clients. Is being deliberate and patient, by nature, an advantage or a disability? It all depends on whether the environment rewards or creates barriers for action.

2. Environmental disability

At the end of the last section, the suggestive notion was raised about disability being environmentally as well as intrinsically focused. Kettlewell's famous experiment underscores this (Kettlewell 1971). The experiment goes like this. Take a region – for example, an industrial region in northern England – where factories have been spewing out soot for years. This soot lands on forests and changes the normal variegated color setting of an unaltered forest into one that is now predominately black. Living in this ecosystem are two subspecies of moth: one subspecies_a has variegated wing color, and the other subspecies_b has black wing color. In Environment_1, the trees that constitute the habitat before pollution, the moths whose wing coloring is variegated dominated in population (meaning could avoid predators and successfully reproduce). In Environment_2, pollution has made the trees black with soot, and so the normal patterns changed.

7 Many of the key distinctions I draw on liberty can be found in Berlin (1969).

8 By support systems, I am referring to the major systems of the body, such as the circulatory, nervous, and digestive systems. These systems allow the conditions for voluntary positive liberty.

Kettlewell noticed that the normally populous $subspecies_a$ (in $Envirionment_1$) were giving way to $subspecies_b$. This was due to industrial pollution (creating $Environment_2$). By cleaning the trees, Kettlewell was able to reverse the trend (making $subspecies_a$ more populous again by recreating $Environment_1$).

Does this mean that $subspecies_a$ is *better* than $subspecies_b$? Certainly not. For in $Environment_2$, $subspecies_b$ flourished and dominated $subspecies_a$. All that it shows is that no traits are "good" or "bad," per se, but are only so within certain environments.

Another example is the gene that expresses sickle hemoglobin. Hemoglobin is the oxygen-carrying protein in red cells, and a specific mutation in the beta polypeptide chain of hemoglobin leads to sickle hemoglobin, so called because the erythrocytes assume a sickle shape in conditions of low oxygen. Not only are such cells more rapidly cleared from the circulation than normal cells, leading to sickle cell anemia, but also especially in individuals who are homozygous for the gene, such sickle cells can aggregate, block blood vessels and organs, leading to the extremely painful and life-threatening sickle cell crises. However, having erythrocytes that contain the sickle hemoglobin in an environment that contains malaria is beneficial. When such cells are infected with malaria, the red cells sickle and the parasites die. In addition, the parasite proteins are released to the circulation, and the body can mount an immune response and abort the infection before full-blown malaria ensues. Thus, although being homozygous for sickle hemoglobin is deleterious, in an environment in which there is malaria, those who are heterozygous for the sickle hemoglobin gene will have a selective advantage and be superior reproducers to those without the gene. However, in an environment in which there is no malaria, the sickle hemoglobin gene will make those who have it less fit for reproduction. Thus, genetic fitness is seen to be a function of a particular gene in a particular environment.

From the perspective of philosophy, phenotypic and genotypic traits are not good or bad. They simply are. Variation in any species is a dogmatic given. This is what allows the species to survive in changing environments.

There is no real good or bad with these cases of environmental disability. It is merely a term that is environmentally relative. However, in human cases, this environmental factor can also be the source of unjust discrimination.[9] What makes this case unjust is that preferment for the more desired positions in the community often go to those with undeserved background qualifications (as judged by work performed by the individual herself – as opposed to privilege given by birth). These so-called accidents of birth or accidents of circumstance are not deserved. For example, when I submitted the manuscript for my first novel, *Far Into the Sound*, it went directly to the publisher (as opposed to going through an agent). This was called the slush pile. A hard-working editor was going through the slush pile one day and then stopped and decided to go to lunch to meet her boyfriend. My manuscript was at the top of the pile when she left for lunch. At the luncheon, the editor's boyfriend asked her to marry him (which was a

9 For discussion of unjust discrimination, see my example of the puzzle maker (Boylan 2004, 139–145; Boylan 2014, chapter 6).

proposition that the editor greeted positively). When she got back to the office, I was at the top of the slush pile. Guess what? She liked my novel and published it.

Did I deserve this good fortune? No. It was out of my control. It is very possible that several manuscripts better than my own were turned down in the morning because the editor might have been in a depressed mood. She looked at my manuscript in an "up" mood. I gained at the expense of other manuscripts that may have been superior.

This is what I am talking about in external environmental factors that can make a positive or negative impact. No environmental factor is deserved. When one's ability to act is accentuated or diminished due to environmental factors that are not within the individual's control, then properly there is no proper praise or blame involved.[10]

However, we all know that the world does not revolve around "properly." This is the battle that ethics faces with prudential factors. One example that I have cited in the past illustrates this paradox in the contrast between positive and negative undeserved environmental factors (Boylan 2014, 187–193). For example, say there are two individuals: Mr. A and Ms. B. Mr. A comes from a very affluent, well-connected background that is rewarded by the mainstream society. Ms. B comes from a poor, discriminated-against background that the mainstream society subjects to unwarranted prejudice. Mr. A's position entering life is to be *en*-abled while Ms. B is *dis*-abled. Neither individual's competitive status in the game of life is fair. Mr. A gets his clear enabled advantage via an accident of birth. Ms. B's disadvantage comes about also via an accident of birth. Thus, if this is a proper paradigm of much of life on earth, then many who are enabled or disabled due to environmental factors are not to be praised or blamed because those factors are out of their power.[11]

3. Disability and stigma

Thus, disability can occur from factors within the agent or from without the agent. In the former case, it is either by genetics (not under the agent's control) or accidents peculiar to the agent (whether they are under the agent's control or not).[12] Let us call this sort of disability clinical individualized disability. It refers to conditions that confront the agent herself in her own personal history. For example, a person may be born with severe curvature of the spine or suffer from a car accident that limits one's ability to commit various sorts of purposive action. In the popular press, most discussion of *disability* refers to these sorts of cases.

In the latter instance, the disability arises from environmental factors that are out of the agent's control. This can be called public health disability, which affects a population

10 Aristotle makes this point in *EN* book 3, chapter 1, 1109b 30–1111a 20–24.

11 I say that desert only follows from what one does himself stripping environmental factors: Boylan (2004, 138–145); Boylan (2014, 187–192).

12 Some would make a distinction here. For example, say you were crippled as the result of a car accident caused by a drunk driver who ran over into your lane and hit you. This would be an example of an injury not in one's control. However, if you were the drunk driver, then you might also be crippled, but the cause of the accident was in your control. This can be a critical distinction concerning "blame" and "desert" but with respect to public policy, it would be impossible to make this distinction. See Smart (2014, 305–312).

differentially. For example, the Love Canal case involved the leakage of toxic chemicals that made its way into the public drinking water so that the citizens of Love Canal (a neighborhood in Niagara Falls, New York) were severely affected (Gibbs 2010). Many were hurt: from children with seizures to adults with cancer. The story here is general with particular people reacting in various ways – some were harmed more than others.

In each case, disability occurs. Disability incurs stigma. Whether a person was disabled due to his own behavior – such as emphysema from smoking – or not (such as a genetic disorder, accident, or falling prey to a public health disaster), there is stigma. This is because most community worldviews (Boylan 2004, 113–136) pretend to a self-description of happiness and prosperity. Even countries that have regular mass starvation, such as North Korea, create songs and public art that present the vision of everything being happy and wonderful.[13] Disability (however caused) gets in the way of this fairy tale.

Stigma is a social term that increases the pain and suffering of the affected individuals (and a fortiori) further diminishes the capability for action. This is because social recognition of a disabled person as the *other* puts him or her into the stream of double consciousness that restricts effective action (Boylan 2011c, 119–131). When one becomes the *other,* then he is saddled with a double consciousness that further inhibits effective purposive action.[14] In double consciousness, one acquires two identities: the agent as he sees himself from his inner consciousness (what I call personal worldview) (Boylan 2004, 21–52; Boylan 2014, 163–170) and a second identity that is the *disabled individual.* This second consciousness comes into play in every life action and can sometimes affect the way one reacts in life. Because another factor is brought into the picture, purposive action becomes more complicated (and a fortiori less effective).

Two examples of this from the interior and exterior vantage points can be set out as follows: *Interior:* the agent has trouble climbing stairs because of damage to his knees. He is always keen on knowing beforehand (if possible) whether there are a lot of stairs and whether there is a handrail to help him navigate the stairs. If he is in a chair or walker, then he needs to know whether there is an elevator. This applies to almost every locomotion decision that he makes beyond his immediate dwelling. *Exterior:* say that I am an African American living in the United States. When I go outside my dwelling by foot or in a motorized vehicle, I must be wary of police and skinheads. (Skinheads are racists of European descent who try to make life difficult for African Americans and others who are different from themselves.) There is no justifiable reason for the loathing of the *other.* I have speculated about this before, but there may be strong strains of desire for homogeneity that is behind this.[15] This is a vain telos. Racial homogeneity (sometimes called purity)[16] is itself a vehicle of disability as we have seen in so-called genetic drift populations (Pierce 2010, chapter 26).

13 For a fictive account, see the Pulitzer Prize–winning novel by Johnson (2012).

14 The originator of this viewpoint can be found in DuBois (1994).

15 Boylan (2004, 85, 170, 187, 245). See my reply in chapter 5.

16 An example of this can be found in the translated phrase "ethnic cleansing" that occurred in the 1990s upon the break-up of Yugoslavia. See Bell-Fialkoff (1999).

There is no objective value to such general exterior judgments that confer disability. As we saw in the Kettlewell experiment, environments' physical characteristics (such as race) are random, and various genotypes perform differentially in these different settings. It is not a value judgment on this level but merely a fact about one individual in her uniqueness within a given set of circumstances.[17] Therefore, those who discriminate against those with interior or exterior disability are engaged in a logical inconsistency. And as per Kant, all consciously held logical inconsistencies are flawed.[18] I also characterize such logical inconsistencies as failures in the personal worldview imperative.[19] In either case, those who freely discriminate against those disabled from within or without are ethically flawed and should alter their personal worldviews.

This and the previous section have sought to set out that difference (whether from interior or exterior factors) is only functionally related to purposive action. It is not *bad*. But socially, so many communities around the world understand physical, mental, or emotional *difference* as a tag of being bad. It does not have to be this way. In the ancient world, epilepsy began as being viewed as *sacred* (as per Cassandra in the *Iliad*, XIII, 366; XXIV, 690) and then took on a double meaning with the early Hippocratic writers (*The Sacred Disease*).[20] Why should we assume that this difference is inherently good or bad? It is a fact that according to the situation may be functionally useful or not. But there is nothing good or bad per se about variations in anatomy or physiology. They just are.

3.1 How should we regard the disabled?

The first thing that is of utmost importance is the attitude that many in most societies take on: if one is disabled in one area of his physiology, then he is to be viewed as totally without positive action capacity. I call this attitude the disability fallacy. Employers seeing a person who cannot walk quickly or climb stairs believe him or her to be fully incapable. Other individuals who are autistic or have Asperger's syndrome are thought to be fit for not good work. The disability fallacy is illogical. Because disability is anatomically or physiologically localized and depends on environment, other powers of the individual must be viewed separately. Of course, a well-known example of this is Stephen Hawking. He suffers from amyotrophic lateral sclerosis and yet he has made some of the most important contributions to cosmology in the past thirty years. His mind is brilliant, although his body faces challenges in normal, daily tasks. Hawking is an example of why we should all resist the disability fallacy.

17 This should not be taken as any agreement on the propriety of the skinheads or any other of the various exterior public health environments, merely a factual description of what happens in the mechanics of environmental disability.

18 See my discussion of Kant and the first and second forms of the categorical imperative in *Basic Ethics* (2009), chapter 13.

19 In my personal worldview imperative, one of the two major mandates is the rational good will, op. cit.

20 "In my opinion this disease is not more sacred than any other" (my translation), from *Hippocrates* vol. 2, ed. and tr. W.H.S. Jones (1923).

Another issue that frequently arises in how we view the disabled is *fault*. I have taken the stance that one should not speculate on *how* one has become disabled. This is irrelevant to the argument on the moral status of basic goods and the table of embeddedness. This argument and its interpretation via the table of embeddedness create positive rights that all people possess.[21] It does not stipulate how one became incapacitated. One has a proportional right according to the level of embeddedness to all goods on the table. Because goods entail duties, it is the duty of everyone on earth to provide access to these goods subject only to the caveat of "ought implies can."

A secondary justification for providing the disabled access to the goods outlined on the table of embeddedness comes from the personhood account within my theory of human rights (Boylan 2014, 163–170). This comes from the personal worldview imperative: "All people must develop a single comprehensive and internally coherent worldview that is good and that we strive to act out in our daily lives." There are four parts to the personal worldview imperative: completeness, coherence, connection to a theory of the good, and practicality. Let's briefly say something about each.

First is *completeness*. Completeness refers to the ability of a theory or ethical system to handle all cases put before it and to determine an answer based on the system's recommendations. This is functionally achieved via the good will. The good will is a mechanism by which we decide how to act in the world. The good will provides completeness to everyone who develops one. There are two senses of the good will. The first is the *rational good will*, which means that each agent will develop an understanding about what reason requires of us as we go about our business in the world. Completeness means that reason (governed by the personal worldview and its operational ethical standpoint) should always be able to come up with an answer to a difficult life decision. In the case of ethics, the rational good will requires engaging in a rationally based philosophical ethics and abiding by what reason demands. Often, this plays out practically in examining and justifying various moral maxims – such as maxim alpha: "one has a moral responsibility to follow through on one's commitments, ceteris paribus." This maxim is about promise making. For example, one could imagine that an employer named Fred hired Olga on the basis of her résumé and a Skype interview that did not reveal her mobility challenges (she needs a walker to get from points A to B for perambulation). Fred promises Olga the job, but when she shows up to work, Fred determines that Olga does not fit the *image* of the company that he wishes to exude: *vibrant, athletic,* and *potent*. A person in a walker is discordant to this image. Even though the job is a desk job (sitting in a cubicle), Fred wants to fire Olga. What should Fred do? The rational good will (as Fred, himself, has developed it via maxim alpha) says that Fred should carry through with his promise to Olga, as there is no conflicting

21 Of course, this is not absolute for ongoing problems. For example, if one were an alcoholic or a drug addict and needed a new liver and there were a shortage of these within a cadre of claimants, then it would seem that unless there were a way to ensure that the claimant would not abuse this new organ, that the scarce organ should be allocated to one who would not abuse the organ. This is not a statement against *past* actions but a statement about the use progressively of organs transplanted from here on out. For a discussion of this, see Smart, op. cit.

moral issue that would invoke the ceteris paribus clause in the maxim. For Fred to act otherwise would be an instance of denying completeness based on the rational good will. Fred should keep his promise to Olga and let her work for him.

Another sort of good will is the *affective or emotional good will.* We are more than just rational machines. We have an affective nature too. Our feelings are important, but just as was the case with reason, some guidelines are in order. For the emotional good will, we begin with sympathy. Sympathy will be taken to be the emotional connection that one forms with other humans. This emotional connection must be one in which the parties are considered to be on a level basis. The sort of emotional connection I am talking about is open and between equals. It is not that of a superior "feeling sorry" for an inferior. Those who engage in interactive human sympathy that is open and level will respond to another with care. Care is an action-guiding response that gives moral motivation to assisting another in need. Together, sympathy, openness, and care constitute love.

In the previous case on promise making, Fred wouldn't be about making and justifying moral maxims such as maxim alpha. Instead, Fred would be developing his capacity sympathetically to connect with other people – call this maxim beta. If Fred sympathetically connected with Olga and her disability that has nothing to do with her ability to carry out the job as advertised, then his caring response would guide him toward maintaining his promise to Olga because to do otherwise would sever the sympathetic connection. Fred would not be acting like a loving person to do otherwise. The shared community worldview of *vibrant, athletic,* and *potent* need not be compromised because these are basically characteristics of the human spirit and not of the physical body. Olga can do her desk job with joie de vivre that reflects the company's shared community worldview. Thus, Fred acting on maxim beta should refrain from firing Olga.

Thus, the two sorts of good will (affective and rational – set out via maxims alpha and beta) work together to promote keeping Olga on the job so long as she can do the work – disability should not be a factor here.[22]

When confronted with any novel situation, one should utilize the two good will dimensions to generate a response. Because these two orientations act differently, it is possible that they may contradict each other. When this is the case, I would allot the tiebreaker to reason. Others demur.[23] Each reader should consider his or her own response to such an occurrence.

A second part of the personal worldview imperative is *coherence.* People should have coherent worldviews. This also has two varieties: deductive and inductive. Deductive coherence speaks to our not having overt contradictions in our worldview. An example of an overt contradiction in one's worldview would be for Sasha to tell her friend

22 Because the affective good will comes from the completeness condition of the personal worldview imperative, the conditions of the imperative also apply to this sort of philosophical love that I have set out. Some detractors think that you cannot order love (as I have done). I give a response to this argument in Boylan (2011a).

23 This is particularly true of some feminist ethicists. See Tong (2009).

Sharad that she has no prejudice against disabled individuals and yet in another context she tells jokes about disabled persons. The coherence provision of the personal worldview imperative says that you shouldn't change who you are and what you stand for depending on the context in which you happen to be: you should either support people with disabilities or excoriate them; waffling between the two is incoherent.

Inductive coherence is different. It is about adopting different life strategies that work against one another. In inductive logic, a conflicting strategy is called a sure-loss contract.[24] For example, if a person wanted to be a devoted husband and family man and yet also engaged in extramarital affairs, then he would involve himself in inductive incoherence. The very traits that make him a good family man – loyalty, keeping your word, sincere interest in the well-being of others – would hurt one in being a philanderer, which requires selfish manipulation of others for one's own pleasure. The good family man will be a bad philanderer and vice versa. To try to do both well involves a sure-loss contract. Such an individual will fail at both. This is what inductive incoherence means. From the point of view of a disabled person, this second form of coherence involves a self-assessment of what can and cannot be done: to seek for both will lead to a sure-loss contract. This creates a reality of the possible in which the disabled person can try to find self-fulfillment (see the next section).

Third is *connection to a theory of the good – most prominent being ethics*.[25] The personal worldview imperative enjoins that we consider and adopt an ethical theory.[26] It does not give us direction, as such, to which theory to choose except that the chosen theory must not violate any of the other three conditions (completeness, coherence, and practicability). What is demanded is that we connect to a theory of ethics and use it to guide our actions.

The final criterion is *practicability*. It is important that the demands of ethics and social/political philosophy (including human rights) be doable and its goals be attainable. This is especially important to consider when one is disabled. One must accept the body one is in at the moment and consider what is possible. This does not mean to "settle" for something less. But it also does not mean that one should hang on scientifically unwarranted dreams of having one's disability reversed. A *utopian* command may have logically valid arguments behind it but also be existentially unsound – meaning that some of the premises in the action-guiding argument are untrue by virtue of their being unrealizable in practical terms. If, in a theory of global ethics, for example, we required that everyone in a rich country gave up three-quarters of their income so that they might support the legitimate plight of the poor, then this would be a utopian vision. Philosophers are all too often attracted to tidy, if perhaps radical, utopian

24 The phrase "sure-loss contract" comes from the notion of betting houses. Say you were betting on the finals of the World Cup: Brazil versus Germany. If you gave 5–1 positive odds for each team, then your betting house will go out of business. A positive assessment of one team requires a complementary negative assessment of the other: failure to observe this rule results in a sure-loss contract.

25 Other aspects of the good can include commitments to aesthetics and religion.

26 My take on the various real and anti-real theories is generally set out in part two of my text *Basic Ethics* (2009).

visions. However, unless philosophers want to be marginalized, we must situate our prescriptions in terms that can actually be used by policymakers. Philosophers involved in human rights discourse must remember that these theories are to apply to real people living in the world. In taxation policy, for example, at some point – let's say at the point of a 50 per cent income-tax rate – even the very wealthy among us will feel unjustly burdened and will rebel and refuse to comply with the policy. Thus, it is utopian to base a policy on the expectation that the rich will submit to giving up 75 per cent of their income. An *aspirational* goal (by contrast) is one that may be hard to reach but is at least possible to achieve (it does not violate principles of human nature or structural facts about the communities that inhabit the world). For the purposes of this chapter, the aspirational perspective will be chosen over the utopian.

The purview of the personal worldview imperative is the individual as she interacts with other individuals in the world. Each of us has to do as much as possible to take stock of who we are and what we realistically think we can and should be. Our personal consciousness is in our power to change what is within our power. Although factors of environment and genetics are not to be dismissed, in the end, it is the free operation of our will that allows us to confront the personal worldview imperative as a challenge for personal renewal. The acceptance of the personal worldview account means that it is in our power to create our ethical selves. The personal worldview imperative thus grounds my theory of personhood that is part of the foundation of natural human rights (of which disability rights is a subset).

Thus, there are two ways to justify public policy that support the rights of the disabled: (1) via rationally based arguments on rights and (2) a personhood account that seeks to integrate rational and emotive dispositions into an integrated good will that dictates people improve upon empathy that can open the opportunity for level sympathy, care, and action (all of which constitute love).

3.2 Disability, health, and self-fulfillment

In the second edition of my text on *Medical Ethics*, I bring together three philosophers (Rosemarie Tong, Anita Silvers, and myself) to write about health.[27] Medicine's mission is to advance health. Disability is connected to health. If we don't know what health is, then medicine is lost without a map, and we have no ground to judge the etiology of disability. In all three of these essays, there are a few common answers to the problem that are in some ways useful but certainly not comprehensive. For example, is being healthy to be at the median within some reference class? Certainly, this is the way medical test results are often presented to the patient. However, there are instances when being far away from the median is thought to be a desirable condition – such as being smart, athletically gifted, or artistically talented. Perhaps there is more to the story? These essays seek to explore this question.

Rosemarie Tong's point of focus is on infertility – especially female infertility. Sometimes, infertility is seen as a disability in which there are potential positive liberty options.

27 Boylan, (2014), Silvers (2014), Tong (2014), all in Michael Boylan, *Medical Ethics* (2014).

Now health care delivery can be seen from at least two critical vantage points: ***clinical medicine*** that focuses on a particular patient seeing her particular doctor about a particular problem and ***public health medicine*** that focuses on groups of people sharing a particular condition that either is itself unhealthy or is a stepping stone to a chronic or fatal disease. For example, smoking and obesity among the general population lead to more respiratory diseases and lung cancer (the former) and diabetes along with muscular skeletal disorders (the latter). Using this bifurcated approach, Tong examines how infertility can be addressed. The clinical approach looks at how in vitro fertilization treatment performs as an answer, along with freezing female eggs before age thirty-five so that they are more viable.[28]

Under the public health approach, various diseases (such as chlamydia) need to be routinely checked and treated to keep women's reproductive tracts in the best possible condition. Also, there are exposures to chemicals in the workplace. Tong makes a strong case for treating infertility first as a public health problem and then as a clinical treatment in order to promote positive liberty and to prevent negative liberty.

In Anita Silvers's essay, the issue of health among the elderly is examined. Being old is often viewed by society as a disability. This is certainly an important segment of the population to look at because elderly people go to the doctor more often and have higher medical expenses. Silvers asks the question whether old people should be thought of as "greedy geezers"? This perception can come about in the United States because Medicare (the social service medical plan that covers most of the elderly in the country) is funded by young people through payroll taxes. But Silvers argues against this charge. People are living longer lives and must adjust what they expect to be able to do. This is important for the personal worldviews of those who may have specific impairments as they age. The health care community must also adjust its expectations about what is healthy among the elderly. Without this adjustment, it might very well be the case that care may be denied "because those relying on prosthetics and mobility devices to locomote is not considered to be healthy enough." Silvers highlights some key issues in clinical medicine and health care policy. If we accept Silvers's argument, then what might be a disability in a person of twenty – for example, limitations on mobility such as stair walking, needing a cane, and the like – might not be considered a disability in someone who is eighty-five. This does return us to the concept of a reference class for a limited application (in a different sense than described earlier) regarding lab tests that are applied to all ages equally.

Finally, in the last essay of this trio, I set out various ways of understanding health: functional approaches (objectivism, uncompromised lifespan, and functionalism/dysfuctionalism). All three are shown to provide several key insights into health but are not sufficient to ground a general theory. Next, I examine the public health approach. Like Tong, I am very interested in this venue, especially because of its ability to be translated into coherent public policy. Finally, there are the subjectivist approaches to health. Many of the subjectivist theories concentrate on well-being. However, there are

28 See my discussion with Tong on this subject: https://vimeo.com/16658981.

some difficulties here. For this reason, I advocate for a self-fulfillment approach that is evaluated by an independent measure (to avoid the circularity problems of the well-being approach). The independent measure involves a particular understanding of personal worldview. It is my contention that, although all of the aforesaid approaches to understanding health have merit, the strongest overall is the self-fulfillment approach that centers around making progress toward what the individual considers to be good in life. Unlike various zero-sum analyses of life where there can be only a few winners, the self-fulfillment approach allows *everyone* to be a winner.[29]

4. Eliminating negative liberty and enhancing positive liberty

Ultimately, public policy approaches require two poles: elimination of negative liberty impediments and the creation of positive liberty capability programs that will assist the disabled to live a healthy life (as defined earlier) in which they can pursue their vision of the good. This was briefly touched on in the last section concerning health.

Negative liberty concerns the impediments that face people with disabilities so that they cannot perform in a setting for which they are entirely capable. One of the most common of these accommodations is the presence of elevators on public transport.[30] Another common negative liberty hurdle is the imposition of health requirements for employment. For example, people with certain diseases (like HIV) have often been discriminated against partly because of an unscientific understanding of how the disease spreads and partly because of homophobic worldviews. In 2014–2015, any travel to West Africa carried the same sort of stigma due to the Ebola epidemic. Often, employers create barriers where they need not be.

Then there are the barriers for government services – such as voting booths, government building design, access to communication devices for the hearing and visually impaired, access to public recreation facilities (especially pools), availability of service animals (such as seeing eye dogs), and so on.

Concerning positive liberty (creating opportunities where they might not presently exist), there is the perspective of the present and the perspective of the future. Concerning the present, various accommodations that do exist can (and should) be publicized to the general public within a given municipality. Also, the use of new technology needs to be integrated into the workplace. For example, there are modern computers that can be operated without the use of hands. This can be a boon to the paraplegic and quadriplegic and can change the nature of so-called white collar jobs. Modern technology that exists right now can be applied to a variety of situations to promote positive liberty.

For the future, it is important for public policy to encourage scientific research into the causes and treatments of birth defects, diseases, and severe accidents. Genetic

29 For a more complete exposition of this, see Boylan (2008).

30 For example, subway systems and buses should be accessible to those who cannot use stairs. This is a real problem in large established public transportation systems around the world.

engineering promises to be a very big player in the future in enabling positive liberty among the disabled.[31]

5. Community support

In a practical way, no public legislation will allow a disabled individual to create a personal life plan that is realistic within the scope of the disability without the support of the community. This means a commitment in the shared community worldview. Community worldviews are viewed variously around the world. My conception of a functioning moral community worldview is one that embraces diversity (subject to the personal worldview imperative).[32] It *requires* participation by all community members. Those who wish to reap the benefits of the community without making their proportional contributions will be deemed to be freeriders (a community parasite that arises from selfish egoism).[33]

The reason that communities should support policies that eliminate negative liberty obstacles and support positive liberty enhancements is because of the characterization of the rational and emotional good will set out earlier. Rationally, set out duties as per the moral right to basic goods and the table of embeddedness ground a logical positive right/duty. Emotionally, level sympathy that leads to care (love) dictates no other response.

Community support at the ground level (micro communities) is the essential practical piece to effective change. You cannot change a person's heart with laws alone.[34] The mechanics of community and personal worldview change require public leaders to come forward to generate overlap with the status quo with some vision of what can be. I call this process "The Way We Confront Novel Normative Theories" (Boylan 2014, 206–213).

6. Conclusion

Although the ancient Greeks honored those with disabilities as being "touched by the gods" – such as Casandra in the *Iliad* – modern societies in their competitive worldviews have often treated the disabled with cruelty. In this chapter, I have tried to set

31 Of course, there are ethical issues here as well. For an examination of some of these, see Boylan and Brown (2002).

32 My version of the shared community worldview imperative is: "Each agent must contribute to a common body of knowledge that supports the creation of a shared community worldview (that is itself complete, coherent, and good) through which social institutions and their resulting policies might flourish within the constraints of the essential core commonly held values (ethics, aesthetics, and religion)" Boylan (2004, chapter 6).

33 Of course, there are unapologetic advocates of selfish egoism, such as Rand (1964) and conservative libertarians like Friedman (1962), who only believe in negative duties; they are advocates of egg carton communities.

34 For example, in the United States, there have been significant gaps between legislation and practical benefit in the case of racial civil rights. The 13th and 14th amendments that were supposed to stop slavery and unequal treatment under the law were a failure at the level where people lived. Racism, lynchings, and other forms of overt oppression continued. Then, a century later, the Civil Rights Act and the Voting Rights Act promised an end to this discrimination. However, although life on the ground improved, it is still the case that police profile and incarcerate and injure (kill) African Americans at a rate far above those of European descent. See Boylan (2011b) and Taylor et al. (2009).

out a shared community worldview in which this will change. By eliminating negative liberty barriers and by investing in the science/engineering that will help extend positive liberty, we can (as societies in the world) extend the range of human agency for all people – which is their basic human right.[35]

7. References

Aristotle. 1995. "Nicomachean Ethics." In *The Complete Works of Aristotle*, edited by Jonathan Barnes, 1729–1867. Princeton, NJ: Princeton University Press.

Bell-Fialkoff, Andrew. 1999. *Ethnic Cleansing*. New York: Palgrave-Macmillan.

Berlin, Isiah. 1969. *Four Essays on Liberty*. Oxford: Oxford University Press.

Boylan, Michael. 1983. *Method and Practice in Aristotle's Biology*. New York: University Press of America.

———. 2004. *A Just Society*. Lanham, MD: Rowman & Littlefield.

———. 2008. *The Good, The True, and The Beautiful*. London: Bloomsbury.

———. 2009. *Basic Ethics*. 2nd ed. Upper Saddle River, NJ: Prentice Hall.

———. 2011a. "Duties to Children." In *The Morality and Global Justice Reader*, edited by Michael Boylan, 385–404. Boulder, CO: Westview.

———. 2011b. "Ethical Profiling." *The Journal of Ethics* 15(1), 131–145.

———. 2011c. *Morality and Global Justice: Justifications and Applications*. Boulder, CO: Westview.

———. 2014. *Natural Human Rights: A Theory*. Cambridge: Cambridge University Press.

———. 2015. *The Origin of Ancient Greek Science: Blood, a Philosophical Study*. London: Routledge.

Boylan, Michael and Kevin Brown. 2002. *Genetic Engineering: Science and Ethics on the New Frontier*. Upper Saddle River, NJ: Prentice Hall.

DuBois, W.E.B. 1994. *The Souls of Black Folk [1903]*. New York: Dover.

Farber, Susan L. 1981. *Identical Twins Raised Apart*. New York: Basic Books.

Friedman, Milton. 1962. *Capitalism & Freedom*. Chicago: University of Chicago Press.

Gibbs, Lois Marie. 2010. *Love Canal and the Birth of the Environmental Health Movement*. Washington, DC: Island Press.

Gould, Stephen Jay. 2002. *The Structure of Evolutionary Theory*. Cambridge, MA: Harvard University Press.

Johnson, Adam. 2012. *The Orphan Master's Son*. New York: Random House.

Jones, W.H.S., ed. 1923. *Hippocrates*. Vol. 2. Cambridge, MA: Harvard University Press.

Joseph, Jay. 1998. "The Equal Environment Assumption of the Classical Twin Methods: A Critical Analysis." *Journal of Mind and Behavior* 9(3), 325–358.

Juel-Nielsen, Niels. 1980. *Individual and Environment: Monozygotic Twins Raised Apart*. New York: International University Press.

Kettlewell, H.B.D. 1971. "Industrial Melanism in Moths." In *Man's Impact on the Environment*, edited by Thomas Detwyler, 667–674. New York: McGraw-Hill.

Owens, Joseph. 2013. "Semantic Comprehension, Inference and Psychological Externalism." *Mind and Language* 28(2), 173–203.

Pierce, Benjamin A. 2010. *Genetics: A Conceptual Approach*. 4th ed. New York: W. H. Freeman.

Rand, Ayn. 1964. *The Virtues of Selfishness*. New York: Signet.

Silvers, Anita. 2014. "Too Old for the Good of Health?" In *Medical Ethics*, 2nd ed., edited by Michael Boylan, 30–43. Oxford: Wiley-Blackwell.

35 I discuss what I consider to be the range of human rights claims in Boylan (2014).

Smart, Brian. 2014. "Fault and the Allocation of Spare Organs." In *Medical Ethics*, 2nd ed., edited by Michael Boylan, 305–312. Oxford: Wiley-Blackwell.

Taylor, Terrance J., David Holleran, and Volkan Topalli. 2009. "Racial Bias in Case Processing." *Justice Quarterly* 26(3), 562–591.

Tong, Rosemarie. 2009. "A Feminist Personal Worldview Imperative." In *Morality and Justice: Reading Boylan's A Just Society*, edited by John-Stewart Gordon, 29–38. Lanham, MD: Lexington Books.

———. 2014. "Ethics, Infertility, and Public Health: Balancing Public Good and Private Choice." In *Medical Ethics*, 2nd ed., edited by Michael Boylan, 13–29. Oxford: Wiley-Blackwell.

United Nations. 2007. *The 2007 Human Development Report*. New York: United Nations Development Program.

12 Afterword

Akiko Ito

"Persons with disabilities as beneficiaries and agents of change in society and development" – the central message of the United Nations' work in the field of disability since the 1980s[1] is increasingly taking concrete forms in its global, regional, and national development agenda. Since the adoption of the Convention on the Rights of Persons with Disabilities (CRPD) by the UN General Assembly in 2006, this global commitment is further enabling new communities of stakeholders to advance a disability-inclusive society and development worldwide.

Recent progress in advancement of the rights of persons with disabilities emerges as a result of the adoption, promotion, and implementation of the international norms and standards relating to disability and development, such as the CRPD. An increasing international focus on the situation of persons with disabilities in development has led to the successful mainstreaming of the disability perspective and the rights of persons with disabilities in global development processes and their resulting frameworks, including the 2030 Agenda for Sustainable Development.

Over the past decade, the UN General Assembly[2] reiterated its commitment to include the disability perspective in the global development agenda, calling for urgent action toward inclusive, accessible, and sustainable society and development. The huge gap between commitment and practice continued in addition to the invisibility of disability in the Millennium Development Goals. Since the entry into the CRPD in 2008, the member states, the UN Secretariat, and the disability community built a new community of stakeholders and steadily strengthened a global platform for disability-inclusive development. Based on several years of concerted efforts in this field, the international community successfully promoted the mainstreaming of disability in the evolving development agenda. For example, the UN World Conference on Disaster Risk Reduction adopted the Post-2015 Framework for Disaster Risk Reduction (Sendai Framework) and recognized persons with disabilities as the essential resource

1 UN World Programme of Action Concerning Disabled Persons (1982) and the United Nations Decade of Persons with Disabilities (1982–1993).

2 A/RES/63/150, A/RES/64/131, A/RES/65/185, A/RES/66/124, A/RES/67/140, A/RES/68/3 and A/RES/69/142.

and agents of change for disability-inclusive disaster risk preparedness, reduction, and reconstruction. Furthermore, the Addis Ababa Action Agenda adopted in July 2015 addresses the needs of persons with disabilities in the global framework for financing the 2030 agenda. These benchmarks led to the historical achievement in September 2015: the adoption by the international community of the 2030 Agenda for Sustainable Development, in which the Sustainable Development Goals include seven targets focusing on persons with disabilities. For example, Goal 10 addresses inequality by making a call to reduce inequality within and among countries. Within that goal, target 10.2 specifically focuses on persons with disabilities by aiming to empower and promote the social, economic, and political inclusion of all, irrespective of disability. This is an entirely new world from the previous global framework with the Millennium Development Goals, where disability was invisible and given limited consideration in the global development processes, institutions, and mechanisms for the implementation of those goals.

This book on *Human Rights and Disability* is a very timely contribution to the historical movement at the United Nations to effect transformative changes through a global framework toward 2030 for inclusive and sustainable development: leaving no one behind. In this regard, the mainstreaming of disability is a central concern to the new global development agenda, and the focus now is on action to implement the 2030 global development agenda also for persons with disabilities.

This collection gives deep insight into how the discourse on disability and human rights could advance an inclusive and sustainable society. In chapter 2, John-Stewart Gordon addressed the lack of cohesion and the inherent tension in the discourse on disability and bioethics. In chapter 6, Holger Burckhart and Bennet Jäger expanded the concept of "inclusion" as applied to persons with disabilities by arguing that promoting human rights and moral obligation is a human duty and that inclusion must be understood and internalized as a guiding principle of society and in all areas of human interaction. In chapter 8, Hans Reinders highlighted the significance of human rights claims to support a moral cause and noted that the interplay of human rights in legal and moral discourses and action for promoting justice is of major significance for effecting change on the ground. These analyses illuminate our minds on inequalities and their complexities faced by persons with disabilities and their exclusion in legal, social, economic, and cultural spheres. The international community must bring disability rights to the front of the 2030 development agenda as a moral and developmental imperative for social justice.

Mainstreaming disability in the development agenda requires a transformative change in both normative and operational frameworks to ensure the equal rights and full participation of persons with disabilities in society and development. In chapter 5, Donato Tarulli, Dorothy Griffiths, and Frances Owen elucidated an emerging paradigm of the rights-based services and supports for marginalized people with intellectual disabilities, commensurate with ideals in disability rights. In chapter 4, Christopher Riddle deftly applied the capabilities approach to justice to reclaim that disability is a human rights issue, in which disability, human rights, and health are integrated into the values of equality, dignity, and autonomy. In chapter 11, Michael Boylan concluded that public policy should be concerned with the elimination of negative liberty impediments and the creation of positive liberty capability programs to improve the lives of persons with disabilities. In this process, creating opportunities through scientific research, as well as through the support of communities on the ground, is important for enabling positive liberty among persons with disabilities. In this context, analyses in this chapter on the interdependence among equality in rights, and of opportunities and outcomes, are of significant importance in contextualizing the holistic integration for persons with disabilities into society.

This volume also brings into policy dialogue the rethinking of disability as a cross-cutting issue. In chapter 3, Johann-Christian Põder sought to identify the rightful place of human rights in the discourse on religion and disability and provided a new discourse on religion, disability, and human rights, in particular as an integral part of the dialogue among civilizations. In chapter 7, Petr Frantik illustrated ongoing efforts to translate the CRPD's commitment to promote inclusive education in Germany, provided a brief overview of the current implementation of the right to inclusive education in Germany, and explored how new forms of teaching and learning can be implemented in schools. In chapter 10, Anita Silvers and Leslie Francis discussed how the civil rights framework advances the engagement for pragmatic efforts for the rights claims by persons with disabilities on the social resources to meet their basic interests, grounded explicitly in acknowledgement of people's differences, such as in health care as part of civil rights rather than human rights. These discussions inform readers that disability is a cross-cutting issue and that multisectoral policies could advance the equal rights and full participation of persons with disabilities in society.

It is crucial to recognize that many challenges still exist in translating commitment into action. Such concern is echoed in chapter 9, where Jerome Bickenbach discussed the limitation of theoretical models in their translation into government action to bring practical changes in the lives of persons with disabilities on the ground. In this chapter, he pursued the argument for the CRPD to move forward to follow a dynamic and realistic process of transforming its goals and objectives into accountable government action for persons with disabilities, striking a balance between the commitment to the inherent values and feasible and progressively realizable social change. He advocated for harnessing the power of social sciences to move beyond the domain of being merely "manifesto rights" and to transform the world. In this context, this collection further brings attention to how commitments can be translated into action that involves measurable goals, practical steps, and tangible government accountability.

To achieve the goal of a disability-inclusive society, good governance, institution, and mechanism are at the heart of action. In March 2016, the international community initiated the first phase of the implementation of the 2030 agenda by adopting specific disability indicators for the Sustainable Development Goals framework. Based on the progress of the Sendai Framework, which included disability in the global disaster risk reduction framework (Sendai, Japan) in 2015, the international community will continue to highlight the multiple challenges faced by persons with disabilities. Furthermore, the third UN Conference on Housing and Sustainable Urban Development (Habitat III) in October 2016 is anticipated to adopt an inclusive New Urban Agenda in Quito, Ecuador. In 2018, the UN flagship report on disability and development will be issued to provide information on the situation of persons with disabilities in economic and social development in line with the CRPD.

While the international community continues to address the persistent gap between policy and practice, the questions arise in every aspect of the implementation of the human rights of persons with disabilities as codified in the CRPD as well as the inclusion of persons with disabilities and their perspectives in the implementation of the 2030 development agenda: What are the practical steps we can take in the immediate period, medium term, and longer term to approach the ideal state of an inclusive, accessible, and sustainable society? How could theoretical models on disability illuminate the current situation of persons with disabilities in society? What action should be taken by different stakeholders? And how could new forms of collaboration, such as multistakeholder partnerships consisting of governments, disability and expert communities, and the private sector and academic communities, accelerate the social transformation for individuals with disabilities, their communities, and their states? In support of the intergovernmental processes to implement the 2030 agenda and to identify responses to such emerging questions, it is essential that persons with disabilities take an active part in the decision making as resource and change agents for inclusive and sustainable society and development, following the motto of the global disability movement: "nothing about us without us."

Bibliography

Allemann-Ghionda, Cristina. 2013. *Bildung für alle, Diversität und Inklusion. Internationale Perspektiven.* Paderborn: Verlag Ferdinand Schöningh.

Beauchamp, Tom L. and James F. Childress. 2009. *Principles of Biomedical Ethics.* New York: Oxford University Press.

Bickenbach, Jerome E. 2009. "Disability, Culture and UN Convention." *Disability and Rehabilitation* 31(14), 1111–1124.

———. 2012. *Ethics, Law, and Policy.* Thousand Oaks, CA: Sage.

Boylan, Michael. 2004. *A Just Society.* Lanham, MD: Rowman & Littlefield.

———. 2014. *Natural Human Rights: A Theory.* Cambridge: Cambridge University Press.

Burckhart, Holger and John-Stewart Gordon. 2014. "Inclusion – A Moral Imperative, But Also Socially Desired?" In *Global Ethics and Moral Responsibility: Hans Jonas and His Critics*, edited by John-Stewart Gordon and Holger Burckhart, 93–101. London: Routledge.

Carey, Allison C. 2010. *On the Margins of Citizenship: Intellectual Disability and Civil Rights in Twentieth-Century America.* Philadelphia: Temple University Press.

Creamer, Deborah Beth. 2009. *Disability and Christian Theology: Embodied Limits and Constructive Possibilities.* Oxford: Oxford University Press.

Eiesland, Nancy. 1994. *The Disabled God: Toward a Liberatory Theology of Disability.* Nashville: Abingdon Press.

Fennell, Phil. 2008. "Human Rights, Bioethics and Mental Disorder." *Medicine and Law* 27(1), 95–107.

Flynn, Eilonoir. 2015. *Disabled Justice? Access to Justice and the UN Convention on the Rights of Persons with Disabilities.* Burlington, VT: Ashgate.

Gordon, John-Stewart. 2013. "Is Inclusive Education a Human Right?" *The Journal of Law, Medicine & Ethics* 41(4), 754–767.

Griffiths, Dorothy, Frances Owen, and Shelley Watson, eds. 2012. *The Human Rights Agenda for Persons with Intellectual Disabilities.* New York: NADD Press.

Harpur, Paul. 2012. "Embracing the New Disability Rights Paradigm: The Importance of the Convention on the Rights of Persons with Disabilities." *Disability & Society* 27(1), 1–14.

Humbach, Martina, Christian Kluwe, Karin Kress, Dirk Schlechter, Jost Schneider, and Rainer Wensing. 2014. *Inklusion in der Schule. Das Praxisbuch.* Donauwörth: Auer Verlag.

Kao, Grace Y. 2011. *Grounding Human Rights in a Pluralistic World.* Washington, DC: Georgetown University Press.

Kayess, Rosemary and Phillip French. 2008. "Out of Darkness into Light? Introducing the Convention on the Rights of Persons with Disabilities." *Human Rights Law Review* 8(1), 1–34.

Koch, Tom. 2004. "The Difference That Difference Makes: Bioethics and the Challenge of 'Disability.'" *Journal of Medicine and Philosophy* 29(6), 697–716.

Lang, Raymond, Maria Kett, Nora Groce, and Jean-Francois Trani. 2011. "Implementing the United Nations Convention on the Rights of Persons with Disabilities: Principles, Implications, Practice and Limitations." *ALTER: European Journal of Disability Research* 5, 206–220.

Langenbach, Anna. 2003. "Human Rights of Persons with Disabilities." http://www.hrea.org/index.php?base_id=152.

Mégret, Frédéric. 2008. "The Disabilities Convention: Human Rights of Persons with Disabilities or Disability Rights?" *Human Rights Quarterly* 30(2), 494–516.

Mladenov, Teodor. 2013. "The UN Convention on the Rights of Persons with Disability and Its Interpretation." *ALTER: European Journal of Disability Research* 7, 69–82.

Nussbaum, Martha. 2007. *Frontiers of Justice: Disability, Nationality, Species Membership*. Cambridge, MA: Harvard University Press.

———. 2011. *Creating Capabilities: The Human Development Approach*. Cambridge, MA: Harvard University Press.

Ouellette, Alicia. 2013. *Bioethics and Disability: Toward a Disability-Conscious Bioethics*. New York: Cambridge University Press.

Owen, Frances and Dorothy Griffiths, eds. 2009. *Challenges to the Human Rights of Persons with Intellectual Disabilities*. London: Jessica Kingsley.

Petman, Jarna. 2009. "The Special Reaching for the Universal: Why a Special Convention for Persons with Disabilities?" In *United Nations Convention on the Rights of Persons with Disabilities: Multidisciplinary Perspectives*, edited by Jukka Kumpuvouri and Martin Scheinin, 20–33. Helsinki: The Center for Human Rights of Persons with Disabilities.

Quinn, Gerard. 2009. "Resisting the 'Temptation of Elegance': Can the Convention on the Rights of Persons with Disabilities Socialise States to Right Behaviour?" In *The UN Convention on the Rights of Persons with Disabilities*, edited by Oddný Mjöll Arnadóttir and Gerard Quinn, 215–256. Leiden: M. Nijhoff.

Quinn, Gerard, and Theresia Degener. 2002. *The Current Use and Future Potential of United Nations Human Rights Instruments in the Context of Disability*. New York and Geneva: United Nations.

Rawls, John. 1971. *A Theory of Justice*. Cambridge, MA: Harvard University Press.

Reich, Kersten, ed. 2012. *Inklusion und Bildungsgerechtigkeit. Standards und Regeln zur Umsetzung einer inklusiven Schule*. Weinheim und Basel: Beltz.

Reinders, Hans S. 2008. *Receiving the Gift of Friendship: Profound Disability, Theological Anthropology, and Ethics*. Grand Rapids, MI: Eerdmans.

Riddle, Christopher A. 2014. *Disability and Justice: The Capabilities Approach in Practice*. Lanham, MD: Lexington Books.

Sen, Amartya. 1995. "Equality of What?" In *Equal Freedom: Selected Tanner Lectures on Human Values*, edited by Stephen Darwall, 307–330. Ann Arbor: University of Michigan Press.

Shakespeare, Tom. 2013. *Disability Rights and Wrongs Revisited*. London: Routledge.

Silvers, Anita. 2009. "The Social Model of Disability." In *Philosophical Reflections on Disability*, edited by Chris Ralston and Justin Ho, 19–36. New York: Springer Academic Press.

Stein, Michael A. 2007. "Disability Human Rights." *California Law Review* 95, 75–121.

Stein, Michael A. and Janet E. Lord. 2010. "Monitoring the Convention on the Rights of Persons with Disabilities: Innovations, Lost Opportunities, and Future Potential." *Human Rights Quarterly* 32(3), 689–728.

Swinton, John, ed. 2004. *Critical Reflecions on Stanley Hauerwas' Theology of Disability*. Binghamton, NY: Haworth Press.

Index

abortion, selective 14, 17n10
accessibility 3
accommodation, reasonable 105–6
ACT Disability, Aged and Carer Advocacy Service 124
Addis Ababa Action Agenda 172
adversarial dyad problem 114
affective good will 163, 163n22
affiliation, as basic capability 41
Agenda for Sustainable Development 171, 172
Americans with Disabilities Act 125
Amnesty International 122
antidiscrimination relief 125
Aristotle 60
aspirational goal 162, 165
Association for Retarded Citizens 52
autism spectrum disorder 104
autonomy *15*; assisted 30, 30n10; capabilities approach 47–8; dignity and 48; executive functioning 134; informed consent 11; notion of 11; right to 120; rise in medical ethics 10–11; value of 123

barriers 1, 167
Berlin, Isaiah 114
Bill of Rights for the Handicapped Child 52
binding legal instrument 100
bioethics: connection to theory of the good 164; deontology 12–13, 14; disability-conscious 4, 9–19; gap between bioethicists and disability rights community 10–15; I-, you- and third-person perspectives 18; resolving conflict between bioethicists and disability rights community 15–19; utilitarianism 12, 14
bodily health, as basic capability 40
bodily integrity, as basic capability 40

capabilities approach 39–48; autonomy 47–8; dignity 40, 45–7; equality 43–5; functionings 39–40; human rights 41–3; list of basic capabilities 40–1
care providers, rights education for 61–2
categorizations in education 82–3, 87
Census Bureau, US 142
chaining of disabled individuals 95–6, 103, 106–7
charity 22–3, 25, 29, 31–3
children rights 55
Christianity *see* theology and disability
civil liberties 102–3, 107–8
civil rights 114–15, 125, 132, 138–40, 143, 148–50
claim rights 17–108, 102–2
claims *in personam* 112
claims *in rem* 112
Cleveland v. Policy Management System Corp. 142
clinical individualized disability 159
coherence 163–4
collective agreement, as basis for rights justification 137–9
Committee on the Rights of Persons with Disabilities 3, 76–7, 77n5, 122
community living 64
community worldview 168–9, 169n32
completeness 162
Conference on Housing and Sustainable Urban Development 174
consciousness, double 160
Convention against Torture, United Nations 122
Convention on the Elimination of All Forms of Discrimination against Women 112
Convention on the Rights of Persons with Disabilities (CRPD) 53–6; adoption 1, 13, 54, 96, 99, 101, 112, 171; Agency Support Group 127; antidiscrimination relief 125; Article 7 55; Article 12 55, 120, 122–4, 134–6; Article 13 55, 62, 135–6; Article 24 55, 75–6, 88, 89; Article 25 55, 62, 136; Article 26 55, 136; Article 31 126; Article 32 126–7; Article 33 126; assisted autonomy and 30, 30n10;

children rights 55; data collection 126; domestic incorporation 127; drafting process 2; enforcement in Germany 76; equal participation 69; guiding principles 2, 58; human rights approach 113–16; implementation 125–8; implementation process 100; inclusion and 29–30, 55, 69; inclusive education 69, 74–6; influence of 56; monitoring of implementation 3; obligations imposed on states under 2–3, 69, 116, 122–3; obstacles to implementation 3, 116–24; paradigm shift 56–60; promise of 113; ratification 4, 5, 74, 88, 98, 100–1, 127; social model 3, 55; structure of 55; translation into German 78; universality of human rights 115–16, 125
Convention on the Rights of the Child 55–6, 112
cost to live 39
court of law 5, 96–7, 99–102, 109
CRPD *see* Convention on the Rights of Persons with Disabilities
cultural rights 114–15, 125, 149

data collection 126
Declaration of General and Special Rights of the Mentally Retarded 52
Declaration of Helsinski 10
Declaration of Independence, US 111
Declaration of Rights of Mentally Retarded Persons, United Nations 52–3, 97, 104–5, 112
Declaration on Social Progress and Development, United Nations 52
Declaration on the Rights of Disabled Persons, United Nations 53, 97, 104–5, 112
deductive coherence 163–4
Degener, Theresia 113, 115
Deohaeko Cooperative 63–5
deontology 12–13, 14
Department of Housing and Urban Development, US 142
dependency, theology and 26
developmental disabilities: historical perspective on 50–3; human rights 50–65
development issues, human rights linked to 101
difference 119–20, 161
dignity: autonomy and 48; capabilities approach 40, 45–7
dilemma of difference 119–20
disability: clashing models of 140–1; defined 97, 132, 141–3, 146–8, 150; meaning of 3; number of people living with 1
disability fallacy 161
disability identity 145–7
disability rights community 13–14, 15, 50
Disabled People's International 53
discrimination: environmental disability 158; prevention of in education 75–6, 84; right to protection from 71
double consciousness 160
dreams 59

earned income 2
economic rights 114–15, 125, 149
education: accessibility 3; categorizations 82–3, 87; classroom arrangement 84; equality of 75; inclusion 68–70, 74–89; in Germany 68–9, 74–89, 78n6; learning by teaching methods 85–6; learning environments 84–8; literacy rate 2; participation in 75–6, 86; rights education 60–2; stigmatization in 75–6, 81–3; teacher opinions on inclusion in Germany 79–80; team-teaching 83–4, 88
elderly, health among 166
emotional good will 163
emotions, as basic capability 40
employment 2; as basic capability 41; disability fallacy 161; good will 162–3; imposition of health requirements for 167; Tallinn Guidelines for Action on Human Resources Development in the Field of Disabilities 53
environment, control over one's 41
environmental disability 157–9
equality 43–5, 75
ethical medicine 166
ethics *see* bioethics
eugenics 13, 15, 17, 51
European Convention on the Protection of Human Rights and Fundamental Freedoms 99–100, 103–4
European Council 100
European Court 99–100
euthanasia, involuntary 17
evolutionary biology 154
executive functioning 134

fault 162
feasibility 104–5
Feinberg, Joel 111–12, 114, 122
Fernald, Walter 51–2
Framework for Disaster Risk Reduction 172
freedom of movement 102–3, 106, 138
freedom of union 102–3
freedoms, substantial 40, 41
freeriders 168
French Revolution 29
friendship 109
functionings 39–40

genetic drift 160
genetic engineering 167–8
genetic fitness 158
genome 135
Germany, education in 68–9, 74–89, 78n6
goods: basic 155–6; capabilities approach and 39, 44–7; duties entailed by 162; fetish 39, 44; hierarchical set of 154–7; justification for providing access to 162; moral status 155–6; non-enforceable 109; purposive action to 154, 157, 161; secondary 156; Table of Embeddedness 155–6
good will: affective 163, 163n22; emotional 163; rational 162–3
group-differentiated rights 140–1, 147
group-specific human rights 120–1

Harpur, Paul 121
Hawking, Stephen 161
health care: accessibility 3; CRPD Article 25 55, 62; deficiencies in 2; for elderly 166; ethical medicine 166; Medicare 166; public health medicine 166
health care rights 139–40
hemoglobin 158
Hobbs, Thomas 111, 114
Hoover, Herbert 52
Howe, Samuel Gridley 51
human exceptionalism 133–7
humanity, as basis for rights ascription 133–7
human rights: capabilities approach 41–3; as equal rights 115; as fundamental not absolute 97; group-specific 120–1; human exceptionalism 133–7; as justice subset 41–3; legal significance of 96, 98–9; linked to development issues 101; as moral claims 97–8, 122; moral significance of 96–8, 106, 122; pluralization 120; promotion of 100–1; protection of 101; second-generation 115, 149; supplements to 42; third-generation 115; universality of 115–16, 125, 127, 132–6
Human Rights and Intellectual Disabilities Conference (2010) 63
human rights approach to disability: Convention on the Rights of Persons with Disabilities (CRPD) 113–16; principles of 113–14; promise and limitations of 2–4; promises and challenges of 4–6
Hunt, Paul 144

ICF *(International Classification of Functioning, Disability and Health)* 117
Ignatieff, Michael 121
impairment 105
implementation: Convention on the Rights of Persons with Disabilities (CRPD) 125–8; of inclusion 3, 71, 74–89, 100, 116–24; policy to practice 57–8
inclusion 68–72; community 64–5; Convention on the Rights of Persons with Disabilities (CRPD) 29–30, 55, 69; in education 68–70, 74–89; implementation of 71, 74–89; integration and 70–1, 78, 80; participation 75; prevention of discrimination and stigmatization 75–6; as responsibility of society 70–2
incompetence, standards of 11, 11n7
Independent Living Movement 144
Individuals with Disabilities Education Act 106
inductive coherence 164
infertility 165–6
informed consent 11
institutionalization 51
integration, inclusion and 70–1, 78, 80
intellectual disability 95–6, 103–8; health care deficiencies 2; historical perspective on 50–3; human rights 50–65; Person-Centered Planning 58–60; rights training for individuals with 60–1; Swedish National Association for Persons with Intellectual Disability 124
International Classification of Functioning, Disability and Health (ICF) 117
International Covenant on Economic, Social, and Cultural Rights 115
International Disability Caucus 54
International League of Societies for the Mentally Retarded 52
International Year for Disabled Persons 53, 112
invisibility 113
I perspective 18

justice: autonomy 47–8; capabilities approach 39–48; CRPD Article 13 55, 62; dignity 45–7; distributive 114; equality 43–5; human rights as subset 41–3; love and 30–1, 33–4; notion of 108–9; obligations, justice-based 42–8; social justice 27, 45, 62, 65, 97–8, 115, 172; theories of 28–34; transformation of compassion into 28
justifiable restrictions 95, 103–7

Kantianism 12–13
Kennedy, John F. 52
kinship 135
Kittay, Eva 135

labels 50
language of love 27–9
language of rights 24, 27–9
learning by teaching methods 85–6

learning environments 84–8
least restrictive environment, principle of 106–7
legal competence 123
legal issues: binding legal instrument 100; court of law 5, 96–7, 99–102, 109; legal significance of human rights 96, 98–9; legal space created by rights 101–2
liberties 102–3, 107–8, 114, 133, 148
life, as basic capability 40
limitations, procedural 108
limitedness 26
literacy rate 2
Locke, John 111, 114
logic, inductive 164
love 109; asymmetry 32; co-dynamic with rights 28–9; as greatest commandment 32n13; justice and 30–1, 33–4; language of love 27–9; as patronizing 31, 33; philosophical 163n22; theology and disability 22, 24–34, 32n13
Love Canal 160
Lucas, John 109

malaria 158
manifesto rights 111–13
marginalization 21, 22, 64
Massachusetts School for Idiotic and Feeble-Minded Youth 51–2
material rights, as basic capability 41
maxims, moral 163
medical ethics: autonomy 10–11; paternalism 10
medical model of disability 117–19, 140–3, 140n3, 146–51
Medicare 140
Mégret, Frédéric 120
mental health disorders 2
mental retardation 50, 52
micro communities 168
Millennium Development Goals 101, 171, 172
minority model 25–8
Minow, Martha 119
mobility disabilities 2
moral claims 97–8, 122
morality, colder part of 109
moral significance of human rights 96–8, 106, 122
moral status, unlinking personhood from 16–17
moth experiment of Kettlewell 157–8

National Monitoring Body 76
natural rights 97, 111
negative liberty 157, 166–7, 169
negative rights 102, 114–15, 125, 138
Netherlands 5, 95–110
New Urban Agenda 174
nonbinding instruments 100
nondiscrimination 41
normalcy, tyranny of 26
normalisation 23
Not Dead Yet 18
"Nothing About Us Without Us" 53
Nuremberg Code 10

obligations: to enforce rights 102–3, 105–7, 112–14; imposed under Convention on the Rights of Persons with Disabilities (CRPD) 2–3, 69, 116, 122–3; justice-based 42–8; reasonable accommodation 105–6; respect-protect-fulfill framework 114
obstacles 3
Office of the High Commissioner for Human Rights 115, 118, 120–1
"ought implies can" rule 103

participation: in education 75–6, 86; Standard Rules on the Equalization of Opportunities for Persons with Disabilities 54
Partnership on the Rights of Persons with Disabilities, UN 127
paternalism 58; in medical ethics 10; theology and 24
patronization: inclusion and 71; love and 31, 33
People First 53
personal worldview imperative 162–5
Person-Centered Planning 58–60
personhood 4, 10, 16; notion of 15; personal worldview imperative 162, 165; unlinking moral status from 16–17
physiology 154, 161
planning, person-centered 58–60
play, as basic capability 41
political rights 41, 114–15, 138
positive liberty 157, 165–9
positive rights 102, 112, 114–15, 125, 138, 149
practicality 164–5
prenatal genetic diagnosis 14, 17n10
President's Panel on Mental Retardation 52
procedural limitations 108
promotional rights 103
promotion of human rights 100–1
property rights 41
protection of human rights 101
public authority 99–100, 102–3
public health disability 159
public health medicine 166
punishment 22, 23, 25, 27–8
purposive action to a good 154, 157, 161
Putnam, Ruth Anna 138

Quinn, Gerald 113, 115

racial civil rights 168n34
rational good will 162–3
rationality 13, 14
reasonable accommodation 105–6
relationships and rights 62–5
resources: capabilities approach and 39, 44–7; equalizing 43–5; mobilization of 59
restrictions, justifiable 95, 103–7
rights: civil 114–15, 125, 132, 138–40, 143, 148–50; claim 17–108, 102–2; collective agreement as basis for rights justification 137–9; cultivating a culture of 62; cultural 114–15, 125, 149; economic 114–15, 125, 149; group-differentiated 140–1, 147; health care 139–40; humanity as basis for rights ascription 133–7; legal space created by 101–2; liberties 102–3, 107–8, 133, 148; manifesto 111–13; natural 97, 111; negative 102, 114–15, 125, 138; obligations to enforce 102–3, 105–7, 112–14, 116, 122–3; political 41, 114–15, 125, 138, 149; positive 102, 112, 114–15, 125, 138; promotional 103; relationships and 62–5; second-generation 115, 149; social 114–15, 125, 148–51; special 120–1, 125; universality of 63; what claims can do 107–8; what disability rights cannot do 108–9
rights agenda, historical context and rationale for 50–4
rights education 60–2; training for care providers 61–2; training for individuals with intellectual disabilities 60–1; training for the community 62
right to life 4, 16–18
Rousseau, Jean-Jacques 138

segregation 145
self-advocacy 53, 58, 64
self-determination 14–17, 30–1, 57–8, 60, 62–4, 71, 134
self-fulfillment approach 167
selfish egoism 168, 168n33
Sendai Framework 172, 173
senses, imagination, and thought as basic capability 40
sickle cell anemia 158
sin 22, 24–5, 28
skinheads 160
slush pile 158–9
social capital 59–60, 63
social Darwinism 51
social justice 27, 45, 62, 65, 97–8, 115, 172
social model 15, 27, 121, 140–1, 140n3, 143–5, 148–51; Convention on the Rights of Persons with Disabilities (CRPD) 3, 55; criticisms of 145–7, 149; fetish 6, 116–19
Social Philosophy (Feinberg) 111
social rights 114–15, 125, 148–51
Social Security Administration, US 142
Social Security Disability Insurance 142
special rights 120–1, 125
Standard Rules on the Equalization of Opportunities for Persons with Disabilities 54
Stein, Michael 115, 149
stigmatization 21, 22; diminishment of capability for action 160; in education 75–6, 81–3; labels 50
suicide: active 14, 17; CRPD Article 12 and 124; physician-assisted 14, 17
sure-loss contract 164, 164n24
Sustainable Development Goals 172, 173
suum cuique (to each his due) principle 98
Swedish National Association for Persons with Intellectual Disability 124
sympathy 163
systematics 154

Table of Embeddedness 155–6
Tallinn Guidelines for Action on Human Resources Development in the Field of Disabilities 53
teachers: opinions on inclusion in Germany 79–80; special needs 79–83, 85–7; team-teaching 83–4, 88; training 83
tenBroek, Jacobus 147
test, divine 22, 23, 25, 27–8
theology and disability 21–34; action and consequences 22; charity 22–3, 25, 29, 31–3; dependency 26; disabling and enabling 34; efforts at rethinking 24–8; historical perspective 21–4; human rights 29–30; love 22, 24–34, 32n13; minority model 25–8; punishment 22, 23, 25, 27–8; sin 22, 24–5, 28; test, divine 22, 23, 25, 27–8; theories of justice 28–34
3Rs Community University Research Alliance 60–1, 65
truth telling 12–13
Tuskegee Syphilis Study 10
Tussman, Joseph 147
Twenty-Four Hour Planning 58

unemployment 2
Union of the Physically Impaired Against Segregation (UPIAS) 143–4
uniqueness 154
United Nations: calorie intake minimum 156; Committee on the Rights of Persons with Disabilities 3, 76–7, 77n5, 101, 122; Conference on Housing and Sustainable Urban Development 174; Convention against Torture 122; Convention on the Elimination of All Forms of Discrimination

against Women 112; Convention on the Rights of Persons with Disabilities (CRPD) adoption 1, 13, 53–6, 96, 99, 101, 112; Convention on the Rights of the Child 112; Decade of Disabled Persons 53; Declaration of Rights of Mentally Retarded Persons 52–3, 97, 104–5, 112; Declaration on Social Progress and Development 52; Declaration on the Rights of Disabled Persons 53, 97, 104–5, 112; Economic and Social Affairs 126; International Year for Disabled Persons 53, 112; Partnership on the Rights of Persons with Disabilities 127; Universal Declaration of Human Rights 112; Voluntary Fund on Disability 54; World Conference on Disaster Risk Reduction 172
Universal Declaration of Human Rights, United Nations 112
universality of human rights 115–16, 125, 127, 132–6
UPIAS (Union of the Physically Impaired Against Segregation) 143–4
utilitarianism 12, 14
utopian vision 164–5

values, non-enforceable 109
vertical-inequality problem 45–6
Vienna Declaration
virtuous suffering 22

Wendell, Susan 147
World Conference on Disaster Risk Reduction 172
World Council of Churches 23, 32
World Health Organization: defining disability 141; *International Classification of Functioning, Disability and Health* (ICF) 116–17
World Programme of Action Concerning Disabled Persons 53, 112
worldview: community 168–9, 169n32; personal 162–5

You perspective 18

FSC
www.fsc.org
MIX
Papier | Fördert
gute Waldnutzung
FSC® C083411

Kolibri 360 GmbH
Ferdinand-Jühlke-Straße 7
99095 Erfurt, Deutschland
produktsicherheit@kolibri360.de